Inequality and Social Policy

For my daughter Lian—
In memory of my mother

INEQUALITY and Social Policy

The Sociology of Welfare

A.W. Djao, Ph.D.
University of Saskatchewan

John Wiley & Sons

Toronto New York Chichester Brisbane Singapore

Canadian Cataloguing in Publication Data

Djao, Angela Wei, 1943-
Inequality and social policy

Bibliography: p.
Includes index.
ISBN 0-471-79867-3

1. Public welfare — Canada. 2. Canada - Social policy. I. Title.

HV105.D62 361'.971 C83-094065-0

Printed and bound in Canada
10 9 8 7 6 5 4 3 2 1

Preface

This book is born out of the experience of many instructors of the sociology of social welfare, an experience that I began to share in 1975 when I taught a course by that title. I had experience in social welfare and community development, but my formal training in sociology was predominantly in industrialization and the sociology of work. Although it would have been logical for me to apply a sociological analysis earlier to the multifaceted phenomenon called "social welfare", the task or, more precisely, the learning process, did not begin until I was confronted with the need to explain it to students. It was then that I discovered the lack of development of published research in the sociology of social welfare. While a great deal of interest in and information on poverty had appeared since the late sixties, the material regarding approaches taken toward welfare, poverty, and related problems was not systematically organized. More important, there were few studies written on the theoretical aspects of the sociology of social welfare and the dynamic processes involved in the formulation, implementation, and consequences of social policy.

Since the late seventies, there has been significant development in the theory and research of the welfare state, both in Canada and abroad, and particularly in Britain. While this is a welcome sign, students of social work and social welfare are often deterred from pursuing certain issues further by the preponderance of publications obviously written for professionals, rather than beginners. Meanwhile, my own research in the area of the sociology of social welfare has revealed that there is considerable confusion regarding particular aspects of welfare. Sometimes the confusion is a matter of semantics. For example, what exactly do "social welfare", "social security", "income security", and "social services" mean? To help clarify this, a section on "Working Definitions" has been included in chapter 1. Often, however, confusion stems from a lack of clarity in conceptualization. The combination of all these factors prompted me to write a book that would clearly summarize the sociological aspects of social welfare within a comprehensive analytical framework and thus provide an information source for the interested audience, including students of sociology and social work.

Among the issues discussed are three that have been the source of major debate. The first is that *welfare recipients or clients are not just those on social assistance*. Because we all benefit from various social welfare programs, we are all welfare recipients. Different social classes and groups benefit from different programs. Moreover, social classes and groups also differ in terms of the degree to which they rely on various programs. In common language, the so called "welfare recipients" are those who depend on public transfers as their sole or major source of livelihood.

Second, *social welfare has been erroneously perceived for too long as the exclusive domain of social workers*. Social work is indeed a crucial component of social welfare. Yet, as will be made clear in the book, social welfare is also an institution in which many groups participate: politicians, social scientists, social workers, nurses, and consumers. While social workers have always written about social welfare, contributions from the social scientists in the academic disciplines have begun to emerge, besides occasional reports they have written for government task forces, commissions, or enquiries. It is useful to bring different perspectives to the same social reality. The analytical approach of this book accentuates the sociological perspective. It also challenges other social scientists, especially sociologists, to apply their professional skills in this area so that there will be better understanding and more people-oriented development in social welfare.

Third, one of the most salient issues lies in the confusion between "ideology" and "theory" that is found not just in the study of social welfare, but in sociology in general. Both students and beneficiaries of social welfare have suffered because of the confusion. An ideology entails a value judgement and an attempt to direct the social and political choices facing members of society. A theory, on the other hand, is the analysis of a situation, closely linked to empirical evidence. A theory may have an ideological basis, but it is not necessarily identical to that ideology. In the past, "theories" have been advanced, with no indication of the ideology to which they were linked. Hence, students and consumers of social welfare have been unable to properly assess the theory or its application in light of its ideological context. This has, in turn, led to a retardation of theoretical development.

By presenting the ideological underpinnings of present-day theories and concepts of social welfare, it is hoped that this book will stimulate clearer and more imaginative theoretical development.

Research for this book was funded by grants from University of Lethbridge and University of Saskatchewan. I would like to thank many of my colleagues and students, and the support staff in the Department of Sociology at both universities for their comments, criticisms, and assistance at various points in my research and preparation of the manuscript. In particular, my thanks go to Dr. B. Singh Bolaria, University of Saskatchewan; Professor Kathy Storrie, University of

Saskatchewan, who read the manuscript and shared with me her insight and experience; Dawn Currie and Rodney Jeffries, who were my competent and conscientious research assistants; and Sheila Harrison, Brenda Roberts, and Sherry Stuber for typing several papers and earlier drafts which were eventually incorporated in the book.

I am grateful to James A. W. Rogerson of John Wiley & Sons Canada Limited for his interest and support. Kathryn Dean and Wiley's editorial personnel provided the best professional editorial services possible. I would also like to express my appreciation for the constructive and useful criticisms provided at the publisher's instigation by D. F. Bellamy, University of Toronto; Dr. Brigitte Kitchen, York University; Dr. John L. McMullan, University of British Columbia; Dr. Cerise Morris, Dawson College; Dr. William G. Vine, George Brown College; and D. Woodsworth, McGill University.

Finally, I thank Anthony B. Chan for his understanding and encouragement throughout the project.

A.W. Djao
December, 1982

Contents

PART I

Ideology, Models, and Theories

1

Sociology of Social Welfare

Introduction

Social welfare is a major institution in Canadian society; at some point, it touches the life of every Canadian. Canadians also believe, by and large, that they know something about social welfare. If asked, most Canadians would likely have some criticism about the present welfare system. In a survey of residents in one medium-sized Western city in the late seventies, over 80 percent of the sample replied that they knew something about social welfare. Yet, from their answers to other questions in the survey, it was revealed that nearly 90 percent of the respondents not only had very limited knowledge but also held some erroneous views about welfare. If this finding is any indication of the general case, it would appear that social welfare is probably the most misunderstood of the major societal institutions. Misunderstanding is not simply ignorance (that is, a lack of knowledge); it is ignorance coupled with wrong information.

This book seeks to provide the reader with some knowledge about social welfare. But more importantly, it provides a sociological analysis of social welfare in Canada: it probes the social factors that have shaped social welfare in this country and the consequences and long-term implications of the present social welfare institution.

Sociological analysis is premised upon one fact of human life: people are social. This fact lies at the core of the discipline that is sociology. From birth to death, humans need other people, and despite individual uniqueness and differences, our existence on Earth is essentially a group experience. Being "social" does not necessarily imply "sociability". Yet our survival depends on many others, known or unknown to us. This interdependence over time falls into identifiable patterns. Thus, the quality of group existence and the patterned way of social living are the main reasons for this book's analysis of the causes and effects of social welfare.

Part I deals with models and theories and their underlying ideologies. The present chapter clarifies a few issues in general sociological theory and their application to social welfare. Four models/perspectives on social welfare are presented: rugged individualism (chapter 2), modified individualism (chapter 3), social democracy (chapter 4), and Marxism (chapter 5). Chapter 5 includes a critique of the perspectives and a presentation of the formal theories derived from them.

Part II discusses social inequality and the state. Social class inequality is analyzed in chapter 6, and income inequality in chapter 7. As social welfare is inextricably linked to social inequality, the analysis of social inequality in Canada in these two chapters prepares the reader for a discussion of the welfare state in chapter 8.

In Part III, the present institution of social welfare and its future prospects are examined. The general features and the main components of the institution as it has developed in Canada are presented in chapters 9 and 10. Chapter 11 focuses attention on the cultural processes through which social inequality is manifested and perpetuated. It also looks at the contradictory impact of social welfare on the lives of the people who depend on it most. Chapter 12 discusses the participants in social welfare. Conclusions about the Canadian welfare state are presented in the final chapter. Throughout the book, analysis focuses on developments in social welfare after the Second World War. Although models and theories of welfare are presented as background in Part I, later in the book they are applied to descriptions of phenomena and programs only insofar as their application is realistic. Obviously, a point-by-point application of each of the theories would lead, in some cases, to a forced interpretation and perhaps even distortion of reality.

Working Definitions

It will be useful to give some working definitions of the terms used throughout this book. However, the reader will derive insights into the reality to which these terms refer as more theories and analysis of facts are presented.

Social Welfare: Income Security and Social Services

Social welfare is a societal institution that provides members of a liberal democratic society assistance in cash or in kind, to assure them a certain standard of living within that particular society. As used in Canada, "social welfare" is a general term that encompasses the provision of "income security" and of "social services".

In addition, the term "social security" is often used to mean "social welfare" and this has led to some semantic confusion, since "social security" has the connotation of monetary aid. The ambiguous meaning of this term has arisen for two reasons. A major Canadian government report on social welfare issued in 1973 was entitled *Working Paper on Social Security in Canada*, although the subjects discussed in that paper pertained to both the income security and social services aspects of social welfare. Second, the term "social security" was first used in the United

States in reference to a public pension plan. In our book, however, social welfare will be considered as consisting of two key units: income security and social services. These are characterized by four points.

First, a societal institution is a pattern of organizational structures and individual behaviour centred around some salient feature of human life, such as economic activities, politics, family, or law. Social welfare as a societal institution touches upon various other institutions—economic life, family, political system, to name a few.

Second, social welfare encompasses programs consisting of either cash assistance or services. The former is known as income security, income support, or income maintenance programs. Throughout this book, we will use the term *income security* to mean a form of compensation, social insurance benefit, or outright grant that can be either unconditional or based on a means/need test, or negative income tax. Social services, on the other hand, refer to any kind of personal or community services other than income support, such as daycare, probation, and legal aid.

Because of the unsavoury connotation that the word "welfare" has acquired in recent years, some governments have changed the name of their departments of social welfare to "Department of Social Services", although these departments are still very much involved in income security programs. In this book we will reserve the term *social services* for those programs that provide services and not income security.

The third point in our definition, while related to the first, is the most difficult to clarify because of the normative element contained in its definition. What constitutes social welfare is really a value judgement because objective standards can indicate only the range of possibilities; any cutoff point can be chosen only on the basis of moral, economic, or other considerations. In any particular society, we can point to a minimum subsistence standard short of which a person cannot live. For example, a person living in Canada must have *x* amounts of food, shelter, and clothing in order to survive. We can also point to average standards that a majority of Canadians seem to have attained; perhaps we can even single out a few exceptional cases that indicate the upper limits of affluence enjoyed by a minority. However, it is an entirely different matter to say what level of living *should* be insured for *all* members of a society. This depends on the overall level of wealth accumulated in the society, as well as the willingness of the richer members to part with some of their material security. Thus, the definition of what constitutes either component of social welfare has purposely been kept vague to avoid the moral dilemma of quantifying what should be ensured at "a certain level". This "ensured level" is usually decided upon by the ministers and senior administrators of governments who initiate and devise the programs. Once chosen, it can be empirically investigated and verified. In Canada, the level of living ensured for all citizens by social welfare is rather low, being close to minimum subsistence standards.

Finally, the above definition of social welfare is used in reference to that category of nation states to which Canada belongs: the advanced capitalist, democratic state. As will be explained later, capitalism continually generates social inequality, and social welfare concerns the distribution of society's benefits to its members in the face of such inequalities. The usual formal channels of distribution are provided in the political, legal, and government bureaucratic institutions and, to a decreasing extent, in private organizations. These operating mechanisms infuse the social welfare institution in advanced capitalist societies with distinctive characteristics.

Analysis of social welfare in this book is limited to that in advanced capitalist societies in general and Canada in particular. The study of social welfare in so called socialist countries merits a separate book. Social inequalities in those countries are of a different kind, and the role of social welfare, although still concerned with distribution of benefits, is also quite different. Suffice it to say that since the means of production are state-owned in socialist countries, there are no social class distinctions based on ownership of productive property, and there is less income inequality in socialist than in capitalist countries. Moreover, social wage, rather than individual wage, is emphasized in socialist countries. Thus, social welfare tends to ensure the optimal standard of living available in those societies rather than the minimum standard in capitalist countries (Drover, 1981).

The Welfare State

Some of the main features of the welfare state have already been alluded to in the definition of social welfare above. A theory of the welfare state is presented in chapter 5 and further examined in chapter 8. Here, we offer a definition from the liberal perspective. The welfare state is "a state in which organized power is deliberately used (through politics and administration) in an effort to modify the play of market forces in at least three directions" (Briggs, 1967, p. 29). These directions are (a) the provision of a minimum income for all; (b) the provision of income for certain contingencies, such as sickness or old age; and (c) the provision of certain social services. As Gough (1978) has noted, the state also modifies the play of market forces by way of legislation, such as that for minimum wages, rather than direct provision of benefits in cash and kind.

When the term "welfare state" is used, the stress is on public provision of assistance. This emphasis reflects the situation that has developed since the Second World War, as the state in capitalist societies has increasingly taken over this role from private individuals and charitable organizations. This book focuses on the Canadian welfare state, but will also give some attention to social agencies in the private sector—charitable organizations, volunteers, and self-help groups—especially as to how these are connected with the welfare state. The welfare state and social welfare in the private sector together make up the institution of social welfare.

Social Policy

Public policy is usually defined as authorized collective intervention. Social policy is that part of public policy undertaken, for a variety of political reasons, to affect some aspect of social life (Yelaja, 1978; Armitage, 1975). Social policy is concerned with the formulation, development, and management of government welfare services at all levels. Inputs to the public administration of services come not only from government, but also from other groups, such as business, labour, voluntary organizations, churches, and interest groups.

Yelaja makes a distinction between social welfare policy and social policy in general. The former "is the expression of the philosophy and programmes concerning the poor, dependent, handicapped (physically and mentally), and other members of society who for a variety of reasons need support (economic, social, and psychological) for their well-being" (Yelaja, 1978, p. 7). It is only one facet of social policy.

Social policy in a broad perspective, on the other hand, is concerned with human resource development, either directly or indirectly. For example, as a social policy, health policy is directly concerned with human resource development because it defines the principles and conditions under which health services are provided to all. But, indirectly, health policy includes public health issues, such as nutrition, family planning, sanitation, education, physical fitness, and recreation (Yelaja, 1978, p. 7).

The narrow definition of social welfare policy carries with it a residual view of social welfare (explained in the next chapter). While the residual view should not necessarily pervade the institution of social welfare, it does reflect, unfortunately, the reality as it exists today. In this book, while the focus is on social welfare policies—for example, those related to income security and social services—every attempt is made to relate such specific policies to social policy in the broader sense, especially with regard to health and education.

Ideology

Ideology, as used in this book, is defined as "a pattern of beliefs and concepts (both factual and normative) which purport to explain complex social phenomena with a view to directing and simplifying socio-political choices facing individuals and groups" (Gould and Kolb, 1964, p. 135, parentheses in the original). This definition is included here because a distinction is made throughout the book between ideology and theory.

Model and Theory

Sociological Theory

A sociological theory is, on the other hand, a system of statements offered to describe and explain some social phenomenon. Where an ideology tends to be prescriptive and entails value judgements, a theory is an explanation supported by empirical evidence. Most sociologists would hasten to add that there is a great deal of variation in the structure of sociological theory. This does not mean that many sociological theories exist in, for instance, the areas of crime and delinquency, population explosion, family, or social change. In fact, some would argue that because of the problem in developing theory, there are few good sociological theories about society in general or any problem in particular. What is meant here is that statements, discourses, and writings that go by the name of sociological theory differ a great deal in their very makeup as theories. They vary in their level of analytical sophistication and degree of explanatory power. They also differ in scope of study (macrosociological or microsociological), factor used (naturalistic or systemic), and focus (social structure or process). Some theories are conceptually clear, logically consistent, and empirically tested. On the other hand, many theories exist that are barely more than descriptions of phenomena, often interspersed with hidden value judgements.

To understand these sociological theories is to look at them as a continuum. At one end of the continuum is the formal theory consisting of abstract and logical propositions about society that are systematically organized and supported by evidence (Zetterberg, 1962, p. 22; Kinloch, 1977, p. 12). At the other end of the continuum is the informal theory that is relatively unstructured, but supported by assumptions from everyday life. Very often it represents no more than a single hypothesis, ideology, or intuition. Some informal theories may have only the rudiments of a paradigm or a model. In sum, formal theories tend to be explanatory, scientific, deductive, and objective; informal theories are more descriptive, ideological, inductive, and intuitive.

Sociological Model and Orientations

There is a difference between a sociological model and a sociological theory. A model is a general mental construct about a social phenomenon: what it is like and how it works. In its more developed form, it is known as a paradigm. Models are constructed to generate propositions (hypotheses) about the relationships between phenomena. Where the hypotheses are tested and found to be true, they become theories. A theory is therefore a more precise and limited explanation of the relationship between two or more aspects of reality. In the hypothesis stage, a theory can also be verified or refuted. A model or perspective may be judged as fruitful, imaginative, partial, or misleading with respect to its capacity to generate testable hypotheses, but it cannot be found true or false because it is not stated as a proposition.

Insofar as models are mental pictures of reality, the approach to any phenomenon is usually taken from a particular angle, as when one takes a picture with a camera. Also, only selected elements are included in the model. Thus, models are sometimes loosely referred to as approaches and perspectives. These characteristics—vantage point and selectivity—also affect the hypotheses and, eventually, the theories that the model generates. A theory may be true; nevertheless, it gives a one-sided and limited explanation of the phenomenon in question. The important point is that all knowledge, particularly social knowledge, "is *perspectival*, that is, acquired from a particular standpoint" (Zeitlin, 1973, p. 57, emphasis in the original).

Within each of the four perspectives (or models) on welfare to be presented later, there have also been attempts at formal theorizing. Therefore, we shall first discuss each model in terms of its philosophy, ideology, and political implications; then we shall present some derived explanatory statements about the determinants, consequences, and implications of social welfare. The theories will be presented in chapter 5.

There are two major theoretical orientations in contemporary sociology: the consensus and the conflict orientations. Each orientation consists of a set of assumptions about human beings and their social systems. The models built on these assumptions and the theories subsequently derived from the models thus bear the imprint of those assumptions.

In the consensus orientation, the fundamental assumption is that members of a social system share common objectives and values. Social structures are, therefore, established on consensus. There is equilibrium among the subunits of the system. Stress in any part of the system is alleviated by adjustments in other parts to restore balance. Thus, the system maintains its boundaries and endures through time. This orientation emphasizes social integration and order.

The conflict orientation does not assume that members of a social system necessarily have values in common. On the contrary, individuals and groups (subunits of a social system) are thought to have different and even opposing interests and goals, which causes social conflict to become endemic to any system. Resolution of conflicts leads to transformation not only of the subunits, but also of the system itself. The emphasis within this orientation is on social change.

Of the four perspectives on social welfare to be discussed in chapters 2 to 5, three are founded, to varying degrees, on the consensus orientation. They are rugged individualism, modified individualism, and social democracy. The fourth, the Marxist approach, is characterized by the conflict orientation.

A Note on Liberalism

The theoretical models or perspectives to be discussed have their origins in political philosophies. In some circles, rugged individualism would be equated with conservatism and modified individualism with liberalism. However, it should be pointed out that these perspectives, especially the first three, are not necessarily the views followed by any of the major political parties in Canada—the New Democratic, Liberal, Progressive Conservative, Social Credit, or Parti Québécois—although each party may profess to adhere to one political doctrine. In fact, the Social Credit, Progressive Conservative, and Liberal parties are essentially similar in their approach to the welfare state in that they all work generally from the standpoint of liberalism. The basic premises of liberal thought cut across the categories called conservatism and liberalism. Hofstadter (1955) sees the roles of the liberal and the conservative so often intertwined and sometimes reversed that it would be difficult to speak of clear traditions. Wolff (1968) argued that there is really no fundamental disagreement in the overall political philosophy between the two. Similarly, strands of liberal thought run through the different models of social welfare. Thus, I have avoided labelling any particular perspective "liberal", "for the term liberalism confuses rather than clarifies discussion today" (George & Wilding, 1976, p. 21). The variants of liberalism differ in individualism to some degree. These differences are discussed in the next two chapters.

Although also influenced by liberalism, social democracy as a political philosophy has a slightly different ideological outlook. The two Canadian social democratic parties, the NDP and PQ, thus hold a somewhat different view regarding social welfare. In principle at least, they are inclined toward greater equality. However, as has been the experience of the Labour Party in Britain and the social democratic parties in northwestern Europe, the Canadian social democratic parties, which have been in power only provincially, have been faced with strictures imposed by the dominant capitalist mode of production. Thus in their *modus operandi*, the social democratic ideals of Canadians are subordinated to the functions of the state in a capitalist society, namely, facilitating the capital accumulation process and legitimizing the existing social order (see chapter 8). Although Canadian social democratic governments may have sought to remain committed to greater equalization, liberalism is nonetheless the view that has dominated the development of social welfare in those provinces.

2

Rugged Individualism

Individualism is a composite ideology with contradictory drifts.[1] On the one hand, it elevates individual initiative and drive; on the other, it presupposes obedience and conformity. Its dominant theme is that people must be as free as possible to pursue their interests and to face the consequences of their actions. At the same time, the power of the government must be limited and dispersed (Friedman, 1962, pp. 2–3). Individualism also postulates that each person is imperfect and should therefore be willing to submit to conventions, the design and justification of which may not be entirely understood by the individual (Hayek, 1949, p. 22). In promoting conformity to existing norms, rugged individualism reveals its conservative nature.

Social Darwinism

The roots of rugged individualism are found in the 19th-century ideology of social Darwinism, which was fervently espoused by business groups at the time (Martindale, 1960). As the name suggests, the social Darwinists borrowed ideas from Darwinian biology and used them to study human society. According to social Darwinism, the principles of natural selection and the survival of the fittest govern the evolution of all species. Charles Darwin himself applied his evolutionary theories to the development of human beings. Through natural selection, the ancestors of human beings developed intelligence, which made possible language, social organization, fire and tools, and eventually, culture. Intelligence and the subsequent development and acquisition of culture by human beings distinguished them as superior (Martindale, 1960, p. 163).

Although the operation of those two natural principles on human ancestors produced superior animals, the superior animals in turn created a civilization that thwarted the further operation of those laws. Darwin noted that medicine and health care kept alive the imbecile, the maimed, the sick, and the weak in civilized societies, thus checking nature's process of eliminating the unfit (Martindale, 1960). On the other hand, the standing army in every country consisted of the finest young men who were exposed to early death in combat, and were prevented from procreating at the prime of life. Moreover, children whose parents died early were likely to marry earlier, and therefore pass on their inferior constitutions to a larger number of descendants. Darwin thus saw in civilized societies tendencies contrary to the laws of natural selection and survival of the fittest. These tendencies resulted in the elimination of the fittest and the proliferation of the weak and the unfit.

While Darwin himself was a "social Darwinist", it was Herbert Spencer the sociologist who systematized the implications of Darwinian evolutionary theory in the study of human life. Some of Spencer's writings on social selection predated Darwin's publication of *Origin of Species*; in fact, Spencer coined the expression "survival of the fittest". More importantly, he converted Darwin's theories from explanations of how things operate in the world into an ideology of how things ought to operate, which became the ideology of social Darwinism (Martindale, 1960).

Spencer was a staunch supporter of classical *laissez-faire* principles. He was opposed to any form of state intervention. In his view, human society was like an organism that inevitably perfects itself. "Progress, therefore, is not an accident, but a necessity. Instead of civilization being artificial, it is a part of nature; all of a piece with the development of the embryo or the unfolding of a flower" (Hofstadter, 1955, p. 40). State interference with the "natural" growth of society was repugnant to him. Poor laws, public education, state regulation of sanitation and housing would only impede the natural process. "The whole effort of nature is to get rid of such (the unfit, the poor), to clear the world of them, and make room for better" (Hofstadter, 1955, p. 41, words in parentheses added).

A third energetic proponent of social Darwinism was William Graham Sumner. Like Darwin and Spencer, he saw the original human situation as a struggle for existence and a process of natural selection. In this respect, Sumner's individualism was extreme. He argued that "individual self-assertion was the only satisfactory expression of the wisdom of nature, and asked of the community only that it would give full play to this self-assertion" (Hofstadter, 1955, p. 8).

From competition for survival Sumner went on to argue for the importance of capital accumulation for civilization. He viewed the captains of industry and capital as the great competitors in modern society and the millionaires as a product of natural selection; their wealth was considered legitimate and justified because they rendered great services to society. Inequality of the social classes was normal to Sumner. He stated that the greatest folly in the world was "to sit down with a slate and pencil to plan out a new social world" (quoted in Martindale, 1960, p. 166).

Social Darwinism has been used to promulgate the conservative outlook in two ways. First, it legitimizes such notions as the following: that the best competitors in the struggle for existence would win, and that competitive struggle would lead to continuing improvement. It does this by elevating these notions to the status of a natural law. Second, it argues that all sound development must be gradual and slow, since evolution took place over aeons (Hofstadter, 1955).

Residual Conception of Welfare

Social Darwinism has been discussed in some detail because it gives expression to rugged individualism in its starkest form. In the present century, proponents of rugged individualism are no less strident, although they seldom use the terms of evolutionary theory. Their views contribute to the residual conception of social welfare. The two leading spokesmen for rugged individualism are F.A. von Hayek and Milton Friedman. The main value they champion is freedom, which is often used interchangeably with individualism. Freedom is defined "primarily in negative terms as the absence of coercion" (George & Wilding, 1976, p. 22).

Hayek concedes that "(only) the coercive measures of the government need be strictly limited . . . that there is undeniably a wide field for noncoercive activities of government and that there is a clear need for financing them by taxation" (1967, p. 239). However, he sees many of the welfare activities of government essentially as a threat to freedom because "though they are presented as mere service activities, they really constitute an exercise of the coercive powers of government and rest on its claiming exclusive rights in certain fields" (1967, p. 240). He sees the government's attempts to bring about a more equitable distribution of income in society and to ensure all its people a given standard of life as examples of government's use of its coercive powers. The attempts constitute an unequal treatment of different people that Hayek declares is irreconcilable with a free society (1967, p. 241).

Friedman believes that competitive capitalism is the best model of a society organized through voluntary exchange, not coercion. When the effective freedom of exchange is maintained, the market economy prevents one person from interfering with another's activities. The market is capable of protecting the consumer, the seller, the employee, and the employer from each other. The consumer is protected because he or she can always buy from other sellers. The seller is protected because there are other consumers who can be his potential buyers. The employee is protected because there are other employers he can work for, and so on. This process is carried out impersonally and without centralized authority (Friedman, 1962, pp. 14–15).

Hayek and Friedman hold the common assumption that income and wealth inequality in capitalist societies is natural. They accept the existence of social inequality; moreover, they obviously do not consider the extent of inequality either excessive or harmful to society (George & Wilding, 1976, p. 26). In fact, they believe inequality to be conducive to economic growth and, therefore, justified. This means that they believe only in the equality of people in one sense: each has an equal right to freedom; one might add that this is the freedom to compete. They would "distinguish sharply between equality of rights and equality of opportunity, on the one hand, and material equality or equality of outcome, on the other" (Friedman, 1962, p. 195). The rugged individualist would accept the former but reject the latter. They would regard "private charity directed at helping the less fortunate as an example of the proper use of freedom" (1962, p. 195). They would even "approve state action toward ameliorating poverty as a more effective way in which the great bulk of the community can achieve a common objective" (1962, p. 195). But this would be done with regret for it would mean having to replace voluntary with compulsory action.

The rugged individualists' attitude toward social welfare is closely linked to their views on government. They see the need for government even in a market economy. But the market greatly reduces the government's decision-making powers, restricting its role to that of "a forum for determining the 'rules of the game' and . . . an umpire to interpret and enforce the rules decided on" (Friedman, 1962, p. 15). Aside from this, rugged individualists would concede to government action in the alleviation of poverty, but not in lessening inequality. Nevertheless, they are quick to add that one major cost of the extension of government welfare activities in recent decades has been the corresponding decline in private charitable activities.

According to Friedman (1962, p. 191–92), two points should be made quite clear in discussing government welfare programs. First, if the objective is to alleviate poverty, then the program should be designed to help the poor. It should help people as people, not because of any special status, such as membership in a particular age group, occupational group, wage-rate group, or minority group. In other words, rugged individualists are opposed to any government attempt to redistribute income or any kind of welfare measure other than outright cash subsidy to the needy. Second, the best method of delivering the needed cash is, according to Friedman (1962, p. 192), the negative income tax.[2] He believes that the scheme specifically addresses the problem of poverty by providing assistance in the most useful form—cash. In addition, although the program operates outside the market, it does not eliminate the work incentive entirely. The defect of price supports, minimum wage legislation, public housing, social insurance plans, and so on, is that they distort the market.

Rugged individualists usually give four reasons for their objection to the welfare state:

1. Substantial increases of welfare programs by government incite dissatisfaction among the minorities and foster animosity among potential recipients. Social disruptions result as various groups clamour for their rights.

2. Government welfare measures waste resources.
3. Government welfare measures promote economic inefficiency.
4. Government welfare measures lead to tyranny and thus obliterate individual freedom (George & Wilding, 1976, pp. 27–30).

Rugged individualists have a basic distrust of the welfare state because, to them, it represents socialism in embryo. In their opinion, although people in western capitalist societies have rejected socialism as a system, they are still attracted to the political ends of socialism, the chief among which is equality. To the rugged individualist, the welfare state is bound to lead back to socialism (Hayek, 1967, p. 239).

In short, rugged individualists believe that competitive capitalism is a natural process. In a capitalist society individuals and families, assured of freedom, should be able to meet their needs through the marketplace. Members of society should be given relief only when the functioning of the normal channels—the family and the market—has broken down. Should a few be unfortunate enough to fall into poverty, the state could provide the needed cash, although private charity would have been more in accord with the ideal of voluntary free action. Aid must not threaten or undermine the operations of the marketplace in distributing benefits, nor should it erode the wage-earners' sense of responsibility for the welfare of their families (Room, 1980, p. 49). The rugged individualists hold a residual and means-tested conception of the welfare state. In this conception, social welfare is "a residual agency, attending primarily to emergency functions, and is expected to withdraw when the regular social structure—the family and the economic system—is again working properly" (Wilensky & Lebeaux, 1965, p. 139).

Although Friedman would like to see public assistance to the destitute restricted to cash subsidy only, the residual concept of welfare has been employed more broadly. The concept can also be found in many other forms of social welfare involving subsidized goods and services to the poor. Public housing and legal aid are two examples. But the underlying principle remains the same: social welfare is provided in times of emergency when the normal channels of procuring goods and services are malfunctioning.

---

1. Chapters 2-4 incorporate many ideas and insights found in George and Wilding (1976).

2. An example of the negative income tax is the Refundable Child Tax Credit (see chapter 9).

3

Modified Individualism

Rugged individualism has been discussed at some length because the basic ideology of individualism shaped the Canadian welfare state from its inception and continues to exert a great deal of influence on welfare programs. However, the ideology of individualism that accompanied the emergence of the Canadian welfare state and that continues to influence its course today is a modified version of individualism. Rugged individualism has given way to a form of individualism that allows for government action to ensure the social security of all the people.

Reluctant Collectivism

The writers who led the process of modifying rugged individualism were John Maynard Keynes, William Henry Beveridge, and John Kenneth Galbraith. They have been referred to as the reluctant collectivists (George & Wilding, 1976). The term not only signifies their collectivist orientation—toward publicly provided welfare—but also implies their basic adherence to individualism. Their thinking, especially that of Beveridge, had a strong impact on Leonard Marsh who, in turn, helped lay the foundation of the welfare state in Canada.

The basic value premises of the modified individualists are the same as those of the rugged individualists. Like the rugged individualists, they believe in liberty, individualism, and competitive capitalism, and are not egalitarian. Inequality is perceived to have social and psychological functions in that enterprising people are thought to heed money-making opportunities in order to avoid turning to cruel and reckless pursuits. Without differences of rewards, it is considered that labour would lose all sense of direction. Lastly, like the rugged individualists, the modified individualists are basically conservative in that they accept the existing social and political order as given (George & Wilding, 1976, p. 45).

The most fundamental common view shared by the rugged and modified individualists is that both endorse the competitive private enterprise system. But the latter are also motivated by a strong philosophy of humanism and are, therefore, concerned about "the human implications of capitalism" (George & Wilding, 1976, p. 43).

Adding to the rugged individualists' definition of freedom as the absence of arbitrary control by governments, the modified individualists insist that people should be free from economic servitude to the five giant social evils: want, disease, ignorance, squalor, and idleness. They seek to eliminate poverty and they see one of its major causes to be involuntary unemployment.

The modified individualists' humanitarian inclinations lead them to some sharp criticisms of capitalism. In a major departure from the view held by the rugged individualists, they do not consider the capitalist economy to be entirely self-regulating. Opposed to classical *laissez-faire* principles, the modified individualists argue that without state intervention, capitalism cannot solve the problems that it has created for itself, such as great imbalances in income and wealth, cyclical recession, structural unemployment, inflation, and technological development. They see that economic growth in advanced capitalist societies has not abolished poverty; rather, by its very nature, capitalism produces and perpetuates inequality and poverty (see chapters 6 and 7). To the modified individualists, the contrast between private wealth and public squalor observable in those societies is not only offensive but also potentially dangerous. It is felt that if the government did not provide certain services for the poor, there would be an increase in crime and social unrest. This theme would be repeated often in the development of the welfare state in advanced capitalist societies.

The modified individualists' second criticism is that unregulated capitalism is wasteful and inefficient. Both Keynes and Beveridge were appalled by the tremendous waste resulting from failure to use productive capacities during the depressed thirties. In more recent years, the powerful multinational corporations have been successful in pressuring the state to meet their requirements. Galbraith (1967) observes that the giant corporations demand defence, roads, airports, port facilities, research, and technological development—and these are met by the state. Basic human needs, on the other hand, are not met or are met inadequately. The powerless and the insignificant ask for care of the old, the disabled and the sick; legal aid; recreational facilities; and other social services. But these are neglected.

Modified individualists set forth a final criticism: in unregulated capitalism, interests of the economically dominant group come to be identified as the national interest. The state's selective response to demands from different groups just mentioned bears this out.

The modified individualists' concern about poverty and unemployment prompts them to ask for more government activities in assistance to the poor: public housing, universal health care, and protection against contingencies. Beveridge (1944), in particular, has argued for government implementation of social insurance plans and other policies securing full employment.

Although their criticisms of capitalism are substantial and their plea for social legislation in various areas, ardent, the modified individualists have no intention of destroying competitive private enterprise. On the contrary, their criticisms and their humanitarian impulses have led them to a defence of capitalism based on pragmatism. They see the faults of the capitalist system as technical in nature rather than fundamental, and thus amenable to correction. Indeed, capitalism generates inequality and poverty but the modified individualists accept inequality. They believe that government regulation of capitalism can eliminate poverty (Galbraith, 1969).

The idea of nonself-regulating capitalism is revolutionary; it allows for the re-entry of politics into the arena of economic activities (George & Wilding, 1976, p. 46). It is wise to examine the views of the modified individualists on government intervention in social and economic matters because the modified version of individualism, more than any other perspective or school of thought, has guided the development of the welfare state in all western capitalist societies including Canada. This does not mean that modified individualism is the best theory in terms of explaining the origins and results of the welfare state. Nevertheless, it does offer the most cogent justification for it. Furthermore, the operations of the welfare state are most closely guided by this variant of individualism.

Unlike the rugged individualists, modified individualists share with the social democrats "a belief in the benevolent potentialities of government action" (George & Wilding, 1976, p. 52). Keynes and Beveridge see the state as having regard only for the public interest. The state sits in independent judgement on the workings of private enterprises and the distribution of the national income, capable of producing sudden and unexpected solutions for human actors who, playing according to the rules of the capitalist game, encounter apparently unsolvable difficulties. Neither Keynes nor Beveridge views the state as the point where an array of conflicting interests and claims converge (George & Wilding, 1976).

Among the modified individualists, Galbraith has a somewhat different and more cynical view of the state. According to Galbraith, the giant multinational corporations have been able to promote their particular interests as the public interest. Nevertheless, he claims that the state can be liberated from this sectional domination by a demonstration of the difference between the particular corporate interest and the real public interest, and by the development of a critical public awareness.

Although the principle of government intervention in social and economic affairs is accepted by the modified individualists, they would still place limitations on government action. Their reasons are that (a) the problems of capitalism are only technical, so once they are solved, the system will function well; (b) capitalism is naturally superior and a source of individual freedom and initiative; and (c) government intervention, although sometimes necessary, is a potential threat to freedom (George & Wilding, 1976).

The modified individualists would like the state to carry out those activities at present not performed by the private sector and would likely be performed by no one at all if not undertaken by the state. Above all, they want the state to eradicate want. Beveridge has forwarded the notion that the government should assure all citizens a subsistence minimum. Galbraith has extended this idea, believing that the state should also eliminate relative poverty. As George and Wilding (1976, p. 53) observe, such ideas imply a qualitatively new, major expansion of government action: it ushers in the principle of partnership between government and business. The government, however, is considered responsible if things go wrong.

The direction taken by the modified individualists signifies a problem-centred, pragmatic approach to welfare. The ultimate concern of Keynes, Beveridge, Galbraith, and others who share their views is that of individualism within the general liberal tradition. The idea proposed is for an individualism with a collectivist tendency (Galper, 1975) that, in turn, reinforces individualism. In this case, the state is responsible for providing assistance, in cash or in kind, "to ensure each person sufficient freedom of expression and a sufficient base of physical well-being to permit active pursuit of that person's self-interest" (Galper, 1975, p. 21). Modified individualists hold the fundamental assumption that collective well-being is the total of individual well-being. Their concern is not about certain specified goals for the whole society, or even particular outcomes for individuals; the welfare state should, in their view, intervene to provide the individual with the opportunity to pursue self-interest.

The modified individualists thus establish "the principle of public responsibility for individual welfare" (Regush, 1972, p. 150). The welfare state is seen as acting with the social purpose of pursuing social values through public law (Schottland, 1967), and it includes all government functions (with the exception of military activity) that intervene to secure and to promote human well-being. This view is summarized by Wilensky and Lebeaux (1965) as the institutional conception of social welfare.

Institutional Conception of Welfare

Underlying the institutional conception of the welfare state is the assumption that industrialization and urbanization are natural forces in human progress. These processes are uncritically accepted by modified individualists as having a momentum and inner logic that lie beyond the control of humankind. While these processes are seen to bring progress to people, they nevertheless have some less desirable side effects that cause social disruption—for example, the decline of the extended family that looked after its members' welfare in the past. Just as industrialization and urbanization have arisen naturally, the welfare state is a natural, automatic, and necessary response to those social developments that have disturbed social harmony. The welfare state is a corollary to the decline of the extended "welfare" family (Briggs, 1967, p. 45). The important point to note is that industrialization, urbanization, and the development of the welfare state, as well as the larger capitalist system within which all these processes take place, are viewed as natural, automatic, and logical developments.

It is further assumed in the institutional conception that there is equilibrium among the various institutions (industries, economic activities, politics, social welfare, and so on) that make up the whole society in the capitalist system. Development in any of the parts that might disturb the equilibrium of the whole will automatically lead to changes in the other parts to restore balance. Since the various developments, such as industrialization, or the decline of the extended family, are necessary and logical phenomena, neither the cause nor the content of these developments is questioned or examined. Furthermore, since the various parts have a tendency to restore equilibrium within the whole capitalist system, the whole will not change but will endure in spite of minor modifications. Going on this assumption, modified individualists would argue that capitalist economies may not have been entirely self-regulating, but the total system is capable of generating new mechanisms (such as social welfare) to deal with poverty, overcrowding, and other less desirable effects of economic growth.

The assumptions of natural developments and automatic adjustments within capitalism that hold up Wilensky and Lebeaux's institutional conception is best illustrated by the writers' discussion of juvenile delinquency:

> The social problem of juvenile delinquency in many ways provides the best illustration of the theme of this book so far: that the technological changes of industrialism lead to changes in the structure of society; these societal changes . . . produce or intensify concern about certain social problems, which creates a demand for welfare services; the supply takes the form of social agencies, public and private, manned by professional social workers and other welfare specialists. On the *demand* side, the social problem of delinquency is linked to industrialization via the changes in stratification and social mobility which industry brings about; it is linked also to distinctively urban conditions. On the *supply* side, an army of specialists has been recruited and sometimes trained to cope with the problem, and both public and private agencies converge on it; police, schools, courts, with their associated detention and probation programs,

child guidance clinics, and youth boards are only the most obvious units in a complex welfare response (1965, p. 181, emphasis in the original).

From this interpretation, it would seem that the "natural" forces of supply and demand operate in juvenile delinquency just as they do in the marketplace!

Since the modified individualist view accepts the existing institutions and dynamics of the capitalist society as given, it projects a future that is essentially an elaboration and unfolding of the present system. It sees the welfare state developing a symbiotic relationship with the capitalist economy. The capitalist economy first creates the need for a welfare state and then uses the welfare state programs "to enable people to 'solve' problems in such a way that they continue, in Wilensky and Lebeaux's terms, to participate in the 'culture of capitalism' " (Galper, 1975, p. 16, quotes in the original).

Wilensky and Lebeaux thus believe that the residual conception of social welfare will become weaker and the institutional conception more dominant. In time, the welfare state will become the welfare society. "Under continuing industrialization all institutions will be oriented toward and evaluated in terms of social welfare aims" (Wilensky and Lebeaux, 1965, p. 147). Whether this statement is true or not is of course an empirical question. Wilensky and Lebeaux do not provide the facts nor the reasons for their belief. (The institutional conception of social welfare is further discussed in chapter 5.)

Development of the Welfare State in Canada

Since the development of the welfare state in advanced capitalist societies is most strongly guided by the modified individualist perspective, it is appropriate to digress here with an account of the emergence of Canadian social welfare. However, the focus is on the impact of modified individualism upon the Canadian welfare state.

Laissez-faire, rugged individualism was the dominant ideology in the early days of industrial capitalism in Canada, around the time of Confederation. It remained influential up to the end of the First World War and is still strong as an official ideology for the common people. But even in the initial years of Confederation, members of the Canadian business community "while protesting their devotion to the principles of *laissez-faire*, have never objected to state intervention in economic matters to benefit industry, and have frequently been clamorous in demanding it" (Wallace, 1950, p. 383). They early looked to the government to supply services and capital in developing natural resources and building roads, railways, and canals. However, adherents of rugged individualism loathed any kind of social legislation. There raged a violent controversy over compulsory, universal, free education, with indignant taxpayers asking "why they should be forced, against their will, to be their brother's teacher" (Wallace, 1950, p. 385).

Although there was support as early as 1881 for the idea that the government should provide for relief of the poor, the frontier mentality with its emphasis on self-reliance was popular. Those who, for any reason, were unfortunate enough to be needy were likely to be regarded as weak or lazy, but "were generally kept from starvation by the efforts of relatives, friends, or private charitable or religious organizations" (Wallace, 1950, p. 386). Local government participation in relief usually took the form of sending the poor, the homeless, and the unemployed to jails and reformatories. In short, up to the beginning of the First World War, the residual conception of social welfare prevailed, although business was successful in its lobby for state assistance in various ventures in the name of furthering trade and industry.

Between the two world wars, especially during the Great Depression and the severe prairie drought of the 1930s, the Canadian federal government—partly in response to agitation by the workers and the unemployed—vastly increased its intervention in social matters by assuming the responsibility of giving relief and cash assistance. This was a departure from the usual practice, as charity to the indigent was traditionally handled by the parish or the local community, a legacy of Elizabethan poor laws. The underlying belief was that only the local authorities could separate the undeserving poor from the truly needy (Adams et al., 1971). This legacy was inherited by Canada insofar as the British North America Act of 1867 gave the provinces, rather than the dominion, jurisdiction over welfare and local affairs (see chapter 9).

The federal government's relief grants and work projects to help the unemployed and the poor in the 1930s were *ad hoc* in nature. They were the federal government's initial attempts to expand its role in legitimizing the social order by promoting social justice and integration, and by providing disadvantaged groups with minimum social security (Stevenson, 1977). From then until now the federal government has, from time to time and depending on its financial capability, tried to extend its legitimization function. But the entry of the federal government into the arena of welfare programs during the interwar years was an important indicator of the arrival of the Canadian welfare state. (The legitimization function of the state is discussed in chapter 8 and federal-provincial relations in welfare are mentioned in chapter 9.)

The flurry of welfare activities before, during, and following the Second World War reflected changes in the prevailing ideological thinking. The decade of hardship and deprivation preceding the Second World War demonstrated to most people that unemployment and poverty were beyond their control, and that the causes for both were structural in nature and could be alleviated only by public effort. Thus rugged individualism was modified, and gave way to the principle of public responsibility for individual welfare. Leonard Marsh crystallized this concept.

Marsh headed the House of Commons Special Committee on Social Security. His *Report on Social Security for Canada*, submitted to the Advisory Committee on Reconstruction in 1943, "was a pivotal document in the development of war and postwar social security programs, the equivalent in Canada of the Beveridge Report in Great Britain" (Bliss, 1975, p. ix). In both his basic ideological orientation and proposed methods for implementation, Marsh was greatly influenced by Beveridge.

Anticipating the end of the Second World War, Marsh was particularly concerned about preventing the massive-scale unemployment that had occurred during the demobilization and return of troops from Europe following the First World War and during the Great Depression. He believed that social legislation in Canada had to be overhauled and extended. He wanted to establish a comprehensive scheme of social security against serious illness, prolonged unemployment, accident, and premature death. This would provide all citizens with a minimum of social security.

The reasons Marsh gave reflected the thinking of Beveridge and other modified individualists. First, he contended that industrialization was an ongoing process necessitating the provision of public welfare. "In modern economic life there are certain hazards and contingencies, which have to be met, some of them completely unpredictable, some of them uncertain as to time but in other ways reasonably to be anticipated" (Marsh, 1975, p. 9). He argued that programs should be "geared closely to consideration of the vast economic and social changes which are going on now, and which must continue only with the difference of changes in purpose and direction, once the war is over" (1975, p. 14). In other words, social security programs would protect people against budget-shattering contingencies and thus prevent poverty—a basic concern, as we have seen, of Beveridge and Galbraith.

Second, social security programs would constitute "one way of realizing nationally a higher standard of living, and of securing more freedom and opportunity through the use of such income as is available once social insurance has taken care of the minimum" (1975, p. 15). Here we see an emphasis on fundamental liberal values of freedom and opportunity.

Finally, like Beveridge, Marsh preferred the method of social insurance based on contribution—it would do away with the means-test, which was particularly painful for the low-income families applying for assistance. Moreover, according to Marsh, the compulsory nature of contribution to insurance would effectively cover the lower-middle income groups unable to provide health services, savings, and so on, to guarantee their own risks, or who would seldom buy expensive individual insurance, but who would also avoid joining the ranks of the destitute by accepting free or charitable services (1975, p. 62). Given the wider extension of pooling principles, greater purchasing power would be mobilized. Resources of the community are not just given to limited cases, as in assistance or relief, but extended to all who might be liable to similar risks (1975, p. 63).

Marsh recommended priority for strengthening unemployment insurance and establishing health insurance. The first would protect people against unemployment and, the second, against universal risks (1975, p. 267). He also made a case for children's allowance for *all* children as the key to consistency in a comprehensive scheme (1975, p. xxv).

When Marsh submitted his report in 1943, the unemployment insurance plan was already established in Canada. The family allowance was established in 1945 and, by 1969, all provinces had some form of health care plan—only British Columbia, Alberta, and Ontario operated their systems on the basis of social insurance. Not all of Marsh's recommendations were followed or implemented in the ways he suggested. But the general contours of Canada's social welfare programs since the Second World War were sketched out in his groundplan and, in the main, the same rationale was used. He emphasized, for instance, the notion of social investment. Social security payments, such as the social insurances and children's allowances, were not money lost but investments in morale and health, in family stability, and in future productive efficiency. The social security system, inasmuch as it demanded personal and community responsibilities from the citizens, would encourage an idea of common effort and foster national solidarity. Marsh concluded that "it has yet to be proved that any democracy which underwrites the social minimum for its citizens is any weaker or less wealthy for doing so" (1975, p. 274).

Development in Canadian social welfare since the end of the Second World War is examined in chapters 9 and 10.

4

Social Democracy

Social democracy stresses the positive role of the state. As a redistribution agent of benefits in society, the state is seen as acting independently of and, at times, in opposition to, the market mechanisms. Thus the state brings about certain changes and promotes an ethic that can reintegrate a society torn by conflicts brought on by market forces. These ideas can be traced to the sociology of Max Weber and Émile Durkheim (Room, 1979). In Britain, social democracy was championed by Richard Henry Tawney, and Beatrice and Sydney Webb. According to their view, social democracy "involved a dialectic between legislation from above and active citizenship from below" (Room, 1979, p. 38). This line of thought was further developed by Richard Titmuss and Thomas H. Marshall, two scholar-reformers who argued that, since the end of the Second World War, there had been a progressive dissolution of the cash nexus through social policy. Although both focused their attention on the British welfare state, their writings stimulated interest in the emergence and development of the welfare state throughout the West. Contemporary social democrats believe that if political leaders act conscientiously, the state will guarantee the citizens their social rights of free access "to an endowment from a common patrimony" (Room, 1979, p. 59). People will then be treated according to their needs, not according to their economic power. Thus the "need nexus" will replace the cash nexus.

Citizenship Rights

A fuller understanding of how the social democrats propose to treat people according to their needs will be gained by examining Marshall's view of the welfare state. Although Marshall's ideas are concerned in particular with the British welfare state, they are generally accepted within the social democratic perspective. Marshall assumes that a society undergoes structural differentiation in the process of industrialization: from a simple, communal society to a more complex one characterized by formal and rational relationships. He sees the origins of the welfare state in the progressive extension of citizenship rights to more groups, and finally to the whole population. He traces the development of civil, political, and social rights in England through the developments in legal institutions in the 18th century, in political institutions in the 19th century, and in the social services in the 20th century, respectively. Civil rights refer to rights of life, equality before the law, and the basic individual freedoms of association, belief, and opinion. Political rights are the democratic rights to vote and to seek political office. Social rights are more difficult to define. They include the rights "to a modicum of economic welfare and security . . . to share to the full in the social heritage and to live the life of a civilized being according to the standards prevailing in the society" (Marshall, 1963, p. 74). According to Marshall, the establishment of the welfare state coincides with the extension of social rights to all citizens.

As Marshall himself has observed, the substantial content of social rights is limited by the quantity of resources available in society and their distribution between competing claims. Typically, in an advanced capitalist society, any number of legal rights may be granted. But the effects of these laws are not felt by the ordinary citizen unless they can be realistically enforced. Social rights legislation seldom constitutes a decisive step toward putting policy into immediate effect; very often it is simply a declaration of policy that the government hopes to put into effect some day (Marshall, 1973, p. 104).

This means that certain social rights cannot be defined precisely; nor can they be enforced easily. What is more, meeting people's needs because they have social rights does not necessarily mean reducing class inequality. Indeed, Marshall recognized early that the welfare state is not an egalitarian endeavour. Equal citizenship status for members of a society does not necessarily entail equality in any other sense. As Mishra notes, Marshall has the analytical insight to see that the idea of the social provision of a basic minimum, even if it tends toward an optimum at times, is quite compatible with a system based on competition and inequality. "Thus equal status as a citizen is quite compatible with inequality . . . resulting from the operations of the market and other structures of capitalism" (Mishra, 1977, p. 22).

Redistribution

In order to provide a social minimum below which no one would fall, the social democrats believe in some types of redistribution in a capitalist society. First, redistribution of wealth, especially inherited wealth, is necessary and desirable because inequality of wealth is grossly unjust in the capitalist society. But the social democrats do not advocate the elimination of inequalities based on private ownership of productive property. They would leave the private sector and the basic structures of capitalism in their present form, but propose a mixed economy. They would like to make the public sector function so well that those who could not benefit from the private sector would be well compensated.

(Chapter 7 discusses wealth and income inequalities further.)

Second, the redistribution of opportunities is also very important to the social democrats, so that all citizens can reach the positions in the social hierarchy to which their natural talents entitle them (George & Wilding, 1976, p. 64).

Third, some form of income redistribution is also deemed necessary by the social democrats. Similar to their view on the redistribution of wealth, income redistribution is not seen as vertical redistribution from the owning class to the working class. The social democratic notion of redistribution of income is limited to horizontal redistribution, mainly within the working class. Redistribution takes place either over different periods in the life cycle of a person (for example, from the younger, productive years to the older, unproductive years, and from periods of employment to periods of unemployment), or from one segment of the working class to another (for example, from the healthy to the sick, from people without children to families with children).

Underlying this attitude toward income redistribution is the social democratic notion of equality. As George and Wilding (1976, p. 66) have noted, the social democrats do not quite answer the question of how much equality is desirable. It would appear that they consider equality to be something more than equality of opportunity, which is the ideal of the modified individualists, but something less than equality of income, which the social democrats consider to be interference with individual initiative and freedom. The social democrats contend that some forms of social and economic inequalities are useful and their reasons are remarkably akin to the functionalist explanation of social inequality advanced by Kingsley Davis and Wilbert Moore (1945). The social democratic argument for some degree of inequality is that once a reasonable provision has been made for all, exceptional responsibilities and talents require and deserve different rewards (George & Wilding, 1976).

Altruism and Community

Social democrats' faith in the political leaders' ethic of responsibility and the beneficent potential of the government is underpinned by a strong moral commitment to the values of compassion, social justice, and, above all, altruism. But altruism is not simply disinterested or spontaneous. Citing the blood donor as an example, Titmuss explains the meaning of altruism. People donate their blood for several reasons: they donate out of a sense of obligation, a need for social approval, a feeling of social belonging, or a general need to help. Many donors seem to realize that their gift to strangers may someday rebound to their own benefit. But this is something they do not desire immediately or ultimately (Titmuss, 1971, p. 238).

What is described here is altruism coupled with a feeling of reciprocity. Altruism and reciprocity together express a sense of caring and responsibility for one another and for the community as a whole (George & Wilding, 1976, p. 67). It is this concern for the community that is, according to the social democrats, the cornerstone of the welfare state.

Altruism and mutual concern are emphasized by Titmuss and other social democrats because they are seen as instruments of social integration. Social welfare provides opportunities for people to express their sentiments of altruism, reciprocity, and social duty. Titmuss (1971, p. 225) admits that the manner a society structures its institutions—particularly its health and welfare institutions—can encourage or discourage the feeling of altruism in people. The organization of these institutions can foster people's sense of integration or alienation.

Social welfare, while providing a context for the expression of altruism, is seen as performing stabilizing, preventive, and protective functions, responding to the changes in the functions and structures of the family. "Interpreted in this way, and not as the modern equivalent of Bismarckian benevolence, the social services become an ally—not an enemy—of industrial and technological progress" (Titmuss, 1958, pp. 117-118).

5

Marxism and Theories of Social Welfare

Marxism

Marxism includes Karl Marx's own writings as well as those of others who have conducted inquiry in and thereby contributed to the intellectual tradition that he founded. If we could cull from this vast intellectual legacy thoughts and ideas about welfare, two broad areas of concern stand out. First, the Marxist school of thought provides a comprehensive theory of society that explains the nature and development of welfare in the capitalist society. Second, it offers a normative view about the transcendence of capitalism and the establishment of a society whose most fundamental organizing principle is promoting human well-being (Mishra, 1977, p. 61).

The first area of concern can be said to comprise the more formal theory aimed at explaining the origin, function, and development of the welfare state in capitalist society. It includes Marx's own work and that of contemporary Marxists. The second is more of a model or perspective, consisting of the values, ideological commitments, and prescriptions of what ought to take place. Here, we are concerned mainly with Marx's own ideas; the theory of the welfare state developed by contemporary Marxists is presented later. The model will be discussed first as it provides the framework within which the formal theory can be better understood.

Marx's basic philosophy is humanism. He was keenly aware of the dignity, worth, and capacity for self-realization of every human being. But with the rise of industrial capitalism, he saw the increasing degradation of the human person in the industrial workers who had no control over their work process or product, and who had to live in squalor, insecurity, and poverty. He argued that workers were deprived of species life, the kind of activity they were capable of and fulfillment they were entitled to by virtue of their being human. People can produce, consume, think, reason, analyze, plan, love, cooperate with others, enjoy drama and music, and so on, as well as eat, sleep, and reproduce (which last three functions lower animals also perform). But in capitalist society, workers and the poor no longer had the opportunities to develop some of their human faculties. They must produce according to the dictates of the industry owners; aside from that, their existence was largely reduced to the animal level. On the other hand, the industry and land owners became enormously wealthy, their lives greatly enriched materially and mentally. Marx argued that this pattern of inequality necessarily developed from a system where productive property was privately owned, production was for profit, wealth was inherited, and resources and benefits were allocated through market operations.

According to Marx, if members of nonproperty-owning classes were to be the species beings they were entitled to be—thinking, producing, loving, and enjoying their work, living as free persons—capitalism must be abolished and communism established in its place. In a communist society, the means of production will be owned by all the people, who would decide what would be produced and how, according to some social criteria rather than profit. The fruits of labour produced through co-operation would be distributed according to the needs of the people. For Marx, social welfare would have been the distribution of all the benefits in society according to the needs of the members. Such a view would be congruent with Marx's basic value orientations: equality and abolition of class exploitation so that people could be truly human. However, his vision of what ought to be did not impair his ability to analyze what existed at that time.

Marx did not specify how communism would replace capitalism, but he suggested large-scale changes that would alter the nature of society as a whole, as well as small-scale changes that would modify existing society or that might cumulatively contribute to its radical change. He was intrigued by the transformation of feudal to capitalist societies in Western Europe, roughly between the 16th and 19th centuries, that produced change in almost every aspect of those societies. Based on his study of the transition from feudalism to capitalism in Europe, Marx argued that tensions between the *forces of production* on the one hand and the *relations of production* on the other in a given society would eventually lead to the transformation of that society.

The forces of production refer to those factors needed for production: materials, energy, technology, as well as the knowledge and skills residing in the human workers and the work relations in which they are involved. The relations of production are legal-formal property relations. In capitalist society, these property relations produce at least two social classes: productive-property owners and propertyless people. The latter usually work for the former. According to Marxist theory, in the early phase of capitalism, property relations foster and facilitate the continual growth of productive forces. In later phases, however, the forces of production are held back and hindered in their growth by property relations. Social class conflicts then ensue. In the process, the propertyless workers acting as a class, try to destroy the restrictions imposed by property relations in an attempt to achieve those ideals stated earlier in the discussion of Marx's humanist values: production according to some social criteria and distribution according to people's needs.

In Marx's scheme, the *mode of production* consists of two parts: static property relations of production and dynamic forces of production (Zeitlin, 1967, p. 67). The former advance, retard, or block the growth of the latter. The potential of the forces of production cannot be based on technological calculations alone, but can be released with the removal of property relations of production that hamper their growth. Only then will the further development of the forces of production and newer forms of human activity again become possible. The mode of production changes as a result of the development in the productive forces and of changes in the relations of production. And changes in the mode of production lead to changes in other spheres of social life as, for example, in the legal, political, ideological, and cultural aspects.

Because he stresses the importance of the forces of production in social change, Marx is sometimes accused of advocating technological determinism. But Marx's theory is not merely technological, since he views the tension between productive forces and property relations as more than merely a lack of adjustment between technical innovations and their social application. According to Marx, one cannot measure productive forces purely in terms of science and technology, apart from the legal-formal property relations in which they are found. One can only guess the potential of a given technology under different relations of production. And the social class interested in maintaining the existing property relations will put up a great deal of resistance to change (Zeitlin, 1967, p. 67). Moreover, Marx's "forces of production" first and foremost refer to the interaction of people with nature and with one another. This is a human-centred view.

A Critique of the Perspectives

Modified individualism was compared with rugged individualism in chapter 2. In this section, the similarities and differences among modified individualism, social democracy, and Marxism will be highlighted, and their implications for social welfare emphasized. The formal theories derived from these perspectives or models are presented in the following section.

Modified Individualists and Social Democrats

The position of the social democrats is often described as lying somewhere between the modified individualists and the Marxists. The boundaries between the social democrats and their counterparts to the left or the right are sometimes blurred (George & Wilding, 1976). This is one way to describe social democratic thinking. But it would be more accurate to say that the middle ground occupied by the social democrats is not so much a stepping stone in the linear progession from individualism to Marxism, as a wellhead of contradictory tendencies. The contradictions lie in the discrepancies between aspects of social democracy's *analysis* of capitalism and the welfare state on the one hand, and the *prescriptions* it offers as to what the welfare state should be, on the other. Parts of social democratic analysis seem to reflect the critical view of the capitalist system that is shared by the Marxists. However, most social democratic ideals for the welfare state are oriented toward legitimizing and supporting the capitalist system, which in effect are the aims of individualists. In the end, it appears that when social democrats come face to face with the dilemmas of choosing radicalism or conservativism, as presented by their own analysis, they have often taken the side of the individualists. Nevertheless, their rhetoric continues to have a collectivist, radical ring.

The normative and prescriptive nature of the social democratic view is nowhere clearer than in (a) their advocating the institutional conception of social welfare which, as will be remembered, is also espoused by the modified individualists; and (b) their concern for the community. We have already discussed the latter in connection with altruism. Here we shall examine the social democrats' support for the institutional conception and its implications.[1]

Institutional Conception of Welfare Re-examined

To begin with, the residual and the institutional conceptions of social welfare are "strongly and explicitly normative, but not markedly theoretical in a sociological sense" (Pinker, 1971, p. 105). Neither derives logically from any major tradition of social theory. Both set forth certain goals of social welfare for which people *ought* to strive. The debate over the residual conception of the rugged individualists and the institutional conception of the modified individualists and social democrats is therefore over values. As Titmuss has observed, there is "no escape from value choices in welfare systems" (1974, p. 132). And he adds that the study of social policy issues is "to expose more clearly the value choices confronting society—whether they relate to medical care, social security, education, and other services which, in essence, involve social relations and systems of beliefs" (1974, p. 136).

That Titmuss's approach derives from ethical rather than sociological theory he himself makes very clear. His insistence on the impossibility of any value-free study of social welfare is shared by other social democrats (Marshall, 1972). But a problem raised by the social democratic approach to social welfare centres not so much on the question of values as on the question of choice. "The problem is that the rhetoric of choice can conceal ambiguities—of reasoning as well as value judgements" (Mishra, 1977, p. 13). In defining and conducting the debate in terms of the residual and institutional conceptions, social democrats ignore other ways of looking at welfare. There seems to be "an implicit value judgement, a tacit understanding of the limits within which the debate on welfare is to be carried out" (Mishra, 1977, p. 11). As a result, value judgements that are made explicit in fact conceal implicit and unexamined value orientations. An example of the excluded alternatives is the critical Marxist conception. Social democrats share with Marxists the ideal of institutionalizing welfare as a normal feature of and central value in society. However, they differ from the latter in asserting that this can be achieved without eliminating capitalism. The Marxists maintain that the profit motive that lies at the core of capitalism is basically antithetical to the ideals of a society founded on equality: producing and distributing goods and services according to the needs of the people. In the institutional conception of the social democrats, institutionalization of welfare is compatible with capitalism. It is not clear why social democrats fail to consider the Marxist conception of welfare which advocates a distribution based on needs and requires a certain type of social action. They have simply made a value choice to focus the debate in terms of a dichotomy, leaving out a third option.

Marshall (1965, pp. 166–83), however, saw all three types of aims as possible for social welfare policies: the elimination of poverty, the maximization of welfare, and the pursuit of equality. These three types of aims correspond roughly to the three general conceptions of welfare: the residual, the institutional, and the Marxist. In Marshall's view, the aim to maximize welfare best expresses the philosophy of the welfare state, a concept which embraces the elimination of poverty. But the third aim—the pursuit of equality—is simply not considered.

As Mishra (1977, p. 13) has pointed out, without including the Marxist conception and the implicit pursuit of equality as a value choice, it is difficult to make real sense of the institutional conception. One can only view the institutional conception as a compromise between the residual and the Marxist conceptions, and that changes the basic nature of the institutional conception, for the institutionalization of welfare causes it to be part of the existing unequal relations of liberal capitalism. The structural constraints posed by capitalism on the development of welfare is likewise accepted.[2] So ultimately the social democratic approach to the welfare state is one of administrative intervention and piecemeal social engineering. It leans toward the residual conception of welfare while holding on to the institutional conception in name. The difference between the two is one of degree, not of quality. How the problem of poverty is researched and studied is a case in point. Mishra notes that poverty is regarded as a central problem for social reform and is therefore singled out as a distinct and separate condition to be studied and perhaps solved administratively, without altering the broad socio-economic structures and organizing principles that generate poverty. This approach gives relief, rather than a treatment of causes. "It could therefore be argued that to label the extreme consequences of stratification as poverty, and to seek a solution through piecemeal social measures, is to accept the structural inequalities of capitalism. Indirectly, then, it is a decision to keep the problem within the bounds of capitalism" (Mishra, 1977, p. 12). This approach to welfare has certain implied values. It is fair to say that a "residual" attitude has crept in and characterized the social democratic approach that essentially follows the institutional conception of welfare.

In summary, the three conceptions of welfare (residual, institutional, and Marxist) mentioned above are all informed by values. The social democrats have in the main advocated the institutional conception. Their vision is of a humanitarian society that not only eliminates poverty, but also redistributes wealth and equalizes opportunities through affirmative programs. Above all, they envision a community where people are free to express sentiments of fellowship and altruism, but where, at the same time, the capitalist system and market mechanisms are also free to operate and produce inequalities. Thus, essentially, the institutional conception has a residual element in that the structural inequalities of capitalism are accepted as being compatible with welfare measures. The prescriptive view of welfare advanced by social democrats is supportive of the status quo, and in the end, this view serves to justify and rationalize social welfare, rather than to explain it, in the capitalist system.

From this discussion of the institutional conception, it is possible to conclude that the social democrats' pragmatic approach is very close to, and at times indistinguishable from, that of the modified individualists. However, some differences do exist. To reiterate, social democrats place far greater emphasis on some types of equitable distribution of resources and benefits in society than do modified individualists. They also attribute a greater potential to government action. Underlying these social democratic ideas is faith in compassion, altruism, and humanitarianism, a moral commitment that is less important to modified individualists.

Social Democrats and Marxists

It has been asserted earlier that social democrats share some prescriptive views of the welfare state with modified individualists. But in their analysis of capitalism and the welfare state, the social democrats are at times close to the Marxists. In this section, the similarities and the differences between social democrats and Marxists are discussed.

Some social democratic analysis of the capitalist system has yielded knowledge from which formal theories explaining social phenomena can be formulated. This critical questioning of various aspects of social welfare in the capitalist society, if carried further, would likely result in a theory on the level of Marxist theory. Marxism certainly argues that capitalism must be absolished if a welfare society is to be established in which distribution occurs according to needs. It appears to be the social democratic view that the existing welfare state can fulfill expectations of redistribution of social benefits and that there is no need for a new social order to realize the ideal community.

But the social democrats stop short in their analysis, so that the latter view, although implied, is never clearly articulated. Instead, they deal with what the welfare state *ought* to do within the bounds of capitalism and declare that the ideals are already being fulfilled within capitalist societies. An example is Marshall's hypothesis of the development of the welfare state corresponding to the extension of social rights to all citizens. As discussed earlier, he sees the equality of status ensured by citizenship rights as the fulfillment of the ideals of the welfare state, a situation which, to his view, is quite compatible with the inequality of capitalism. In his analysis, he rightly sees welfare as legitimizing inequality. But contrary to the Marxists, Marshall sees nothing problematic in this. "It [welfare] represents the convergence without which the composite social system would have had little chance of stabilizing itself. . ." (1972, p. 26). This emphasis on social integration is of course shared by Titmuss. This functionalist approach is further transmuted into a normative stance. Marshall sees the social change sought by the discontented as one of values and attitudes rather than one of basic structures. "I see no reason why their aims should not be achieved—if they can be achieved at all—within a social framework that includes representative government, a mixed economy, and a Welfare State" (Marshall, 1972, p. 32).

This elucidation by Marshall summarizes the irreconcilable differences between the social democrats and the Marxists. The latter seek the transformation, not just of values and attitudes, but of the basic structure of society as well. To the Marxists, true welfare is impossible in a mixed economy; it requires instead a society where private ownership of productive means is abolished.

Theories of Social Welfare

Five theories of social welfare can be derived from the models discussed above. The *economic theory* of social welfare is predominantly based on rugged individualism. The *theory of technological determinism and convergence* stems principally from modified individualism, although its main thesis is probably acceptable to many social democrats. As modified individualism and social democracy do share several similar views, two closely related theories—the *functionalist* and the *pluralist*—derive from both these perspectives. Finally, the *Marxist* theory of the welfare state develops from Marxism.

The Economic Theory of Welfare

The economic theory of welfare, based on the philosophy of rugged individualism and welfare economics, does not so much explain the welfare state as provide criteria for evaluating government social policy and guidelines for the future (Gough, 1978). As has been discussed above, the basic premise of rugged individualism is that individuals must be free to pursue their own interests, especially economic goals, with as little government intervention as possible. The unrestrained operation of the market will maximize welfare for everyone. Of course, the economic theory of welfare as a derivative of the model espouses the same notions. It uses "an individualist methodology which is profoundly unsociological" (Gough, 1978, p. 34). As Gough (1978) notes, the theory posits an atomized society that consists of individuals, where there are no classes or class interests. State expenditures and social policies are considered to be ultimately determined by the electorate, as voters' choices are assumed to be autonomous and unaffected by any social influence such as the mass media. The state is equated with the legislature. Finally, the theory also assumes near-total consensus among the members and, conversely, the absence of coercion in the liberal democratic society.

This theory's normative stance on freedom precludes any real explanation of the role of the state in the development of welfare. Thus no explanatory propositions can be stated here. Instead, the theory specifies a number of functions the government must fulfill. It must

1. Act as a rule-maker and umpire;
2. Define and enforce private property rights;
3. Provide a stable monetary framework;
4. Prevent the formation of monopolies;
5. Provide those necessary goods and services that cannot be consumed individually but necessarily benefit all members of the society as, for example, defense and national security; and
6. Compensate for the effect of gross "externalities" that occur "when the production or consumption of goods imposes costs (or provides benefits) to persons other than those doing the producing or consuming," as in government intervention in cases of severe environmental pollution by private industries (Gough, 1978, p. 33).

The economic theory of welfare is essentially an informal theory of social welfare: it is largely ideological and prescriptive. In many ways, it is more a perspective than a theory.

The Theory of Technological Determinism and Convergence

Modified individualists see industrialization and urbanization as natural and inexorable processes in human development, and a theory of social welfare can be derived from this perspective. Various welfare activities are established first by individuals and private organizations, and then increasingly by the state, to soften and redress the undesirable side effects of progress. As societies advance technologically, the differences in ideology and material conditions between the free enterprise capitalist system and the centrally planned socialist system may diminish and, perhaps, even disappear some day (Kerr et al., 1960). In other words, the logic of industrialism carries both kinds of societies toward a common institutional arrangement, the development of social welfare policy by the state being only one component of this commonality.

To cast the ideas of the modified individualists into a formal theory, we can state the technological determinism/convergence theory thus:

1. Industrialization is a natural process in the development of the human race.
2. State social welfare policy is a natural feature of industrialization, which lessens the personal and community upheaval generated by industrialization and its concomitant process, urbanization.
3. Industrialization may take different routes in different societies initially, but the logic of industrialism leads to common institutional patterns in all societies.

The technological determinism/convergence theory draws our attention to the interconnections between industrialization, society, and social welfare. Any perceptive analysis of social welfare or of modern industrial societies cannot ignore these interconnections. However, the deterministic nature of the theory reduces its usefulness in applications to the real world. Since social welfare policy is seen "as an adjunct to industrial development, virtually everything that happens appears as necessary and inevitable" (Mishra, 1981, p. 48). A major problem with the technological determinism/convergence theory is that embedded in its notions of inevitability is an ideological bias toward accepting the existing social arrangements as naturally given. Such an ideological bias is an "endorsement of the institutional pattern of welfare as the most 'appropriate' for advanced industrial society" (Mishra, 1981, p. 48, quotes in the original). The bias leads logically to apathy because no purposeful human action to change the present course of industrial development can be considered. Similarly, no alternative kinds of welfare provision could even be envisioned.

Also, whether or not convergence has taken place remains an empirical question. The limited comparative data that do exist point to real differences between the capitalist and socialist systems in both basic social structures and the function of social welfare within them.

The Functionalist Theory of Social Welfare

Despite the differences between the modified individualists and social democrats discussed above, the functionalist theory of social welfare encompasses ideas and sentiments that are present in both.

According to the functionalist theory, every social system must meet four functional prerequisites in order to persist:

1. *adaptation* to the external environment to provide members with a means of livelihood;
2. *goal attainment:* co-ordination of collective activities to reach certain goals;
3. *integration* of members to maintain cohesion, solidarity, and harmony; and
4. *pattern maintenance,* through which basic social values are perpetuated.

According to the perspectives of both modified individualism and social democracy, the function of social welfare is integration, a process which occurs in two ways. First, the state establishes welfare measures to minimize tensions among various groups or social classes, thus enhancing harmony within the larger society and contributing to the stability of the social order. Second, social welfare programs offer members of society opportunities to express concern for each other. Expressions of altruism strengthen solidarity within the community, the sense of being a part of a community.

Functionalists also propose that, in simpler societies, provision for people's needs and expression of solidarity typically take place within the family and kinship groups. In more complex societies, structural differentiation takes place such that specific institutions arise to perform specialized functions.

The functionalist theory of social welfare can be summarized in three statements:

1. Social welfare activities perform the integrative function in society;
2. Social welfare activities contribute to sentiments of communal solidarity; and
3. Formal social welfare activities develop as a society becomes more complex and undergoes structural differentiation.

The major criticism that is made of the functionalist theory is that it emphasizes continuity and stability of the present system and offers no hypothesis on social change. The conservative bias in functionalism makes it an inappropriate tool for the analysis of social welfare in relation to change.

The Pluralist Theory of Social Policy

This is a political theory that has roots in liberalism. Its basic premises are congruent with the ideas and value assumptions of both modified individualists and social democrats and, as a result, it has been used by both groups.

According to the pluralist theory, conflict exists within Western democratic societies but it is not a structured conflict between groups with particular and enduring socio-economic interests, such as between social classes. Moreover, the pluralist theory posits that power is widely diffused in these societies. There is, therefore, "a series of shifting coalitions" (Gough, 1978, p. 36) among various interest groups in advancing common causes. Because of this constant shift in the alignment of pressure groups, no single group can rise to a position of dominance. Any group attempting to do so will be checked by other groups. This constant interplay of power is acted out in public, and "the state is seen as a neutral arena within which interest groups can compete on an equal footing" (Gough, 1978, p. 36). This view of society and the interest groups in it assumes that preferences of individual voters or consumers are autonomous and not socially determined. This assumption is of course open to question. However, available empirical evidence shows that public opinion and attitudes, especially in regard to social policy, are influenced by the dominant social class values (Gough, 1978).

The pluralist theory of social policy has been used to explain the emergence and development of specific welfare policies and programs. As Gough (1978) notes, none of these applications have moved beyond the case study approach, with the possible exception of industrial relations, in which employers and employees are seen as two institutionalized pressure groups in opposition to each other, with the state acting as mediator. By its very nature, the pluralist theory is not a general theory of the welfare state. Its main proposition is this: every individual welfare program or policy is a unique event determined by the interplay of various interest groups with the state acting as the neutral arbiter (Gough, 1978).

The Marxist Theory of the Welfare State

Marx himself did not address the issue of social welfare directly. However, his views on factory legislation in England reveals two things. First, he considered it to be the result of agitation from the working class and, therefore, saw it as a working class victory in class conflict. Second, he saw the reforms in working conditions then required by factory legislation as a useful strategy in the elimination of capitalism.

Many contemporary Marxists would disagree with Marx on the second point. They would argue that while reforms have brought some benefits to the propertyless workers and to the subordinate classes in general, their real consequence has been to strengthen and reinforce the capitalist system. However, the contemporary Marxists (Miliband, 1969; Poulantzas, 1960; O'Connor, 1973) have contributed to the theory of the welfare state by developing Marx's ideas on the state in capitalist society. The Marxist theory of the welfare state identifies three sets of contradictions. The first contradiction lies in the role of the state. On the one hand, the capitalist state protects and furthers the interests of the economically dominant class, that is, the productive property owners. On the other, the state must pay some attention to the interests and demands of other social classes to avoid overwhelming discontent with the regime. This is the contradiction between the capital accumulation and legitimization functions of the state (further explained in chapter 8).

The second contradiction is linked to the first, and has already been alluded to earlier. In discharging its legitimization function, the state provides welfare to its citizens. Yet, as with the factory reform laws in 19th century Britain, reforms are not merely concessions by the state but also represent the victory of the working class in its concerted struggle for changes. This is the contradiction between the legitimization function of the state and the class struggle activities of the subordinate classes.

The third contradiction is a corollary of the second. Social welfare programs, insofar as they are instituted by the state in order to legitimize the regime, can be seen as a measure of social control, regulating and controlling the behaviour of the subordinate classes. On the other hand, these same programs are also the fruit of much struggle by the subordinate classes, who do derive some benefit from the programs, although the final state-established program usually falls far short of the aims of the subordinate classes. This is the contradiction between social control for integration by the state and social benefit for the subordinate classes. The contemporary Marxists have largely emphasized the social control aspect of the welfare state and neglected the class struggle aspect. This book attempts to redress this imbalance by calling for a more dialectical approach to the analysis of social welfare.

The Marxist theory of the welfare state proposes that the general phenomenon of the welfare state arises out of these three contradictions in capitalist society, and that its development in any particular capitalist society depends on how these contradictions are resolved. More specifically, the Marxist theory explains the welfare state thus:

1. The capitalist state uses its power (a) to lower the cost of reproducing labour power, and (b) to maintain the nonworking population, thereby ensuring peace and harmony in society.
2. Nevertheless, specific welfare policies and programs may be introduced or established partly as the outcome of class conflicts.

3. Thus, welfare programs are not only measures of social control, but also means by which the subordinate classes can acquire social benefits.

An Assessment of the Theories

Four major approaches to social welfare were presented in the last four chapters in an attempt to draw the reader's attention to the values and ideology that characterize each approach or model. This has been undertaken in order to communicate the fact that it is legitimate for social theorists and researchers to have values or even ideologies; all social knowledge is in fact grounded in some particular point of view, chosen not purely according to reason, but because of values and norms as well. The proper procedure in scientific inquiry is to make this choice of values as explicit as possible. This has been done with respect to each of the models discussed.

No theory of social welfare is a formal theory in the strict sense. At least I have not presented them in the form of lawlike propositions. Some are, of course, more amenable to reformulation to that effect than others. In chapter 1, it was mentioned that the principal task of a theory is to *explain* some phenomenon. To explain the welfare state adequately, a theory should deal with three features:

1. the emergence of the welfare state in all advanced capitalist countries in the 20th century;
2. the similar trends in state welfare intervention in all these countries; and
3. the diversity in the nature and scope of state welfare policies and programs among these countries (Gough, 1978).

In light of these three criteria, the technological determinism/convergence theory and the functionalist theory can explain the emergence of the welfare state and similar trends in all advanced capitalist countries. But they cannot account for the important differences among those countries. For example, since the Second World War, all the advanced capitalist countries (in North America, Western Europe, and Japan) have developed minimum income security programs, largely in the form of social insurance schemes. The establishment of these programs can be explained in terms of structural differentiation as a society becomes more complex (functionalist theory) and as automatic, natural responses to industrialization and urbanization (the theory of technological determinism). Yet the United States and Japan still have no comprehensive health insurance system or family allowances. Neither theory can explain such important and immense differences.

A number of modifying factors can be cited to explain these discrepancies: the "traditional" cultural factor, the different government structures, the salience of the labour movement, and so on. All these points could enhance the explanatory power of the theories, but they are contingent and *ad hoc*. In fact, they all undermine the original framework of functionalism and determinism/convergence (Gough, 1978, p. 31). Moreover, in their determinant stance, these two theories leave no room for the creative role of human actors in history.

On the other hand, the economic theory of welfare and the pluralist theory of social policy can explain the differences but not the similar trends in the welfare state observed in all advanced capitalist societies. These two theories have certain features in common: emphasis on the individual actors, and the action-orientation of the individuals. (Pluralist theory posits that even when individuals form pressure groups to advance their interests through democratic processes, their alliances are temporary and issue-oriented, not likely to form permanent unions and deepen group awareness.) Both theories analyze the welfare state "in terms of human *subjects*—their *interpretation* of reality in light of their values, and their responses to it. Thus, explanations of social policy focus on the subjective interpretation of what constitutes a social problem, rather than on the objective determination of the problem as with functionalist theory" (Gough, 1978, p. 38, emphasis in the original).

These two theories have the merit to emphasize the subjective content of human creativity, and hence the diversity in the welfare state phenomenon, but do not allow for structural causation. "There is no recognition of a material reality [such as social classes, class interests, and conflicts] outside the heads of the 'actors' which shapes their values and behaviour" (Gough, 1978, p. 38, words in parentheses added).

As the rest of this book will demonstrate, only Marxist theory can explain both the common phenomenon of the welfare state observed in all advanced capitalist societies and the important differences in social policies among them. Marxist theory explains the general common phenomenon in terms of structural problems encountered in the capitalist system, two major ones being (a) the requirement of the capitalist class to increase productivity in order to maximize profit, and (b) the maintainance of harmony in society in the face of the tremendous inequalities produced in the capitalist system. The welfare state has emerged precisely to tackle these two problems, especially the second.

Marxist theory can also account for diversity because it sees human beings as capable of initiating and directing action, including group action. Diverse social policies in different countries are the result of different human activities: historical backgrounds, class struggles, and other decisions made by people.

Earlier in chapter 4, it was mentioned that the social democratic school of thought contains contradictions between its analysis and its prescriptions. We see that these contradictions are unresolved in social democracy when two seemingly opposite theories, the functionalist theory based on structural determinism and the pluralist theory with its emphasis on individual action, are both traceable to social democracy. Functionalist theory objectifies reality, while pluralist theory subjectifies it, but the two are reconcilable. In Marxist theory, the contradictions between the two are resolved in such a way that the objective and subjective elements are both recognized and accounted for. The result is a theory that is adequate and general.

---

1. Wilensky and Lebeaux's institutional conception of social welfare corresponds to Titmuss's institutional redistributive model of social policy (see Titmuss, 1974).

2. In his study of blood donors, Titmuss points out the constraints imposed by institutional arrangements, such as the buying and selling of blood in the United States, on the exercise of altruism. (*The gift relationship*. New York: Pantheon Books, 1971.)

PART II

Social Inequality and the State

6

Social Inequality I: Canadian Class Structure

The Concept of Social Inequality

Social Inequality and Social Stratification

There are two notions of inequality, the descriptive and the prescriptive (or the objective and the normative). Social inequality, or social stratification as it is termed by many social scientists, means an objective difference in people's access to social rewards as a result of their personal or group characteristics (Robertson, 1981) without involving any evaluation. However, the definition offered by social scientists does not account for the fact that "any distribution of rewards can be legitimately challenged as to its fairness, since it involves a selection of one particular measure of the inequality of reward and this selection inevitably introduces some normative considerations" (Jordan, 1980, p. 65). In other words, the degree of inequality cannot be measured without introducing evaluative assumptions as to what constitutes equality or inequality (Atkinson, 1975, p. 47). Thus, in studies of social stratification or inequality, social scientists actually employ both objective and normative criteria, and the appropriate procedure is to recognize this explicitly. Sociologists use the term "social stratification" to refer to investigations into "the differences in social rank and the institutionalized arrangements underlying the distribution of privileges" (Jordan, 1980, p. 66). These usually entail a description of the differentials in the distribution of social rewards, such as income, wealth, social status, privileges, and so forth. However, all too often "social stratification" is used in these studies not only as a descriptive term to refer to those differentials, but also as a normative term to refer to the evaluations of those differentials according to some standard of social equality. Studies of stratification fail to note or to resolve the problem of relating statements about differentials to the evaluative statements about those differentials that involve, explicitly or implicitly, some criteria of social inequality (Jordan, 1980, p. 66). These studies often confuse facts with values by combining what is, with what ought to be. This classic fallacy of deriving value judgements from statements of fact is all the more likely to be made in sociology where value statements often are not merely prescriptive, but also descriptive and informative (Jordan, 1980, p. 66).

To avoid such a fallacy, one should distinguish between the order of categories used in the examination of social stratification and inequality. The categories of stratification theories are constitutive: they are required in order to acquire knowledge of stratification, or knowledge about the objective differences in social rank and their underlying structures. The categories of social inequality theories, on the other hand, are regulative: they regulate those evaluative statements made on the basis of knowledge gained through the constitutive categories. We use the constitutive ideas of social stratification as knowing subjects. We use the evaluative ideas of social inequality as moral agents. It follows from this distinction that there is no logical relation between statements of social stratification and those of social inequality (Jordan, 1980, p. 75).

Value Assumptions

Bearing in mind the duality of facts and values, we shall use the term "social inequality" in this book to include the meanings of stratification and inequality as distinguished by Jordan. In our discussions of social inequality, we shall be describing and analyzing social stratification, that is, differential distribution of resources and rewards, and so on, and the structures producing these differentials. But our discussion of these differentials and their sources will be premised on two value judgements. First, that the distribution of resources and rewards should be as just as possible, and, second, that exploitative inequalities should be removed.

Let us discuss each of the two value judgements in greater detail. The reference to justice in the first statement demands a rule or canon of distributive justice, and the one that is chosen here is distribution according to need. At the subsistence level, we all need food, air, water, clothing, and shelter in order to survive. So at the very least, the resources and rewards in society should be shared or distributed in such a way as to assure everyone the basic necessities for survival. However, the canon of need can also be interpreted in a relative sense. Needs are relative to the standard of living of a given society and are determined in relation to the average income of that society (Caskie, 1979; Jordan, 1980). In this sense, needs can include such resources required for personal dignity and social well-being as comfort, education, and health and recreation, that are in accord with the average standard in that society.

Distribution according to need seeks to provide every member of society with a certain standard of living. This does not mean that everyone would receive the same amount of identical items. On the contrary, people have different endowments and differ in individual needs. Thus, distribution should be according to the varying needs, natural and social, of individuals and groups. Families with children have different needs from single individuals or childless couples. The elderly and the disabled have special needs. Certain ethnic groups have preferences for certain kinds of clothing and foods.

But these differences cannot be based on or lead to an exploitative relationship between individuals or groups. For example, if Jennifer has mathematical talent and Ernesto shows musical talent, both should have the opportunity to develop their respective talents. But the resources required to train Jennifer in mathematics and Ernesto in music must be given in such a way that others with different or less talent are not denied their respective opportunities. Moreover, once Jennifer and Ernesto have been able to develop their talents and reached a certain level of achievement, they should not use the power derived from their talents to dominate others.

In our society, distribution according to need is obviously an ideal that is difficult to attain. Yet this ideal has been and continues to be the guiding principle for most of the delivery of social welfare. As an ultimate goal, it can be reached if certain conditions are met. To bring about a distribution according to need, a necessary though not sufficient condition is that the ownership of the means of production (also known as productive property) must be socialized, that is, owned by all the people and not by private hands. Other important conditions would require changes in the culture (the laws, political system, customs, and values) that are compatible with the socialized ownership of productive means, and the distribution of resources and rewards according to need.

The second value judgement pertaining to social inequality is the abolition of exploitative inequalities. The primary inequality lies in the capitalist relations of production through which the surplus value produced by the workers is expropriated by the capitalist. This exploitative relationship underlies and continually generates a variety of other secondary inequalities, such as differential distribution of income, opportunities, information, privilege, and influence. As a result, certain individuals and groups become enormously rich on grounds that are not justifiable, while many are unable to attain a standard of living that is materially possible within the society. Both the primary and secondary inequalities will be discussed shortly. The fundamental premise for this value judgement is that unless exploitative inequalities are removed, it would be impossible to distribute resources and rewards according to need.

Taken together, these two value statements describe a society that differs from the existing capitalist society in several important aspects: the basic social structures, the organizing principle, and the social relationships among people as producers, consumers, and simply as people. This book does not make prescriptions for this envisioned new social order; it does not provide a blueprint for societal change. However, it does offer a means of analyzing social welfare that is fundamental to any attempt to progressively eliminate social inequality.

This analysis of social welfare and the method upon which it is based are important because the institution of social welfare in advanced capitalist societies has been, at least in part, a response to the existence of inequalities. As we have seen, our views about social inequality are linked to our value assumptions and ultimately to our moral commitment. Thus, it has been necessary to explain the author's personal value assumptions about social inequality as these same values will influence not only the way in which social inequality and social policy is analyzed, but also proposals regarding the direction in which the development of social welfare should take place.

This intellectual honesty is indispensable in a researcher, for if value assumptions and moral commitment are not openly stated, it does not mean that they do not exist, but rather that they are concealed. Very often, these hidden values and commitments will influence the researcher's work in such a way as to create confusion and distortion. In investigating social welfare, the outcome may likely be a rationalization or justification for existing inequalities, and a recommendation of solutions that will help to maintain the status quo.

Definition of Social Inequality

Most sociology textbooks define social inequality as the patterned differential distribution of rewards among members of a society because of their different positions in the social hierarchy. Insofar as the hierarchy of rewards relates to opportunities, resources, power, privilege, and other societal factors, the definition includes the differential distribution of opportunities, resources, power, privilege, information, and influence. This is the definition that has been used in the chapter so far. However, before analyzing the various dimensions of social inequality in Canada, a different definition will be developed: social inequality is a differential limitation on the behaviours of members of society. "Structures of social inequality consist of limitations which are differentially imposed on system members" (Baldus, 1975, p. 189) and restrict their behaviours to different degrees. Stated in this way, inequality is a form of "structural violence" (Galtung, 1971, p. 81) and not the result of unequal rewards for varying contributions to common goals. As Baldus explains:

> . . . differential limitations can be imposed in the form of normative regulations or by the differential distribution of goods or services. While often accompanied by regulatory rules, the possession of material goods must be considered as a separate and independent determinant of behaviour parameters. This is, in particular, the case with differential access to productive, surplus-yielding goods which can become the basis for characteristic forms of dominance and subordination (1975, p. 189).

This definition is used here because the determinant of social inequality is traced to the objective social structures, whereas the basis for the differential distribution of rewards is the subjective evaluation of varying contributions to shared objectives by members. This point will be made clearer in the following section.

With this concept of the structural causation of social inequality in mind, we shall discuss inequality in Canadian capitalist society and class structure.

Social Inequality in Capitalist Society

Canada is a class society, that is, a society divided by social classes. Social classes are not merely groups of people having similar socio-economic positions, although many sociologists use the term in that sense. Such a definition is based on their peers' subjective perceptions of individuals' status as the basis for social classes. Thus, although there are usually three social "classes"—upper, middle, and lower—according to these sociologists, the criterion for class division allows them, in theory, to have as many class categories as there are individuals in society and as many classification systems as there are evaluators; the possibility exists that no two individuals are perceived by their peers to belong to the same socio-economic group.

In contrast, the social classification system used in this book, generally known as the Marxist social class scheme, does have external objective criteria: categories or social classes are defined by the objective relationships of the individuals studied. These relationships centre around the economic processes in society[1] of which two are the most important in a capitalist society: (a) individuals' relationships to productive property, that is, whether or not they own or control productive property; and (b) their relationships to work, that is, whether they sell or buy labour-power. Productive property, or means of production, refer to such things as the land, factories, tools, machines, equipment, raw materials, and so on, used in the production and distribution of commodities. It does not include consumer property, such as homes, cars, and home entertainment systems for private use by owners (Bowles and Craib, 1979). Labour-power, the capacity for labour, consists of "the aggregate of those mental and physical capabilities existing in a human being, which he exercises whenever he produces a use-value of any description" (Marx, 1972, p. 164).

Social inequality in a capitalist society is based on the ownership and nonownership of productive property. As first analyzed by Marx, it is established when individuals or groups of individuals who own the means of production buy labour-power from other individuals who do not own such means.

Individuals who sell their own labour-power must be in possession of their own persons in order to be able to dispose of their labour-power as they will. But those who sell labour-power do not own the raw materials or the instruments of labour needed to activate their capacity for labour and to earn a living. Labour-power is therefore sold as a commodity to the owner of productive property, the capitalists, who use a portion of their capital to buy this labour-power in the form of wages.

The wage a worker receives from the capitalist is payment for allowing the latter to dispose of labour-power for a definite period of time. In working for the owner of productive property, the worker during one part of the labour process produces goods and services the value of which when sold is the equivalent of the wage earned. During the rest of the labour process, the worker still expends labour-power, but is not paid for the labour. In other words, the worker's wage constitutes the equivalent of only part of the total value he or she produces. The other part accrues to the capitalist as surplus-value or profit. The worker is paid for only part of the labour, while the value of the unpaid part is reaped by the capitalist as income, and as replacement and additions to the existing pool of capital for further production. The added capital to buy new means of production (new machinery, factories, transport, and so on) or to employ more workers is also derived from surplus-value created by unpaid labour. This process is known as the accumulation of capital. With the further employment of workers who produce surplus-value, the process is then repeated. It is, therefore, through the accumulation of capital that social inequality is continually generated. Thus "the exchange of equivalents, the original operation with which we started, has now become turned round in such a way that there is only an apparent exchange" (Marx, 1972, p. 547), for wages, by their very nature, always imply the performance of a certain quantity of unpaid labour on the part of the labourer (Marx, 1972, p. 580). This is exploitation: those hours of labour expended by workers over and above the hours necessary to produce their own wages but appropriated by the capitalist.

The worker's wage (the value of the worker's labour-power) is based on what is necessary for him or her to produce and reproduce labour-power, and that of others to succeed the worker. The limit of the wage is very elastic. It is determined chiefly by a physical element. To continue physical existence and to reproduce labour-power, the labourer must have food, clothing, and shelter for himself or herself and for any dependents, who are potential workers. But the limit is also influenced by a historical or social element. In addition to meeting the needs of physical life, the labourer needs to satisfy certain wants in accordance with the standard of life prevailing in the society in which people are born and reared. However, this element can be expanded, contracted, or altogether eliminated such that only the physical element remains (Marx, 1970, p. 222).

Whatever the limits of the worker's wage, simply by working for the capitalist the worker produces surplus-value for the capitalist. Furthermore, the process of creating surplus-value is by no means clearly understood by either the capitalist or the labourer. The labourer is often unaware that under the wage system he or she hands over all material benefit but subsistence to the capitalist. This ignorance works in favour of the capitalist, the most ostensible benefit being the worker's submission to the conditions of employment. The benefits and the surplus-value produced are collectively termed the surplus-benefits to the capitalist. As for the workers, when they are separated from the means of production, though their labour-power is the living source of all revenue, they are left with "absolute poverty: poverty not as shortage, but as total exclusion of objective wealth" (Marx, 1973, p. 296). When they do produce goods and services of value, as when they are employed by the capitalist, they are dependent on their own product, part of which they receive as their wages. This exclusion from the ownership of productive property and, hence, from the product itself, along with the subsequent dependence on the product from that property, structures the relations of social inequality in a capitalist society. It is also this exclusion and the limit of the workers' wages that ultimately imposes restrictions on their behaviour.

By using the two criteria of (a) ownership or nonownership of productive property, and (b) buying or selling of labour-power, we can distinguish four basic sets of relationships to productive property and work:

1. the capitalist class, or bourgeoisie, which owns productive property and purchases the labour-power of others to operate it;
2. the petite bourgeoisie, that is, independent commodity producers, such as farmers and small entrepreneurs who both own and operate their productive property;
3. the proletariat, or the working class, which owns no productive property and is, therefore, forced to sell its labour-power; and
4. the underclass members who neither own the means of production nor sell their labour-power.

This concept of structured social inequality between classes is essentially different from the notion of social inequality or social stratification popular in contemporary sociology, in which the term is used to mean merely a differential distribution of rewards, resources, status, and information. However, these differences are the most observable extensions of the basic structure of domination and subordination, exclusion and dependence. Inasmuch as there are such differential distributions, they are due to the underlying differential limitations on the behaviours of the different classes imposed by the primary structure of social inequality.

There is also social stratification within the working class. The differential distribution of money, social prestige, information, and influence within the working class, and the differences between the working class and the underclass constitute a secondary inequality. Secondary inequality may account for the persistence of the primary structure of domination. Members of the working class or the underclass who strive or manage to move upward along any dimension of the formal or informal rank differentiations may inadvertently come to approve and trust the established social order, including the primary inequality structure. Contrary to the Davis and Moore thesis (1945), social stratification as a phenomenon of the lower classes is not an expression of a functional division of labour; in fact, it is largely nonfunctional. Its only functional value is in the legitimization of the basic structure of inequality by members of the lower classes (Baldus, 1975).

Class Structure in Canada

Class divisions in any concrete society are never so clear-cut as described above. Nor are the four classes exhaustive or all-inclusive. In Canada, we can identify the four main classes. Moreover, there are fragments within each social class inasmuch as members of the same class may behave differently, or have different and, at times, even conflicting ideas and interests. But by and large, because of their objective economic position in society, their behaviour, ideas, values, and interests are more or less similar. This view of Canadian society is very different from the popular misconception that Canada is essentially a "middle class" society.

The manner in which the four main classes have developed under historically specific conditions in the last century shaped the kind and degree of social inequality in Canadian society. Johnson (1972) has shown in his analysis of class development that the capitalist class has gained preponderant power over the economy through concentration of ownership of productive property by a small minority. The size and influence of the petite bourgeoisie declined over time, resulting in the polarization of the two major social classes: the bourgeoisie and the proletariat.

The Petite Bourgeoisie

Up to the mid-19th century, Canada did not have a capitalist mode of production. It was made up mostly of small-scale producers. The family farm was the unit of production, producing not only its own food, but also many other household items, such as clothing, soap, candles, ploughs, and harrows. Other necessities were provided by local artisans and merchants. While wheat was grown as a cash crop, there was usually not enough surplus to sell after meeting household needs. Thus, the link between agricultural production and the market was tenuous.

Social life revolved around the small village. There were also independent craftsworkers—coopers, blacksmiths, tailors, shoemakers, wheelwrights, and so forth—who set their own production goals and patterns of work. At the time of Confederation, Canada was essentially rural in character with 50 percent of the labour force engaged in agricultural pursuits (Rinehart, 1975).

The independence and small-scale production of the earlier self-employed producers still characterize the petite bourgeoisie today. However, with the emergence of the capitalist mode of production, especially after Confederation, the number of independent producers declined considerably, as many among them became members of the working class. Moreover, their links with the market system became more extensive and intensive. Not only did they purchase most of their consumer goods from the market (a sign of continuing erosion of their self-sufficiency); their production was also mostly destined for the market.

Today, the petite bourgeoisie in Canada consists of three categories of people: the small-scale capitalists, the independent commodity producers, and self-employed professionals.

The small-scale capitalists own or control small businesses that they operate themselves. They include independent owners of small service establishments, such as cafes, motels, rooming-houses, and retail outlets; proprietors of businesses, such as garment workshops and construction companies; and owners of other revenue-yielding property. They derive the main portion of their income from the businesses, and they personally participate in the day-to-day operations, often in the actual physical activity of producing goods or services themselves. The number of hired workers in these establishments is small compared to that employed by the large-scale capitalists. In many cases, the owner and family members are the only workers.

The independent commodity producers include the farmers, fishermen, loggers, and craftsworkers. These producers own their means of production: land, livestock, machinery, equipment, and materials. They combine their own labour and that of their family members with the means of production to produce commodities. Most of the commodities are sold on the market for cash; in other words, they are not producing merely for subsistence.

Both the small-scale capitalists and independent commodity producers are subject to great insecurity as fluctuations in market conditions have an almost immediate impact on their businesses. Moreover, all of their activities are also carried out in ways other than those of small-scale production. Large corporations do produce the same goods and services as those produced by the petite bourgeoisie. In fact, the latter is increasingly dominated and displaced by the large-scale capitalists for access to valued resources, such as land, minerals, or markets. The petite bourgeoisie is then absorbed either as labourers (wage labour) or as managers of the large corporations (salary labour) to perform some of the tasks of capital in supervising production (Clement, 1981).

Within the petite bourgeoisie, also known as the middle class, there is another category of people, the self-employed professionals. These are self-employed people trained in the elite professions, such as medicine, law, and dentistry. They have maintained their independent status and ensure enormous increases in their incomes through careful restrictions of new entrants into their ranks. However, the proportion of other professionals in independent practice—nurses, engineers, architects, and others—has declined significantly in the 20th century. This is part of the process known as proletarianization.

The Capitalist Class

The capitalist class is made up of the large-scale capitalists, that is, those individuals who own and control large enterprises. Most of the means of production are owned by a few giant corporations. But corporations also have owners. In the final analysis, after stripping away the intermediary holding companies and a large number of small shareholders, there emerges a restricted group of individuals who control the corporations on the basis of owning a controlling interest (Johnson, 1972).

It has been suggested sometimes that ownership and control of large corporations have been separated in advanced capitalist societies; these organizations are run by hired professional managers, while ownership is dispersed among a vast number of shareholders. But the majority of shareholders hold insignificant proportions of shares that exclude them from the decision-making circles. In some cases, the individuals who own the controlling interest are also the chief executives in their corporation. By and large, while we can distinguish between owners and managers, the control is in the hands not of the small shareholders but the few wealthy shareholders owning the controlling interest. The latter make the major decisions that affect not only their corporations, but also other segments of society. On the other hand, the managers who can be hired and fired are responsible for implementing the goals and policies established by the owners. Thus, one can say that there is no separation of ownership and control of the major corporations.

Who are the large-scale capitalists? Social scientists have produced various lists naming these individuals. While there is no strict consensus on the exact number—"from a high of 922 down to the proverbial 50" (Johnson, 1972, p. 154), there is general agreement that a small group of individuals, predominantly male, controls the main components of the economy, "and that they are linked together in complex patterns of intercorporate ownerships, cross directorships, and social relations" (Johnson, 1972, p. 154).

The high degree of concentration of share ownership by a small group of people also enables them to have an almost total control over the economy, "not merely because of the huge proportion directly owned, but the extreme concentration allows easy manipulation of those shares for decision-making purposes" (Johnson, 1972, p. 157). We can see how the capitalists' power applies to the economy, not just to their respective corporations, when we examine the consequences of their decisions. Their decisions determine the level of economic activity in society, the direction of development, and the rate of labour force participation. They also largely determine the wage structure and thus fundamentally establish the living standards of the working class. Furthermore, the large-scale capitalists have a pervasive influence over the state and the entire political system. Thus, directly or indirectly, they have played a major part in shaping other societal institutions, such as immigration, family life, urban development, education, health care, and social welfare. In a very real sense, the decisions of the capitalists touch the lives of almost everyone, for they can and do determine the quality of the air we breathe, the water we drink, the food we eat, the house we live in, and so forth.

Just as the petite bourgeoisie is made up of different fragments, the capitalist class is not homogeneous, consisting of the industrial capitalists, the financial capitalists, and the commercial capitalists. Whereas the different groups have certain common interests, for example, a stable social and political environment in which they can accumulate capital unhindered, they do have diverging and, at times, conflicting interests arising from the nature of their specific pursuits. Thus, although they may hold a similar general outlook toward the state, their specific relationships with the state may differ from time to time.

One important fragment of the capitalist class consists of the foreign capitalists, also known as multinational or metropolitan capitalists. They are called "multinationals" because their corporate activities extend across national boundaries. They are referred to as "metropolitan capitalists" because Canada serves as an economic hinterland offering essentially raw materials. Throughout this country's history, there has always been a group of large-scale capitalists located outside of Canada, and long before the capitalist mode of production was established in Canada, they had played an important part in the economic and social development of this country. Capitalists in France and later those in Britain accumulated profit by extracting and trading in raw materials found in Canada: fish, fur, timber, and wheat. As the capitalist mode of production eclipsed the mode of production by independent producers in Canada (approximately after Confederation) as well as in the world as a whole, other natural resources such as minerals, lumber, oil, natural gas, and hydro-electric power, became of greater interest to the metropolitan capitalists. At the same time, capitalists located in the United States began to own and control many Canadian businesses, especially in the natural resources and manufacturing sectors.

Since the end of the Second World War, the influx of American direct investment in Canada increased significantly. By the end of 1977, of the top 400 industrial, retailing, and financial corporations in Canada, 208 had the largest single shareholder from a foreign country, and of these, 154 were from the United States. Among the top 20 petroleum and mining corporations in Canada, the top three were wholly owned by Americans and another nine were 50 percent or more, but less than 100 percent, owned by Americans; only four were wholly owned by Canadians (Smucker, 1980, p. 116).

Foreign capitalists have made decisions that have had a significant impact on Canadian society. Moreover, because of their influence on the Canadian government as well as their own governments, they have helped to shape important international and national policies affecting Canada. Hence, in our understanding of the Canadian class structure, it is not enough merely to look at Canadian society alone; we must also look at the group of powerful capitalists located outside of Canada.

While the important position of foreign capitalists could not be gainsaid, it would be an oversimplification to say that Canadian capitalists are simply hangers-on or lackeys of American imperialism. The relationship between Canadian and foreign capitalists is quite complex. Most Canadian capitalists are deeply involved in foreign multinational corporate business in Canada, either as their senior executives, or as suppliers or distributors of their goods and technology. A few Canadian capitalists are, at least for now, still members of the national bourgeoisie operating independently of foreign corporations. Another minority group became multinational capitalists themselves or partners of other multinational interests (Johnson, 1972, p. 159).

As has been mentioned before, the capitalist class in Canada comprises a small group of people. A point to emphasize is that we must distinguish between the capitalist class made up of individuals with names, identities, and individual as well as class interests, on the one hand, and the means of production, that is, the technology and organizations, that they control on the other (Johnson, 1972). For in locating the causes and effects of social inequality, the alienation, low wages, health and safety hazards, and insecurities experienced by the working classes are effects of social inequality. However, their causes are not to be traced only to the factories, mines, or other means of production in which they work, but also primarily to the system of ownership and exploitative structures, and to the class of individuals who defend and benefit from the system. Unless otherwise stated it is to these large-scale capitalists that we will refer when the term "capitalist" is used throughout the rest of this book.

The Working Class

Members of the proletariat do not own significant productive property, but sell their labour-power to their employers for a wage. Thus, they are dependent on their employment, and most of them do not derive significant income from sources other than employment.

The occupational structure. The size of the working class has grown tremendously in the twentieth century as a result of the decline and absorption of the petite bourgeoisie, especially the farmers. In 1901, the farmers made up 40 percent of the work force; by 1975, only five percent were farmers. A more drastic change occurred in the composition of the working class. From 1901 to the mid-1970s, manual or blue-collar industrial workers declined slightly from 28 percent to 27 percent of the total labour force. By contrast, white-collar workers (professional, managerial, technical, clerical, and sales) rose from 15 percent to 49 percent during the same period.[2] Service workers (e.g., waitresses and gas station attendants) rose from eight percent to 12 percent in the same years (Crysdale and Beattie, 1977). Furthermore, in recent years, there has emerged a significant proportion of people employed in public administration: state employees made up 7.1 percent of the total labour force in 1978.

These changes in the occupational structure led to an emergence of a category of people about whose class position there is considerable controversy. This category encompasses salaried managers, senior public administrators, professionals, and technicians. Some of them are highly paid; most others are well paid. Objectively speaking, insofar as they sell their labour-power, they are part of the working class. However, they manage the subordinate working people for the capitalist class, they defend the class interests of the capitalist class, they propagate the ideology of the capitalist class, or in other ways, they serve the capitalist class with their knowledge and expertise. Because of their position within the hierarchy in corporations or the state, and also because of the high social prestige and status of the professionals and technicians, their outlook, values, and attitudes approximate those of the capitalist and/or the petite bourgeoisie. Thus, they occupy a contradictory class location (Wright, 1978). This category of intermediate occupations is sometimes referred to as the "new" middle class.

The ambiguity of this new middle class should alert us to two things. First, in any concrete society class boundaries are not clear-cut, although with increasing proletarianization, loss of skills, and control over jobs by more and more workers, the polarization into the two major classes—the bourgeoisie and the proletariat—is taking place. Second, political, ideological, and cultural factors also intervene in determining class positions in any particular society.

The debate over these intermediate groups should not obscure a basic fact that the majority of the white-collar workers are part of the proletariat. The typist, the bank teller, the nurse, the school teacher, and the engineer are similar in that they sell their time and ability to work to their employers in the same way as the factory worker and the construction labourer, although the types of labour-power sold are different. None of them own productive property. They all have little control over their work process and working conditions. They are all insecure in their jobs as they are subject to the vagaries of the capitalist economy, just like blue-collar workers.

As we have seen, the working class is by no means homogeneous; within it are many different strata defined according to occupation, income, education levels, or social prestige. There are further fragments within the Canadian working class: the unionized and the nonunionized, and groups characterized by racial, ethnic, religious, and sexual differences. But the most important division within the working class is probably the dual labour market.

The dual labour market. To understand the dual labour market, we should begin with the notion that our economy consists of three different sectors: the monopoly, the competitive, and the state sectors. The monopoly sector is formed by the giant corporations that have been successfully circumventing the vicissitudes of the market system by expanding their operations so that more spheres of activity would be brought under their own control. For example, a manufacturing establishment will expand backward into raw material extraction to ensure supplies, and forward into marketing and retailing to ensure reliable outlets; it may also gain control over transportation to ensure steady flow of commodities. This kind of expansion is known as vertical integration. On the other hand, there may be horizontal integration, whereby one corporation takes over other firms in the same industry. Furthermore, giant corporations may even move across industries to take over companies in other industries and thus form conglomerates. The important consequence of this kind of extreme concentration of capital is that one corporation or a few together control or receive large proportions of total assets, total profits, total sales, or total values added. The corporation(s) with the monopoly (oligopoly) is (are) usually in a position to set the prices.

The sector controlled by monopoly or oligopoly (for convenience, the term "monopoly sector" is used to indicate both kinds of control) is predominantly represented by such industries as mining, steel, automobiles, utilities, forestry, petrochemicals, and transport and communication. These industries are characterized by high capital-labour ratios (high amounts of investment and output per worker), and these high levels of capitalization create very high fixed costs. Any unnecessary work stoppage will lead to tremendous losses. Besides, it is usually difficult, if not impossible, to move operations in industries without great loss of capital. To prevent large losses when there is no production, jobs in the monopoly sector are well paid and relatively stable. There are also fringe benefits, good working conditions, and promotion prospects. Moreover, there are usually workers' organizations—unions and professional associations—that promote workers' interests and protect their job security.

The jobs in the monopoly sector make up the primary labour market, also known as the normal market. Professional, managerial, technical, supervisory, skilled (both white-collar and blue-collar), and middle-level sales jobs are part of the primary labour market. Some better paid semiskilled and unskilled jobs (both white-collar and blue-collar), usually in large corporations with a unionized labour force, also belong to the primary labour market (National Council of Welfare, 1977). Monopoly sector employers can afford to pay wages by virtue of their price-making position. They then pass the increased labour costs to the consumer in the form of higher prices. However, the share of new jobs provided by industries in this sector has been declining in recent years. This means that an increasingly large proportion of the labour force is looking for work in the competitive sector of the economy (Economic Council of Canada, 1976).

The competitive sector is made up of industries that are more labour-intensive: the capital-labour ratios are low and so is productivity. The firms in this sector are predominantly located in the service, trade, and some manufacturing industries (such as electronics, garment, and textile), and also in construction. They are usually owned by small-scale capitalists, although some are owned by giant multinational corporations. Since most of these firms have little fixed capital for permanent facilities, they tend to move to low-wage areas when labour, land, and other production costs increase.

Workers in this sector generally have low levels of skill and, except for some construction workers, are paid low wages. They are in a weak bargaining position for higher wages, better working conditions, fringe benefits, and job security; they have seen their employers move to other areas or go out of business because of a downturn in the economy or pressure from competitors. Most of the workers are not unionized.

The jobs in the competitive sector belong to the secondary or the marginal labour market. Jobs in the marginal labour market are rarely organized

> according to ladders of ascending levels of pay, skill, and responsibility. Nor do (the industries) provide for advancement through training acquired on the job, or reward good performance by promotions or raises in pay. Instead, the single most important determinant of the wages of low-income earners is the amount of time they work (NCW, 1977, p. 10).

Since the wages of these workers are based on the amount of time worked (regardless of whether they are calculated at piece-, hour- or daily-rate), the number of working hours per day and working days per year have a marked impact on the workers' annual income. Workers with jobs in the secondary labour market are noticeably poorer and have a below average standard of living.[3] Yet the choice to work full time and year-round or to work part time is not entirely up to the workers. Rather, it is the jobs that are subject to seasonal interruptions, economic fluctuations, and general insecurity. In other words, the marginal labour market is characterized by periodic unemployment and underemployment.

The third sector of the economy is the state sector. As has been noted above, state employees now comprise a significant portion of the Canadian labour force. Between 1961 and 1974, 8.3 percent of the new jobs were created in public administration (Economic Council of Canada, 1976, p. 98). Jobs in the state sector can be in either the primary labour market (professional, technical, and skilled jobs) or the secondary labour market (semiskilled and unskilled). However, as mentioned earlier, some low-skilled and low-paid workers protected by strong unions have been able to win higher wages, better working conditions, and some measure of job security from their employers. State employees working in clerical and janitorial and other low status jobs would fall into this category, as public service unions have grown considerably in size and militancy in the last two decades. On the other hand, the state, because of its tax base, is better able to assume higher labour costs than employers in the competitive sector.

The discussion of the dual labour market in relation to the monopoly, competitive, and state sectors makes one point clear: dualism cuts across industrial sectors, industries, occupations, and companies. Therefore, it is sometimes difficult to distinguish between the primary and secondary labour markets. Identifying the two labour markets is not simply a matter of drawing up separate lists of companies or types of jobs. For example, forestry is one of the industries in which the increases in capital-labour ratios have been the highest. Yet some of its casual, seasonal labourers are poorly paid. In other words, many industries, firms and the state combine some jobs in the primary labour market with others in the marginal labour market (NCW, 1977; Clement, 1980).

1. Class definitions and relations differ from society to society where the means and modes of production are different. The section on Canadian class structure is based on the work by Johnson (1972), and Craib and Bowles (1979).

2. The figures on white-collar workers also include the proprietors who, by the definition of social class used here, should be classified as the petite bourgeoisie. The proprietors together with managers made up four percent and ten percent of the labour force in 1901 and 1973, respectively.

3. Poor or low-income Canadians are those whose income is below the Statistics Canada poverty line. The wage-earning poor are those Canadians

living below the poverty line who derive more than 50 percent of their income from employment. (See chapter 7 on Income Inequality).

While identifying the two labour markets is problematic, the separation between the two is a real one. Those working in the marginal labour market face great barriers that keep them away from the primary labour market. Conventional wisdom has it that they are locked into their unrewarding jobs "because they lack the education, work experience, aptitudes, and skills that are needed in the normal labour market—the same factors frequently offered to account for their low wages" (NCW, 1977,p. 23). Although such factors may describe the condition of some individuals, the implication that the workers themselves are responsible for this situation is invalid. Structures of social inequality impinge upon some individuals and groups, creating conditions of deprivation (such as the lack of education, skills, and opportunities) and thus barring them from the normal labour market. Chapter 11 will examine the "culture of poverty" hypothesis that has often been used to explain the "deprivation" of the poor.

The Underclass

It is difficult to draw the boundary line between the underclass and the proletariat, particularly those whose jobs are in the marginal labour market. As discussed earlier, there are hundreds of low-income workers who work on the fringes of the capitalist economy in Canada. The wage-earning poor serve as an industrial reserve army, and when the demand declines, they lose their jobs. Women, the elderly, youth, and members of some ethnic minority groups usually make up this reserve that has the overall effect of reducing labour costs, especially in the competitive sector.

To some writers, the terms "underclass" and "industrial reserve army" are synonymous. However, within the industrial reserve army there is, at bottom, what Marx calls the "lowest sediment" of the relative surplus-population that dwells in the sphere of pauperism. "Pauperism is the hospital of the active labour-army and the dead weight of the industrial reserve army" (Marx, 1972, p. 603). It is in this sense of pauperism that the term "underclass" is used in this book. Those who belong to the underclass are not the seasonally or the casually employed, but the permanently unemployed. Among members of the underclass are those who are able to work but are "demoralized and ragged" (Marx, 1972, p. 603) because they are unable to adapt to the labour market with its ever more complex division of labour. The underclass also includes those who are unable to work, among whom are the victims of unsafe workplaces, the disabled, and the chronically sick. The production of the underclass is included in the production of those fragments of the working class known as the industrial reserve army. Along with the industrial reserve army, the underclass forms a condition of capitalist production, and of the capitalist development of wealth (Marx, 1973,p. 603).

That the underclass is fully integrated into the capitalist class structure can be seen in the important function it fulfills for the capitalist economy. First of all, members of the underclass play the role of ideological scapegoat. Because they are permanently unemployed and subsist, for the most part, on state handouts, they become an identifiable group upon which the wrath of society is vented. This is particularly true of many of the native peoples of Canada. Because of historical discrimination and isolation (both geographical and social structural), from the larger society, they are reduced to pauperism in many cases. And because they are racially distinct, their dependence on welfare is made even more noticeable. Their underclass position is explained in racist ideologies, thus obscuring the class origin and nature of their plight (Elias, 1975; Kellough, 1980).

A second benefit to the capitalist economy is the role of consumer that underclass members play by contributing to the circulation of money within the economy. For example, although white entrepreneurs may complain about problems caused by "drunken Indians," they are willing to accept their welfare dollars spent in stores and taverns (Kellough, 1980).

Lastly, the underclass has political utility value as it provides an excuse for state intervention (Spitzer, 1975). By their behaviour, personal qualities, and/or social position, members of the underclass threaten the social relations of production in a capitalist society. The threat is posed when they impede or undermine the legitimacy of any of the following:

1. capitalist modes of appropriating the product of human labour (theft violates these modes of appropriation);
2. the social conditions under which capitalist production takes place (these conditions are threatened when members of the underclass refuse or are unable to perform wage labour);
3. patterns of distribution and consumption in capitalist society (these patterns are altered by those who use drugs for escape, rather than adhering to the values of sociability and adjustment);
4. the process of socialization for productive and nonproductive roles (this process is partially invalidated by youth who refuse to be schooled or by those who deny the validity of "family life");and
5. the ideology that supports the functioning of capitalist society (this is done by members of the underclass who propound alternative forms of social organization)
(Spitzer, 1975, p. 642).

Summary

Since the duality of fact and value influences all concepts of social inequality, the values of the researcher should always be stated before a study is undertaken. According to the stance taken in this book, studies of social inequality should not only investigate the reality of social stratification, but also further the desirable value of greater equality through the mechanism of distributing the wealth of society according to members' needs. Social inequality is defined as differential limitation on behaviours of members of a society. The origin of social inequality is traced to the process of capital accumulation by capitalists. The class structure in Canada today consists of four main classes: the bourgeoisie, the petite bourgeoisie, the proletariat, and the underclass.

7

Social Inequality II: Income Distribution

Wealth and Income

Class structure is the most fundamental social inequality, as people obtain different kinds and amounts of resources and rewards depending on whether or not they own productive property. Although this seems apparent, data on social class differences are scarce and difficult to collect for several reasons. First, members of the large-scale capitalist class are few, often invisible, and very inaccessible; money secures privacy. Second, social class differences are qualitative and difficult to assess quantitatively. Even the distribution of wealth and income (discussed below) fails to reveal the kind of socio-economic power, or lack of it, attached to various classes. Third, while most Canadians have a general though imprecise knowledge of the differences between the rich and the poor, they in fact recognize and understand little of the social classes as defined in the preceding chapter. Most Canadians consider themselves middle class, although the term is often left ambiguous. The prevailing ideology is that people may be rich, of average wealth, or poor but that there are no social classes based on exploitation in Canada.

Nevertheless, it is important to have some means of measuring social inequality; not only are there differences among social classes but, as discussed in the previous chapter, there are significant differences *within* classes, especially within the working class. One measurement used is the distribution of wealth. The more frequently used measure is that of the distribution of income.

Distribution of Wealth

Wealth is defined as total assets minus total debts, or net worth. It consists of deposits, cash, bonds, stocks, liquid assets, mortgages, real estate, automobiles, and equities in business and practice. Information on distribution of wealth is not as complete as the data on income, as Statistics Canada does not conduct regular surveys of wealth. In wealth distribution, all units (families and unattached individuals)[1] are placed in one of ten equal groups with each group containing ten percent of all units. Assigning units to each of the groups, called deciles, is done according to that unit's ranking by size of wealth held. The first ten percent, the bottom decile, own the least amount of wealth. The next ten percent form the second decile, and so forth up to the highest ten percent of wealth owners in the tenth decile.

In the 1977 distribution of wealth, the top ten percent of all units (the tenth decile) owned 50.6 percent of Canada's wealth, that is more than the wealth held by the rest of the population put together. The top 20 percent (ninth and tenth deciles together) held 68.1 percent, or more than two-thirds, of all wealth. The bottom decile held -0.6 percent of all wealth; in other words, their net holdings were negative and they were in debt overall (Ross, 1980, p. 35).

The Gini Coefficient for the distribution of wealth in 1977 was 0.686; in 1970 it was 0.716 (Ross, 1980,p. 35). The Gini Coefficient measures the inequality of any distribution, whether of wealth or of income. Its values range from 0 to 1. The higher the value, the greater the degree of inequality. Thus, a value of 0 indicates that everyone in the population gets equal share, while 1 indicates that one person gets everything while everyone else has nothing.

It is obvious that the distribution of wealth in Canada is quite unequal. Although we know that ownership of wealth is concentrated at the top, the distribution itself does not reveal the nature or extent of economic power that such concentration gives the owners. One important point to keep in mind is that not everyone who owns some form of wealth is a capitalist. Most people classified as wealth holders in surveys own no more than their homes and an insignificant amount of stocks and shares. They do not own controlling interests.

Distribution of Income

Most studies of social inequality have focused attention on distribution of money income. Money incomes are relatively easy to measure. In Canada, Surveys of Consumer Finances conducted since 1951, by the federal government and directed specifically at measuring incomes have produced comprehensive income distribution data (Canada, Statistics Canada, 1980, p. 99). Income inequality is also less provocative ideologically because class inequality is traced to social structures (the class system, controlling interest,) whereas under capitalism, income differences are mostly attributed to personal responsibility, or motivation and achievement.

Since no distinction between social classes is made in income distribution data, one cannot locate differences in distribution among the various social classes. However, large-scale capitalists would probably be among the top five percent or even one percent of income recipients, unless they had little or no income at all, deriving huge profits from property and wealth since capital gains are not considered to be income in Canada. Nevertheless, most Canadians do depend for their livelihood on income, whether in the form of salaries or government transfer payments. Income distribution could therefore indirectly indicate the range of differences within the working class and the underclass.

In collecting data on income distribution, Statistics Canada defines income as cash income before taxes but after transfer payments. It consists of all money incomes from the following sources:

1. wages, salaries, sales commissions, and tips (before deductions for taxes, pensions, and so forth);
2. net income from self-employment (for example, income after expenses from farming, independent professional practice, roomers and boarders);
3. investment income (such as interest, dividends, rental income);
4. government transfer payments (such as Old Age Security, Family Allowances, Workers' Compensation, Training Allowances);
5. pensions (retirement pensions, annuities, and superannuation); and
6. miscellaneous income (such as scholarships or alimony).

The following are not included in income: gambling gains, money inherited in a lump sum, capital gains, and receipts from the sale of property or personal belongings. Nor does income include income in kind (such as meals and accommodation) or fringe benefits (such as holiday pay).

The usual measurement of income inequality is income distribution by quintile. This is similar to the distribution of wealth by decile discussed earlier. Income units (families and unattached individuals) or individuals with incomes are divided into five equal groups, each containing 20 percent of units or individuals. The placement of units or individuals in each group is done according to the ranking by size of income of every unit or individual. The first 20 percent are those with the lowest incomes, and they form the bottom quintile. The next 20 percent form the second quintile, and so forth. The fifth quintile includes the 20 percent with the highest incomes (Ross, 1980).

Table 7.1 gives the distribution of income among families and individuals for selected years between 1951 and 1979. Table 7.2 gives the percentage distribution of total income of individuals with incomes by quintiles.

It can be readily seen from these two tables that income distribution is unequal, although less so than the distribution of wealth. In 1979, 4.2 percent of all income went to the poorest 20 percent of income units, while 42.3 percent of all income went to the top 20 percent of income units. If the accounting is done for all individuals with incomes, the distribution is even more unequal: 2.7 percent of all income for the

Table 7.1 Distribution of Income Among Families and Unattached Individuals for Selected Years, 1951–1979

	All Units								*1979*	
	1951	*1961*	*1967*	*1971*	*1973*	*1975*	*1977*	*1979*	*Families*	*Unattached Individuals*
Average Income	$ 3 185	4 815	6 519	8 845	10 694	13 805	16 764	17 123	20 554	8 891
Median Income	$ 2 703	4 262	5 859	7 832	9 441	12 179	14 969	15 499	19 214	7 509
Gini coefficient[2]	0.3904	0.3679	0.3789	0.4001	0.3924	0.3917	0.3878	0.387	0.315	0.379
Upper limit of:[3]				current dollars						
Bottom quintile[1]	1 260	1 930	2 592	3 110	3 980	5 038	5 973	7 331	11 851	3 777
Second quintile	2 310	3 586	4 824	6 275	7 620	9 793	12 013	14 148	19 214	5 820
Middle quintile	3 180	4 950	6 807	9 395	11 286	14 565	17 993	21 380	25 512	10 500
Fourth quintile	4 320	6 630	9 468	12 941	15 943	20 598	25 598	30 400	33 963	16 000
Shares of total income going to:[3]				percentage						
Bottom quintile	4.4	4.2	4.2	3.6	3.9	4.0	3.8	4.2	6.1	4.6
Second quintile	11.2	11.8	11.4	10.6	10.7	10.6	10.7	10.6	13.0	8.9
Middle quintile	18.3	18.3	17.8	17.6	17.6	17.6	17.9	17.6	18.4	15.8
Fourth quintile	23.3	24.4	24.6	24.9	25.1	25.1	25.6	25.3	24.3	25.1
Fifth quintile	42.8	41.3	42.0	43.3	42.7	42.6	42.0	42.3	38.3	45.6
Total	100.0	100.0	100.0	100.0	100.0	100.0	100.0	100.0	100.0	100.0

[1] Farmers not included before 1967. All data shown are in current dollars.

[2] The Gini coefficient measures the inequality of income distribution. Its value ranges from 0 to 1. The higher the value the greater the degree of inequality.

[3] Each quintile contains one-fifth of all units; for example, the lowest quintile contains the fifth of families and unattached individuals with the lowest incomes.

SOURCES: Statistics Canada, *Perspective Canada III*, 1980, p. 103; and *Income Distribution by Size in Canada*, 1979. Reproduced by permission of the Minister of Supply and Services Canada.

Table 7.2 Percentage Distribution of Total Income of Individuals with Income by Quintiles

Year	*Bottom Quintile*	*Second Quintile*	*Middle Quintile*	*Fourth Quintile*	*Top Quintile*	*Total*
1951	3.2	9.2	17.4	25.2	45.0	100.0
1954	2.8	8.6	17.0	25.6	46.0	100.0
1957	3.3	9.5	17.5	25.4	44.3	100.0
1959	3.4	9.1	17.3	25.8	44.4	100.0
1961	3.1	8.9	17.2	26.0	44.8	100.0
1965	2.5	7.9	16.8	26.0	46.8	100.0
1967	2.7	8.4	16.8	25.8	46.3	100.0
1969	2.1	7.4	15.9	25.8	48.8	100.0
1971	2.0	7.2	15.5	26.0	49.2	100.0
1972	2.4	7.8	15.7	26.1	48.1	100.0
1973	2.3	7.9	15.7	25.9	48.2	100.0
1974	2.6	8.1	15.8	25.5	48.1	100.0
1975	2.5	8.0	15.9	25.7	47.9	100.0
1976	2.2	7.7	15.4	25.4	49.2	100.0
1977	2.5	8.2	16.1	26.4	47.0	100.0
1978	2.2	7.8	15.6	26.2	48.3	100.0
1979	2.7	8.3	16.0	26.0	47.1	100.0

SOURCE: David P. Ross, *The Canadian Fact Book on Income Distribution*, 1980, Table 2; and Statistics Canada, *Income Distribution by Size in Canada*, 1979.

bottom quintile as compared to 47.1 percent of all income for the top quintile. "Obviously the pooling of several family members' earnings . . . helps to narrow the greater inequality of individually received incomes" (Ross, 1980: 11–15).

The income shares of all income units in the bottom two quintiles in 1979, totalling 14.8 percent, even fall short of the 17.6 percent of the income share of the middle quintile (Table 7.1). This strongly suggests that the bottom two quintiles, and not just the lowest quintile, of the Canadian population are doing poorly. If any shift toward greater equality in Canadian incomes is to take place, it would have to occur between the top and the two lowest quintiles (Ross, 1980, p. 15).

The most alarming feature of tables 7.1 and 7.2 is that the pattern of distribution has remained quite stable over a period of almost three decades. All the more disturbing, it was during this period (especially in the 1960s) that the Canadian state, led by the federal government, greatly expanded its legitimization function and established or expanded many cash transfer payment programs such as Old Age Security, Family Allowances, and Unemployment Insurance. Thatcher (1982, pp. 30–31) argues that the establishment and liberalization of transfer payment programs at that time could be seen as a defensive response by a relatively weak federal government to challenges from the provincial governments as to the legitimacy of Confederation itself. The legitimization function of the state will be discussed in the next chapter. For now, the discussion will centre on the impact of these programs on income distribution.

Government Budgetary Policy

A government through its budget policy can affect income distribution in two ways: through the tax system and through the expenditure system (Ross, 1980). In the tax system, the government decides how to raise revenue; that is, whom to tax and by how much. In the expenditure system, the government decides how to spend its money: on whom and by how much. Transfer payments are amounts that the government collects from some people and transfers to others. "If, for example, low-income Canadians receive proportionally more of all spending, and pay proportionally less of all taxes, then we should expect the overall impact to reduce income inequalities" (Ross, 1980, p. 49). Of course, how much inequality is tolerable or desirable is a moral and political question.

Although the rhetoric of the Canadian state may at times include terms such as "redistribution" and "equalization" (Canada, Government of, 1969, p. 60), to redistribute income more equally has never been its serious or explicit goal (Gillespie, 1978). Rather, reflecting the ideology of modified individualism, the aim of the Canadian state is to eliminate poverty at the same time as preserving the status quo. In other words, a certain pattern of income inequality is to be maintained as long as no significant segments of the total population are living in poverty. This is accomplished through the tax and expenditure systems.

The Tax System

A tax system can be progressive, proportional, or regressive. It is progressive if the rich pay a greater percentage of income than the poor, that is, if the rich are taxed at a higher rate. The reason behind progressive taxation is that the rich are better able to pay. A progressive tax system has a redistributive impact in that it tends to equalize income between the rich and the poor. A regressive tax system takes a greater percentage of income from the poor than from the rich; the tax rate for the poor is higher than that for the rich. A proportional system has the same tax rate for all income groups; it takes equal proportions from the rich, the middle-income, and the poor.

The Canadian tax system is complex. To find out whether it is progressive or not, one has to look at its four major components: (a) personal income tax, (b) tax expenditures, (c) other taxes, and (d) "fiscal" welfare and "occupational" welfare.

Personal income tax. Personal income taxes in Canada are progressive in principle. The higher the income, the higher is its tax rate; that is, the greater the percentage amount paid to the government. It would therefore be expected that personal income taxes would have a redistributive impact in favour of low-income groups. However, when the pretax income distribution is compared with the posttax distribution (see Table 7.3), the changes brought about by income taxes are quite modest. The top quintile's share of income dropped about two percentage points as a result of personal income taxes. The bottom and middle quintiles gained by about half a percentage point, while the second quintile gained the most by almost a full point. The fourth quintile's share was virtually unaffected.

If the ability-to-pay principle of progressivity were really operational, how could the changes in the income shares of various groups resulting from personal income taxes be so modest? The answer lies in the tax loopholes provided in the personal income tax that negate the intent of progressive taxation.

Tax expenditures. The Income Tax Act provides for tax expenditures that ensure a tax break to some income recipients who can then save substantial amounts of money that progressive taxation would otherwise have required them to pay (National Council of Welfare (NCW), 1976).

The savings can be made in the form of deductions and exemptions from income, tax deferrals, tax reductions, credits against tax, and preferential tax rates, which are collectively called "tax incentives" or "loopholes". But these savings for some individuals are in fact revenue lost (spent) by the government. Thus, these deductions and exemptions would more accurately be called "tax subsidies" (to some individuals) or "tax expenditures" (by the government) (NCW, 1976, p. 6). It should be noted that tax expenditures are distinct from the more commonly known government expenditures, such as those on welfare programs.

That these tax expenditures are government subsidies to individuals is demonstrated by an example given by the National Council of Welfare. A person earns $20 000 in a year: $19 000 in wages and $1000 in interest from a savings account. The tax on $20 000 is $5020, based on the 1976 tax and exemption rates applicable to an Ontario resident. Provisions in the Income Tax Act, however, allow this income taxpayer to deduct up to $1000 of interest income before arriving at taxable income. In other words, $1000 of the taxpayer's interest income is tax free; he pays tax on only $19 000. This amounts to $4640, which is less than the tax on $20 000.

> The entirety of this $380 tax savings is due to the special deduction for interest income. In a very real sense, then, the government has spent—by not collecting the tax—the amount of $380. From the point of view of the taxpayer, he has received a subsidy of $380—a reward, as it were, for

Table 7.3 Pretax and Posttransfer Income Distribution Comparisons by Quintile, Selected Years

	1971			*1974*			*1975*			*1977*			*1979*		
	Share of Total Income			*Share of Total Income*			*Share of Total Income*			*Share of Total Income*			*Share of Total Income*		
*Income Quintile**	*Before Taxes %*	*After Taxes %*	*Change %*	*Before Taxes %*	*After Taxes %*	*Change %*	*Before Taxes %*	*After Taxes %*	*Change %*	*Before Taxes %*	*After Taxes %*	*Change %*	*Before Taxes %*	*After Taxes %*	*Change %*
Bottom	3.6	4.2	+ .6	4.0	4.6	+ .6	4.0	4.6	+ .6	3.8	4.4	+ .6	4.2	4.8	+ .6
Second	10.6	11.5	+ .9	10.9	11.7	+ .8	10.6	11.5	+ .9	10.7	11.6	+ .9	10.6	11.5	+ .9
Third	17.8	18.2	+ .6	17.7	18.2	+ .5	17.6	18.2	+ .6	17.9	18.4	+ .5	17.6	18.1	+ .5
Fourth	24.9	25.0	+ .1	24.9	24.9	0	25.1	25.1	0	25.6	25.5	− .1	25.3	25.2	− .1
Top	43.3	41.1	−2.2	42.5	40.6	−1.9	42.6	40.6	−2.0	42.0	40.2	−1.8	42.3	40.3	−2.0

*The unit in each group is a family or an unattached individual.

SOURCES: Statistics Canada, *Income After Tax, Distribution by Size in Canada*, various years. Reproduced by permission of the Minister of Supply and Services Canada.

> having saved enough money in the bank to have gained $1000 in interest.
> The government could have chosen to collect the full tax on $20 000 and then paid this person, through a direct transfer, a grant of $380 as the means for giving him this "reward." The government would have ended up with the same net revenue and the taxpayer with the same net income. Furthermore the government accounts would have shown that it has spent $380. However because the subsidy is accomplished through an exemption from taxes, in never appears as a government expenditure (NCW, 1976, p. 13).

The concealment of subsidy in a tax exemption does not make it any less a government expense. It has been estimated that in 1974, 17 out of approximately 60 tax subsidies in the personal income tax system cost Canadians $6.4 billion.[2] This sum was "equal to well over one-fifth of the entire federal budget in 1974. . .(and) four and a half times the cost of the Olympic games" (NCW, 1976, p. 16). The sum was also 12 times the total amount of funds transferred from the federal government to the ten provinces and the territories for all the social welfare expenses incurred in 1974 (Canada, Statistics Canada, 1977, p. 977). By 1976, the total amount of government revenue lost due to 20 such tax expenditures rose to 7.1 billion (NCW, 1979a:2).[3] In 1979, the Canadian government finally made public some estimates of federal tax expenditures in 1976 and 1979 for the individual income tax, the corporate income tax, and commodity tax. It was shown that tax expenditures are numerous, the values of some of which are large in terms of renounced tax revenues. In some areas, "the amounts involved are comparable to or even larger than related direct spending programs" (Canada, Department of Finance, 1979, p. 28). It was estimated that in 1979 federal tax expenditures made up 60 percent of all direct expenditures (Ross, 1981, p. 102).

Tax subsidies benefit Canadians differentially: the higher their income, the greater their benefit (Table 7.4). The poorest, whose incomes fall below the income tax paying threshold, receive no benefit at all.

Deductions and exemptions always give those with higher incomes greater benefit: they take money out of the income bracket taxed at the highest rate applicable to their income. Thus, income tax rates may be progressive, but the intended purpose of distributing the tax burden according to the ability to pay is defeated by allowing incomes to be taxed at lower rates; more simply put, subsidies are granted to those with higher incomes.

The best known deductions are contributions to the registered retirement savings plans, registered home ownership savings plan and registered pension plans, interest income deduction, and child care deduction. Even if these tax subsidies were intended as incentives to foster national savings among ordinary Canadians, their implementation makes them both arbitrary and unjust because the wealthy derive

Table 7.4 Estimated % Distribution of Total Benefits from the 20 Tax Subsidies and Average Benefit per Taxfiler, 1976

Income Group (Decile)		*% of Total Benefits from the 20 Tax Subsidies*	*Average Benefit per Taxfiler ($)*
(Bottom 10%)	1st	0	0
	2nd	1.0	59.57
	3rd	3.1	179.23
	4th	5.4	312.29
	5th	6.5	372.09
	6th	7.8	445.93
	7th	10.0	570.15
	8th	12.8	735.57
	9th	17.3	992.04
(Top 10%)	10th	36.1	2068.40

SOURCE: National Council of Welfare, *The Hidden Welfare System Revisited,* 1979, p. 7.

the greatest benefit from them, while low- and middle-income tax payers receive only modest benefits.

It may be argued that the purpose of most exemptions, such as those for wholly dependent children, for blind and disabled persons, and for students, is to lessen the financial burden of specific categories of people with special needs. While such an aim is of course reasonable and socially justifiable, it may be more equitably met by means of tax credits (see chapter 9). However, the tax exemption mechanisms now in use always guarantee the greatest benefit to those who already have the most income (NCW, 1976).

Other taxes. Personal income taxes, federal and provincial, constitute the largest single source of government revenue, but account for only one-third of all tax revenues collected by all levels of governments (Ross, 1980, p. 52). Other taxes that provide revenues are corporate tax, municipal property tax, sales tax (federal and provincial), selective excise taxes (such as those on liquor and tobacco), natural resources taxes, and income security and health insurance taxes. Property and sales taxes together make up 30 percent of all government tax revenues.

While tax expenditures undermine the principle of progressive taxation, personal income taxes remain the only part of the Canadian tax system that reduces income inequality in any way. The Report of the Royal Commission on Taxation in Canada published in 1966 found that the personal income tax is the only progressive component of the entire tax system. The other taxes are largely regressive. As a result, the total tax system has poor families paying larger percentages of their pretransfer payment income in taxes than richer families. For the 1961 tax year, families with incomes of $10 000 over paid 38.4 percent of their income in a variety of taxes, while families with incomes under $2000 paid 60 percent of their pretransfer income. For families in income groups between these two amounts, the total tax system is proportional: about one-third of their income was paid in taxes (Ross, 1980, p. 52).

The most recent available data for 1969, and that provided by Maslove (1972) found that the poorest Canadians still paid the highest overall tax rate. In the main, the heavy tax burden borne by the poor is composed of corporate taxes, part of which is passed on to them as higher prices; property taxes passed on to them by the landlords in the form of rent; and sales and excise taxes passed on as higher prices. Moreover, the nonincome taxes used to fund social insurance programs (such as contributions to Canada Pension Plan, and premiums on unemployment insurance and health care) are regressive because (a) contributions to social insurance programs are tax deductible, which means that they, like the other tax deductions and exemptions, accrue the greatest benefits to the highest income earners; and (b) the fixed maximum contributions would constitute a decreasing percentage of income as earnings rise. Yet pension and unemployment insurance benefits paid to those with higher incomes are greater (NCW, 1978 a).

"Fiscal" welfare and "occupational" welfare. In sum, the principle of progressive taxation contained in the personal income tax is thwarted first by tax expenditures and then by other regressive taxes. The overall effect of the total tax system is regressive, and these regressive features constitute what is known as "fiscal" welfare for those with higher incomes. Yet its beneficiaries typically view this form of welfare as having been earned. "More is heard of their complaints concerning the taxes they pay than is heard of recognition of the value of the taxes from which they are exempt" (Armitage, 1975, p. 121).

Related to "fiscal" welfare and the tax system is "occupational" welfare, which also seems to confer the greatest benefit to those in the top quintile of income recipients. While permanent employees of large corporations may be given some fringe benefits, such as dental care and subsidized meals, it is the wealthy who enjoy the bulk of "occupational" welfare. It includes residences; company cars; chauffeurs; personal expenses for travel, entertainment, and dress; and holiday expenses, among other things. There is little systematic knowledge about "occupational" welfare, yet it is tacitly recognized insofar as it is excluded from the definition of income for tax purposes. Although employers (mainly the large corporations) provide "occupational" welfare, the cost nevertheless falls on the entire body of taxpayers because the various items are tax deductible (Titmuss, 1974, p. 139).

"Fiscal" and "occupational" welfare are referred to in quotation marks because they are not intended by the state to be welfare programs: they are not recorded in government accounts as welfare payments. It is true that they stem from the tax system, but they certainly extend beyond the usual sense of social welfare, which is the provision of the minimum or basic living standard.

The Expenditure System

The second component of government budgetary policy, the expenditure system, will be discussed under (a) Cash Transfers and (b) Health and Education Benefits.

Government cash transfers. Cash transfers, also known as income security programs, can be administered by the federal, provincial, or municipal government. Four federal programs—Old Age Security, Old Age Security Guaranteed Income Supplement, Family and Youth Allowances, and Canada/Quebec Pension Plans—account for over three-quarters of all government spending in income security programs. The main cash transfers are discussed in chapter 9. Here, we are concerned only with their effect on the redistribution of income.

Data on the redistributive impact of government cash transfers are available for the 1970s alone. A close look at the distribution of benefits of the total income security system shows that, overall, it provides benefits in a progressive manner (see Table 7.5). The bottom quintiles receive greater shares of benefits than the top quintiles. Consequently, there is a tendency toward reducing income inequality (Ross, 1980, p. 65). However, two points should be kept in mind.

First, the higher income groups have maintained, and perhaps even improved, their proportion of transfer payments, at least in the early 1970s (Ross, 1980). Second, the differences are not large. In 1975, the top quintile received only six percent less than the bottom quintile. The top two quintiles received, in fact, one-third of all benefits. The reason for this pattern of cash transfers is that not all income security programs are progressive. For example, Social Assistance, by virtue of the means-test required of all applicants, benefits almost exclusively the low income groups. Similarly, Canada/Quebec Pension Plans, Old Age Security, and OAS Guaranteed Income Supplement are open only to those who are over 65 years of age, and the elderly on the whole are heavily concentrated in the bottom quintiles. Thus, these programs have a progressive impact. Family Allowances, on the other hand, are distributed regressively. In 1975, the bottom quintile received only 5.7 percent of all Family Allowance benefits mainly because many unattached individuals, especially the elderly without eligible children, made up the bottom quintile. The Child Tax Credit introduced in 1979 might have a more equalizing effect, but no data on its impact on income distribution is yet available. Unemployment Insurance benefits seem to be proportional or somewhat regressive. Unemployment Insurance gives little assistance to the bottom quintile (only 8.1 percent of all benefits in 1975) because many people in that quintile fail to qualify for benefits due to underemployment, intermittent employment, or permanent unemployment (Ross, 1980). In the final analysis, the redistributive impact of the cash transfers is less than what might have been expected.

Statistics Canada data on income distribution reveal that the major source of income for the bottom quintile today is government cash transfers. Also, if one recalls that, over the years, the bottom quintile has consistently received only about four percent of posttransfer income, while the top quintile has received about 42 percent (Table 7.1), it would appear that in order to lessen the overall income inequality in any meaningful way, a much more progressive benefit structure than that shown in Table 7.5 is necessary (Ross, 1980). On the other hand, if it were not for government transfer payments, the shares of income received by the two bottom quintiles would be even less.

Health and education benefits. The impact of cash transfers on reducing income inequality is discernible, although limited. It is sometimes claimed that if the free and subsidized services available to all Canadians

Table 7.5 Distribution of Total Benefits[1] of Government Cash Transfers Across All Economic Families, Ordered by Total Income After Tax[2]

	1971	*1973*	*1974*	*1975*
Quintile	*Total Benefits (%)*	*Total Benefits (%)*	*Total Benefits (%)*	*Total Benefits (%)*
First	25.1	24.4	24.0	23.4
Second	28.9	26.4	25.1	25.2
Third	17.5	17.4	17.1	18.2
Fourth	14.2	15.8	17.1	16.2
Fifth	14.3	16.0	16.7	17.0
Total	100.0	100.0	100.0	100.0

[1] Benefits includes Family and Youth Allowance, Unemployment Insurance, Canada and Quebec Pension Plans, Old Age Security, Guaranteed Income Supplement as well as Workmen's Compensation, pensions and assistance to veterans and the indigenous population, assistance to blind and disabled persons. Benefits are on a before-tax basis.

[2] All family units are divided into five quintiles each containing 20 percent of the family units. The first quintile contains the family units with the lowest total after-tax income, while the fifth quintile contains the highest after-tax incomes.

SOURCE: With permission from J.E. Cloutier, *The Distribution of Benefits and Costs of Social Security in Canada 1971-1975*, Economic Council of Canada Discussion Paper No. 108, Ottawa, 1978, Table 3, p. 6.

were translated into dollar values, it could be shown that those in the bottom quintiles would be receiving numerous benefits and that the distribution of income would therefore be more equal. However, it is not easy to determine the redistributive impact of social services. Existing studies have produced conflicting results, especially with regard to health services. Here, only the two largest social services, health care and education, will be mentioned.

Statistics Canada conducted a survey on the use of education and health services in 1974 (Canada, Statistics Canada, 1974). Dollar values, based on the net cost to the government, were assigned to the use of these services. The dollar values were then added to income. It was found that 70 percent of all income groups used physicians' services in 1974 and that the usage was quite evenly spread across all income groups. More low income than high income units made use of hospital services, whereas a greater number of high income than low income families made use of education services, especially at the postsecondary level. When the dollar values are assigned to health and education benefits, the higher income families do in fact receive larger dollar benefits—more than double the share received by low income families. Yet it can be said that the benefits are progressively distributed; as proportions of income, they are larger for low income than for high income families.

On the whole, the elderly, who are disproportionately concentrated in the low income groups, are the heaviest users of health care services. On the other hand, there appears to be a strong positive correlation between the size of parental income and children's attendance at university and other postsecondary institutions.

Overall Effect of Government Budgetary Policy

At the beginning of this chapter, we mentioned that the government can redistribute income more equally through the tax system and the expenditure system, that is, through budgetary policy. In terms of broad categories, the greatest redistributive effect is made through cash transfers (Social Assistance, Old Age Security, and so on), followed by personal income taxes, health and educational services, and finally other taxes (such as the sales tax and property tax). However, it should be recalled that some cash transfers, such as Family Allowances and Unemployment Insurance benefits, are not progressive, and that the higher income groups derive greater dollar value benefits from health and education services. Thus, many transfer programs in cash or in kind established in the 1960s did give the poor a small relative gain. But other features of the tax and expenditure systems (federal and provincial) have counteracted the redistributive impact. Consequently, income inequality in Canada has virtually remained unchanged in the last 30 years

(Gillespie, 1976; Ross, 1980). Government redistribution efforts at best have prevented the gap between the rich and the poor from widening.

Poverty in Canada

Poverty and Poverty Lines

Just as the word "welfare" is deemed to have an image problem, there has been a tendency since the 1970s to avoid the use of such terms as "poor", "poverty", and "poverty line". Statistics Canada, which collects and provides most of the data on income distribution, uses two specific terms in discussing the poor: "low income" is used to mean "poverty" and "low income cutoff" is used instead of "poverty line".

There are two approaches to defining poverty or low income: the absolute and the relative (Ross, 1981, p. 4). In the absolute approach, poverty status is determined in terms of the basic subsistence needs of the family. If the basic necessities of life (food, clothing, and shelter) cost $6000 per year for a family of four, a family earning less would be considered poor. The relative approach considers not merely a family's subsistence needs, but also the living standards of other families in the community. If in a year the cost of basic necessities of life is $6000 for a family of four, but the average income in the community is $20 000 per family, a family with an income of $7000 would not be poor in the absolute sense (because it could afford all the necessities), but would be relatively poor because its standard of living would be a bit lower than the average. "The relative approach does not imply, in its extreme, that all incomes should be equal. . .(but) it places a floor on just how low incomes should be relative to the community average" (Ross, 1980, p. 5).

There are three poverty lines, or low-income cutoffs, in use in Canada, which are devised by Statistics Canada, the Canadian Council on Social Development, and the Special Senate Committee on Poverty. None of these are completely absolute or completely relative (Caskie, 1979, p. 3).

The Statistics Canada line. Although Statistics Canada does not regard its low-income cutoff as the official poverty line, it is the most widely accepted and used. This line comes closest to being based on the absolute income and subsistence concept of poverty. It has been established by Statistics Canada that Canadian families spend on average 42 percent of their income on basic necessities. Since poor families must allocate an above-average proportion of their limited income to basic necessities, families that spend 62 percent or more of their income (at least 20 percentage points above the average) on the subsistence necessities are considered poor. This family income figure corresponds on average to a low-income cutoff.

Before June 1980, Statistics Canada based its low-income cutoffs on

1969 information of family expenditures. In June 1980, it revised them based on 1978 information on family expenditures. The lines are updated each year according to changes in the cost of living as measured by the Consumer Price Index. For example, as the inflation rate was 12.5 precent in 1981, the 1980 lines were increased by 12.5 percent to give the 1981 low income cutoffs (NCW, 1982a and 1982b).

Since family size and place of residence affect the cost of living, Statistics Canada adjusts its low-income cutoffs to these two factors (see Table 7.6). There are seven categories of family size ranging from a single person to seven or more persons. Communities are divided into six groups according to population size.

The Canadian Council on Social Development (CCSD) line. This is a more relative poverty line because it is based on a measure of income inequality. Families and individuals are considered poor if their income is less than 50 percent of the average Canadian income. The CCSD line is adjusted to family size but not to the size of the place of residence.

The Senate Committee line. This line was devised by the Special Senate Committee on Poverty when it prepared its report on poverty in 1971. It is somewhat complicated to calculate, as it combines some elements from both the Statistics Canada and CCSD lines. Based on a measure of expenditures (as in the Statistics Canada line) rather than simply on income (as in the CCSD line), the Senate Committee line is also adjusted for family size but not for community size. By means of a complex technique, it is updated each year to account for changes in average living standards. Since it was first computed, the Senate committee line has consistently corresponded to 56 percent as compared to CCSD's 50 percent of average family income. The Senate Committee line is usually considered to be the most relative. It was also the most generous of the three before Statistics Canada revised its low-income cutoffs in June 1980. But the Senate Committee line is infrequently used.

The Poor

Who are the poor in Canada? At the end of the 1970s, it was estimated that about ten percent of all families, 35 percent of unattached individuals, or 17.4 percent of all income units, had low incomes (Ross, 1981, p. 6). Although those living in poverty would be found in the lowest income group (bottom quintile), the fourth quintile receives only about ten percent of Canada's income (Table 7.1). Members of this group do in fact share many of the problems faced by the bottom quintile. Thus, in discussing the poverty population, one could reasonably group the bottom two quintiles together.

There are several characteristics that have been persistently linked with poverty, the greatest single determinant being labour force status. The incidence of poverty is much greater for those not in the labour force (Table 7.7). "The absence of employment and the resulting shortfall in

Table 7.6 Statistics Canada Revised (1978) Low Income Cutoffs, 1980 and 1981

Family size	*500 000 and over*	*100 000 - 499 999*	*30 000 - 99 999*	*Less than 30 000*	*Rural*
			1980		
1	$ 7 152	$ 6 792	$ 6 371	$ 5 890	$ 5 289
2	9 436	8 955	8 355	7 753	6 912
3	12 622	11 961	11 179	10 398	9 256
4	14 545	13 823	12 922	12 020	10 699
5	16 949	16 047	14 966	13 943	12 441
6	18 511	17 490	16 348	15 206	13 583
7 or more	20 375	19 293	18 031	16 769	14 966
			1981		
1	$ 8 045	$ 7 640	$ 7 167	$ 6 626	$ 5 949
2	10 614	10 073	9 398	8 721	7 775
3	14 198	13 455	12 575	11 697	10 412
4	16 361	15 549	14 536	13 521	12 035
5	19 066	18 051	16 835	15 684	13 995
6	20 823	19 674	18 390	17 105	15 279
7 or more	22 919	21 702	20 283	18 863	16 835

SOURCE: National Council of Welfare, *Revised 1982 Poverty Lines*, 1982.

Table 7.7 Characteristics of the Poor, 1977

	*Families**		*Unattached individuals*	
	Low income	*Other*	*Low income*	*Other*
		Percentage		
Province of residence:				
Newfoundland	3.0	2.0	1.7	0.8
Prince Edward Island	0.5	0.5	0.5	0.4
Nova Scotia	3.7	3.3	4.0	2.9
New Brunswick	3.5	2.7	2.7	2.1
Quebec	30.5	26.6	26.3	22.2
Ontario	32.1	37.5	33.5	37.3
Manitoba	5.3	4.2	6.2	4.4
Saskatchewan	4.3	3.9	4.6	4.6
Alberta	7.1	8.3	7.2	10.2
British Columbia	10.0	10.9	13.3	15.0
TOTAL	100.0	100.0	100.0	100.0

Table 7.7 (cont'd.)

	*Families**		*Unattached individuals*	
	Low income	*Other*	*Low income*	*Other*
	Percentage			
Population of area of residence:				
500 000 persons and over	32.2	32.7	36.1	37.5
100 000 - 499 999 persons	21.1	23.4	24.8	27.0
30 000 - 99 999 persons	7.9	7.6	9.7	7.2
15 000 - 29 999 persons	6.0	6.5	7.2	8.1
Small urban areas (less than 15 000) persons	11.4	11.2	12.6	10.3
Rural areas	21.2	18.6	9.5	10.1
TOTAL	100.0	100.0	100.0	100.0
Weeks worked by head in the year:				
None	52.0	11.6	67.5	17.3
1-9 weeks	4.0	0.8	4.2	1.6
10-19 weeks	5.4	1.8	8.3	3.1
20-29 weeks	5.6	3.4	5.5	4.9
30-39 weeks	4.0	3.5	3.0	5.1
40-49 weeks	4.5	4.6	2.1	5.5
50-52 weeks	24.5	74.2	9.3	62.5
TOTAL	100.0	100.0	100.0	100.0
Age of head:				
24 years and under	8.1	5.6	23.8	25.2
25-34 years	25.0	26.2	7.5	25.5
35-44 years	17.7	21.9	4.0	9.2
45-54 years	13.4	20.7	7.9	10.5
55-64 years	13.0	14.8	14.1	11.7
65-69 years	8.7	4.9	10.6	5.8
70 years and over	14.2	6.0	32.1	12.0
TOTAL	100.0	100.0	100.0	100.0
Current employment status of head:				
Employee	31.7	75.9	21.2	74.6
Employer or self-employed	12.8	8.9	4.6	3.3
Not in labour force	55.5	15.1	74.1	22.2
TOTAL	100.0	100.0	100.0	100.0
Education of head:				
0-8 years	44.8	27.5	42.0	16.9
Some high school and no postsecondary	39.3	43.0	32.6	40.9

Table 7.7 (cont'd.)

	*Families**		*Unattached individuals*	
	Low income	*Other*	*Low income*	*Other*
	Percentage			
Some postsecondary	6.7	8.2	13.0	13.1
Postsecondary certificate or diploma	5.7	10.5	7.2	13.5
University degree	3.6	10.8	5.2	15.5
TOTAL	100.0	100.0	100.0	100.0
Nonfarm and farm residence:				
Not-resident of farm	92.3	95.3	98.2	98.3
Resident on farm	7.7	4.7	1.8	1.7
TOTAL	100.0	100.0	100.0	100.0
Major source of income:				
No income	1.8		8.5	
Wages and salaries	27.0	84.0	23.3	76.5
Net income from self-employment	8.0	5.6	2.0	2.3
Transfer payments	57.5	6.5	61.0	9.2
Investment income	2.4	2.0	2.9	6.8
Pension and miscellaneous income	3.4	1.9	2.3	5.1
TOTAL	100.0	100.0	100.0	100.0
Number of children under 16 years:				
None	41.0	45.7	100.0	100.0
One child	19.6	21.7		
Two children	20.7	21.3		
Three children	11.6	8.1		
Four or more children	7.1	3.3		
TOTAL	100.0	100.0	100.0	100.0
Sex of head:				
Male	67.6	93.3	33.9	50.5
Female	32.4	6.7	66.1	49.5
TOTAL	100.0	100.0	100.0	100.0
ESTIMATED TOTAL NUMBER	659	5207	842	1458

*Family units were classified by the head's employment status at the time of the survey. This is not necessarily the employment status during 1977.

SOURCE: Statistics Canada, *Perspectives Canada III*, 1980, Table 6.9. Reproduced by permission of the Minister of Supply and Services Canada.

income is the major element separating the poor from the non-poor" (Caskie, 1979, p. 27). The incidence of low-income families and unattached individuals decreases as the number of weeks worked by the principal income earner increases. However, about one-quarter of the low-income families and nine percent of low-income unattached individuals are employed full time the whole year round (50 to 52 weeks). These are the wage-earning poor (see Ross, 1981).

Related to labour force status is the number of earners in the family (not shown in the tables). According to Caskie (1979), the largest percentage of low-income families has only one income earner, whereas the largest percentage of other families has two. This again points to the importance of pooling of incomes by family members in attaining an average or near-average standard of living. Transfer payments provide most of the money income for those in the low income group, while wages and salaries are the main sources of those with high income.

A large number of the poor live in the four Atlantic provinces, and the largest percentage of both the poor and the nonpoor reside in cities with a population of 500 000 and more. The largest percentage of both low-income and other families are headed by males. However, the percentage of female heads is much greater among low-income families. Females constitute about two-thirds of low-income unattached individuals. The low-income families have a higher percentage of heads ages 24 and under, and 70 and over, than the nonpoor families. The largest single group of low-income unattached individuals is in the age category of 70 years and over. It is clear that the age and sex of the head of the family are important factors related to family income.

Life Cycles and Composition of the Poverty Population

After examining the income distribution and some of the characteristics of the poor, an important question remains. Do the same persons live below the poverty line year after year or do Canadians move from one income quintile to another? This type of questioning is based on the assumption that a person's income varies according to the different stages in the life cycle, and the annual income is a poor measure of income inequality in society. According to the "life cycle" hypothesis:

> . . .young people are apt to earn low incomes and have little wealth because they undergo an initial training period in life and earnings are highly experience related. Also, at this time, family responsibilities are low. During mid-life, earnings reach their highest levels, wealth starts to accumulate, and family obligations are generally at their highest level. During the later stages of life, earnings are again low, the stock of wealth has reached its maximum, and family obligations are again at a much reduced level (Ross, 1980, pp. 32–33).

On the basis of limited evidence, Ross (1980) concluded that most of the families in the bottom quintile are likely to remain at the bottom if the present income distribution factors and policies continue. Two-thirds of the heads of families in the bottom quintile are not young (24 years and under) or elderly (65 years and over) but are in their prime. Their low-income status cannot be accounted for by the life cycle hypothesis. Furthermore, 44 percent of families living below the poverty line have heads in the labour force. It would seem that for the poorest families, whether they are in the labour force or on social assistance, their incomes are insufficient or too insecure to move them into higher income groups. Although "some of the young. . .temporarily earn low incomes while undergoing training and some of the old have low incomes but substantial wealth" (Ross, 1980, p. 34), there appears to be little significant shifting among quintiles on account of changes in individual income, although there is possibly more due to changes in family composition.

---

1. In presenting data on income or wealth, four categories are commonly used: families, unattached individuals, all units, and all individuals with income (or wealth). The *family* is a group of individuals related by blood, marriage, or adoption who share a common dwelling unit. An *unattached individual* is a person living alone or in a dwelling place where he or she is not related to other members of the dwelling place. *All units* is a category that includes both families and unattached individuals. *An individual with income* (or wealth), or *income recipient* (wealth holder), is any person 15 years or over who has received some money income (wealth). In income distribution, all incomes received by members of a family are assumed to be pooled together to form one family income. It should be pointed out that the pooling of incomes in families is an assumption. In fact, the extent of pooling varies from family to family. Members of a family do not necessarily have equal access to the "pooled" family income; in some case, one or more members may have no access to it at all.

2. The 17 tax subsidies on which the National Council of Welfare estimate is based are those about which there is sufficient information. They do not include (a) personal exemption and the deductions for expenses directly related to earning an income; (b) tax reductions through "dummy" companies set up by high-income earners such as managers and professionals, or tax reductions through other exotic loopholes; (c) revenue lost because some individuals with very, very high incomes paid no income tax at all (NCW, 1976, p. 18); and (d) revenue lost because of fraudulent tax returns.

3. The 20 tax expenditures are: the married or equivalent exemption; the age exemption; the exemption for wholly dependent children; the exemption for other dependents; the deductions for Canada/Quebec Pension contributions, Unemployment Insurance premiums, Registered Retirement Savings Plan contribution, Registered Pension Plan contributions, Registered Home Ownership Savings Plans, tuition fees, child care expenses, medical claims, and charitable donations; the interest and dividend deduction; the pension income deduction; the education deduction; the disability deduction; the standard deduction; eligible deductions transferred from spouse; and the dividend tax credit (NCW, 1979, p. 28).

8

The State and Social Welfare

Social inequality in our society does not spring from differences between individuals in terms of height, weight, colour of skin or eye, ability, intelligence, or talent, although all these have been used at various times in human history to justify or rationalize social inequality. Social inequality is generated by social structures. In the discussion of social inequality in Canada in the previous two chapters, two trends have been made quite clear. First is the widening gap in income between the capitalist class and the working class. In the drive for capital accumulation, capitalists usually resort to labour-replacing technology that renders many workers redundant; this enlarges the pool of potential but unemployed workers and depresses wage rates. Accumulated capital is reinvested, while control of production is centralized in the hands of the capitalists. Moreover, in corporate capitalism the larger corporations, especially the multinationals, have a competitive edge over smaller companies. The small enterprises either go out of business or are bought out by the larger ones; capital becomes concentrated in the hands of a few giant corporations. The overall consequence has the small number of capitalists becoming enormously rich, with the large majority of workers becoming relatively poorer over time.

A second trend in Canada related to social inequality is the fragmentation of the working class. Cleavages in the working class appear along lines of occupation, education, ethnicity, race, sex, and age. There are also differences between the primary labour market and the secondary labour market, between the unionized and the nonunionized workers, and between the employed and the unemployed. These differences within the working class are often reflected in income differentials to the extent that those with higher salaries and wages and higher socio-economic status often regard themselves as the "middle class." The differences in the objective economic conditions and self-perceptions by members of the working class have resulted in the absence of unity within the class. In fact, there are often tensions and conflicts among the various fragments of the working class. Consequently, there is no concerted line of action by the working class toward the capitalist class.

These two trends—inequality between capital and labour, and

inequality within the working class—stem from the very nature of the capitalist system, and are closely linked to the array of programs and services known as welfare activities. In the early years of small-scale, competitive industrial capitalism, which in Canada roughly covered the 30 years after Confederation, principles of *laissez-faire* were the dominant ideology. The free enterprise system allowed individuals to look after their own well-being, and no need was seen for the government to meddle in people's private affairs. While these notions lingered until the 1930s, in practice the Canadian state was never a *laissez-faire* state in the economic sense (Panitch, 1977). Furthermore, the state was involved in legislating social laws and in implementing social programs both before and after the First World War. During the Great Depression of the thirties, the pace of devising and carrying out social policies by the various levels of government accelerated. But it was not until after the Second World War that the welfare state came to its own in Canada and the principle of state responsibility for individual welfare was generally accepted.

In this chapter we shall discuss the role of the state in developing social welfare in the midst of continually generated social inequality. The functions of the state in capitalist society will be treated first, one function being the provision of social welfare. Then, the activities of the welfare state will be delineated. Here we should clarify that the state is the power structure of the government. But as Miliband (1969) has pointed out, the state is far more than just the government. The power structure consists of a complex of institutions: government (at central and sub-central levels), the bureaucracy (civil service, public corporations, regulatory agencies, central banks, and so on), the military, the judiciary, and the representative assemblies.

Functions of the State

It must be stressed that discussion of state functions does not validate a functionalist explanation of the welfare state. As Gough (1979, p. 50) states, functionalism contains the implicit assumption that analysis will reveal the causes of state action and responses to the functional requirements of capital. But this assumption is quite unjustified: stating the requirements for the accumulation or reproduction of capital does not give any indication as to whether the state fulfills those requirements or how it meets them. Such issues call for an empirical study of the manner in which those requirements are translated into political demands and state responses are formulated into policies. Although it is useful to specify the functions of the welfare state, we do not use the logic inherent in the structural-functionalist theory of society. According to that logic, whatever exists is necessary to bring about some consequence. In place of the functionalist logic, we use a Marxist methodology which postulates (a) a hierarchy of social phenomena, and (b) the existence within any society of internal contradictions that counteract the tendency of the system to maintain itself as a going concern. These two conditions in Marxist theory explain why and how societies change and transform themselves (Hobsbawn, 1972).

As has been mentioned earlier, the state is not a neutral arbiter between different social classes, but acts to ensure the political domination by one class over other classes (Gough, 1979, p. 41). Acting in the interest of the capitalist class, the state tries

> to fulfill two basic and often mutually contradictory functions—accumulation and legitimization. The state must try to maintain and create the conditions in which profitable capital accumulation is possible. However, the state must also try to maintain or create the conditions for social harmony (O'Connor, 1973, p. 6).

Panitch lists four tasks that the state performs in its first function—that of facilitating the capitalist class to accumulate capital:

1. The state provides a favourable fiscal and monetary climate for economic growth by private enterprises. This is reflected, among other things, in the fiscal policies presented in the national budget and in other economic policies intended to provide capitalists with incentives to invest. The state also promotes foreign trade by sending trade delegations abroad.
2. The state underwrites the high production risk faced by some private enterprises. For example, the Canadian state finances some private developers in building inexpensive housing for low-income families, considered to be high risk projects that yield low profits. Thus, the developers are ensured a profit. Such financing in housing is done through the Crown corporation Canada Mortgage and Housing Corporation, or through finance institutions that are guaranteed by CMHC.
3. The state has provided for capitalist development such physical infrastructure as railroads, airports, and port facilities, that are too risky or costly for private capital to undertake on its own. State construction, ownership, and operation of these facilities "were never undertaken as ends in themselves with the aim of managing or controlling the economy, but always with a view to facilitating further capital accumulation in the private sphere to the end of economic growth" (Panitch, 1977, p. 14).
4. The state has played a key role in creating and maintaining a sizeable amount of the social cost of production of capitalist enterprise through such mechanisms as immigration, public education, health care, and unemployment insurance.

The state carries out these four tasks (within its capital accumulation function) through public security, economic, and social policies.

The second function of the state, legitimization, encompasses those social policies aimed at integrating the subordinate classes within the capitalist social order. Labour legislation protecting workers' and unions' rights, governmental consultation with labour leaders, grants and subsidies to citizen action or dissident minority groups, and social assistance programs are some examples of the legitimization function. The aim of this function is social control by promoting social harmony. This is done through the introduction of reforms, or through the co-operation with leaders of labour, welfare, or ethnic groups by offering them a semblance of power and participation (Panitch, 1977).

Welfare Activities of the State

The welfare activities of the state can best be broached by examining how the state spends its money. Corresponding to the capital accumulation and legitimization functions of the state, nearly all state expenditures have a twofold character: social capital and social expenses. Furthermore, social capital can be subdivided into two types of activities: social investment (constant social capital) and social consumption (variable social capital). Thus, there are altogether three categories of state expenditure[1]:

1. *Social investments*: services and projects that raise labour productivity (constant social capital).
2. *Social consumption*: services and projects that lower the costs of reproducing labour-power (variable social capital).
3. *Social expenses*: services and projects that maintain social stability and promote social harmony.

Social capital expenditures, that is, social investment and social consumption, are indirectly productive for the capitalists in that they contribute to economic growth in the private sector. Social expenses, on the other hand, consist of various programs designed to maintain social order so that production and capital accumulation can proceed unhindered. They encompass assistance to the nonworking population and various ideological or coercive activities of the state concerned with controlling groups within that population that threaten social stability. "This would include the activities of some social workers, community workers, and race-relations bodies as well as the more obvious work of police, prison, and probation staff" (Gough, 1979, p. 52). Social expenses are necessary but unproductive for capital.

Almost every state agency performs both functions—capital accumulation and social control. Also, elements of social investment, social consumption, and social expense are found in almost every state expenditure. For example, education can be seen as social investment in that it raises labour productivity. Yet much of public education consists of socializing the young in values and ideas that support the capitalist system. Thus, education falls within both capital accumulation and legitimization functions of the state.

Most of the activities associated with social welfare are similar to education in that they have a dual function. Welfare activities are a social expense insofar as they fulfill the legitimization function; for example, social assistance that defuses the discontent and frustration of the poor helps to maintain social order. But they can also be seen as part of the capital accumulation function. Insofar as welfare programs more often lower the cost of reproducing labour-power than raising labour productivity, they are items of social consumption rather than social investment.

Reproduction of Labour-Power

The twofold function of welfare programs can be better understood if we first probe the meaning of the welfare state. According to the Marxist theory of the welfare state, the state uses its power to modify the reproduction of labour-power and to maintain the nonworking population (Gough, 1979, pp. 44–45). As has been mentioned earlier, labour-power is defined as a person's capacity to work. It is, therefore, necessary in all human societies to reproduce this capacity continually, a process which takes two forms: the daily and the generational. In capitalist societies, the daily reproduction of labour-power takes place in two stages. First, workers sell their labour-power to earn a wage or salary, which provides the means to buy consumption goods and services, such as food, shelter, clothing, transport, and entertainment. These are the items workers need in order to replenish their capacity to work. The second stage of daily reproduction comprises the various tasks in planning and budgeting for the purchase of consumption goods and services; in actually buying these items; and in further processing and preparing these items. The tasks include planning, shopping, cooking, laundry, cleaning, and so forth. In working class families, tasks in the second stage are usually performed by the housewife, who is not paid.

The generational reproduction of labour-power refers to physical procreation, which provides a new generation of workers whose labour-power will be available for sale in the future. In addition, child care and socialization duties must be considered part of the generational reproduction of labour-power. Again, the tasks associated with them are performed by the housewife.

As mentioned earlier, the state undertakes social consumption expenditure in order to lower the cost of reproducing labour-power. It does this by providing certain goods and services either free of charge or at lower price, so that they are available to the working class. Low-cost housing, medicare, public education, retraining programs, and community services are examples of social consumption that help to lower the cost of reproducing labour-power. The state also intervenes in another way, that is, by directly providing the working class with amounts of money to spend on consumption goods and services through the income security system, such as family allowances and unemployment insurance benefits. Furthermore, the state also regulates the standard and quality of goods and services sold on the market. Particular goods and services are subsidized, such as certain kinds of housing, foods, and transport.

Finally, since children make up the future labour force, the state has increasingly expanded its role in modifying the generational reproduction of labour-power. "Almost all social policies have a direct bearing on the capacity of the family to bring up children" (Gough, 1979, p. 46). The entire field of child welfare seeks not only to protect the physical well-being of children, but also to ensure their proper rearing and socialization. The most extreme measure is to make the children temporary or permanent wards of the state because the parents are judged to be unable or unwilling to care for them. In addition to family allowances, refundable child tax credit, education, specific health services (such as Saskatchewan's free dental care for children), and housing policies are all aimed at providing special benefits to families bringing up children.

Maintaining the Nonworking Population

The second major activity of the welfare state is maintaining the nonworking population. All societies contain categories of people who are not economically productive and must depend on others for their living. They are the young, the old, the sick, the mentally disabled, and other unemployable people. In most nonindustrial, noncapitalist societies, the dependent members share in the fruits of labour (called social product) of the productive members through the mechanisms of the nuclear family and extended kinship. In other words, family and relatives usually assume the responsibility of providing for and looking after the dependent members. But in capitalist societies, family and kinship structures are increasingly replaced or regulated by a variety of state measures. Old age security, social assistance, and a variety of social welfare services provide different kinds of support or supplement to the elderly, the sick, the unemployable, and the casual labourer, "gradually usurping the role of kinship and community in the past, and of charitable and voluntary bodies in the more recent past" (Gough, 1979, p. 47). These programs comprise social expenses because the basic aim is to promote social harmony with the effect of controlling the nonworking population. The effect of social control is institutionalized: it stems from the very structures of providing assistance to the nonworking population. This effect is produced, regardless of any altruistic motives of social workers and others who provide the actual assistance.

Just as elements of social investment, social consumption, and social expenses exist in state expenditures, the boundaries between the working and the nonworking populations are not always distinguishable. For example, children are part of the nonworking population, but they form the future labour force. Hence, the cost of their maintenance at present cannot be separated entirely from that of reproducing future labour-power. Another example is that of social assistance. O'Connor (1973) assigns welfare assistance programs to the category of social expenses on the assumption that welfare clients exist outside the capitalist mode of production whose subsistence nevertheless must be provided for by the state in the interest of social order. While this may be true to a certain extent, as in the case of assistance to the underclass, it is also true that social assistance clients move through a "revolving door" between short periods of employment and short periods of assistance (Butler & Buckley, 1978). They are the job-seekers on the marginal labour market, usually in the competitive sector of the capitalist economy. In a sense, then, social assistance is the marginal worker's unemployment insurance (Adams, 1978). These groups—the young, the unskilled seasonal worker, the working-age sick but not chronically sick—constitute the reserve army of labour; their maintenance can, therefore, be seen as a measure of reproducing labour-power. What these examples show is that the two activities of the welfare state, that is, reproducing labour-power and maintaining the nonworking population, cannot be distinguished clearly from one another.

Contradictions within the Welfare State

We have shown that state expenditures, whether as social capital (in capital accumulation function) or as social expenses (in legitimization function), ensure the political domination of the working class and the underclass by the capitalist class. Social capital expenditures are indirectly productive for private capital: the state assumes the cost of preparing the appropriate and useful labour-power for the capitalists. Social expenses, on the other hand, provide the stable social environment required by the process of private capital accumulation. The capitalist class, therefore, stands to benefit the most from the activities of the welfare state.

These same activities also have the effect of manipulating and controlling the working class and the underclass. To end the analysis here would be to submit to the logic of structural-functionalism. This means, first of all, simply accepting the view that various societal institutions, including social welfare, exist for the survival and maintenance of the system; secondly, denying the existence of internal contradictions which counteract the self-maintaining tendency of the society; and, finally, denying the possibility of societal change. However, in the Marxist theoretical framework we use in this book, it is important to explain the internal contradictions within a society, which are the seeds of change. In dealing with the activities of the welfare state it is, therefore, also important to stress that their effect on the subordinate classes is not merely one of social control. To focus only on this "negative" aspect of the welfare state is to neglect the fact that the welfare state is a contradictory phenomenon and that years of class conflict have resulted in some real gains for the subordinate classes.

Many, though not all, of the welfare programs provide real benefits to workers and their dependents by improving their standard of living. This is to say that the development of welfare activities has two aspects. On the one hand, an increasing part of the social capital costs of production and the expenses of ensuring capitalist relations is met through the state. The function of social expenses of the state in maintaining harmony in the capitalist relations of production is particularly important. The mechanisms for carrying out this function include the coercive apparatus (army and police), the judiciary, the state bureaucracies, and the ideological apparatus (the public school system and state controlled media). On the other hand, the wage system has also been increasingly socialized in the sense that the state has taken over from the private capital sector the responsibility of providing for the production and reproduction of labour-power. "Put differently, the worker's standard of living depends not only upon what he or she takes home in his or her paycheck, but also upon the goods and services provided by the state" (Adams, 1978, p. 47). These state-provided goods and services, which help to produce and reproduce labour-power, constitute the social wage. The social wage is, of course, distinct from both the wage paid by the employer (money income and employee benefits) and other types of state activities (for example, policing and nonlabour social capital expenditures). Moreover, the social wage is not synonymous with government social welfare expenditures. The latter include a variety of activities that may have a "social control" function (for instance, policing the existing social order) or a "social wage" function (for instance, health services), which improve the living standard of the working class. Social welfare expenditures may also be a combination of both functions.

The combination of both functions is especially noticeable in education and personal social services. These services may provide real benefits that enhance the recipients' standard of living; conversely, cutbacks in these areas would lead to a decrease in the standard of living. On the other hand, teachers and social workers who provide these benefits may act as policing agents vested with coercive power or as ideological agents for the socialization of clients with values and norms supportive of the capitalist relations of production (Adams, 1978).

What is delineated here are the contradictions within the welfare state. The roots of these contradictions lie within the capitalist mode of production. As we have seen above, the capitalist mode of production is a way of organizing production in which the capitalist class acts in pursuit of one goal: maximization of profits. In the process, it is compelled to accumulate capital. Such a way of organizing production "differs utterly from an economic system which serves to meet human needs, yet this is exactly where many orthodox studies of social policy begin and end" (Gough, 1979, p. 12). Parenthetically, many social welfare and social work textbooks prefer to point to meeting human needs as the primary goal of social welfare. They tend to ignore such harsh realities as the class structure and the profit-maximization motive of the capitalist class. Such a benign neglect of the facts is a grave disservice to social work and social welfare students, as they will encounter these realities again and again in their practice later.

As social control and social wage are two sides of the same coin, or in more technical terms, the two opposites of a dialectic, the distinction between them in specific welfare programs is difficult to draw. The differences between them should, nevertheless, be kept in mind for analytical purposes. If social services and income security programs have intrinsically only the social control function, then there would be no more reason for opposing cutbacks in social wage expenditures than for opposing cutbacks in military or intelligence expenditures. However, for those who are concerned with social inequality in class societies, there are reasonable grounds for opposing cutbacks in social wage expenditures. The reason is that these cutbacks are in fact a disguised wage cut. They are part of a strategy of the state to lower personal and social consumption, in order to facilitate capital accumulation. The concept of social wage highlights the fact that transfer payments, health programs, and various social services are as much part of the real income of working class families as the paycheque. "The income is disposed of by the capitalist state on behalf of those families who exercise neither individual nor collective control over it, but a cutback is a reduction in real income for all that" (Adams, 1978, p. 50).

The social wage has become such an important feature in advanced capitalist societies since the Second World War, that there is a tendency for class conflicts to extend from the economic sphere to the political sphere. The working class, in safeguarding its standard of living, is not only engaged in the struggle with the employers over wages and working conditions, but it is also increasingly involved in a struggle over social policy, that is, "over what proportion of the social product should go to what purposes and who should decide" (Adams, 1978, p. 51). While the underclass is excluded from many forms of social wage that are employment-related, it nevertheless shares in some social benefits. For example, unemployment insurance is employment-related, while medicare in Canada is not. This kind of development potentially questions the basic social structures of the class society.

Summary

The state in capitalist society has two major functions: capital accumulation and legitimization. In its capital accumulation function, the state socializes the cost of producing and reproducing labour-power, while in its legitimization function, it maintains the nonworking population. These tasks of the welfare state are translated into social policies. The contradictions in the welfare state have consequences for the subordinate classes. Welfare programs are often experienced by them as measures of social control, yet they do derive social benefit from some of these programs.

---

1. This section relies a great deal on Gough's (1979) analysis of the British welfare state.

PART III

Welfare Processes

9

Welfare Institution I: Income Security

The institution of social welfare in Canada is complex. Although the welfare activities of the state are visible enough, complemented by private welfare, the various programs do not make up one coherent and systematic institution. In fact, the entire institution consists of many systems and components, some of which are not connected to each other at all. Others are only partially related or even contradict each other. This and the following chapters will present some schematization of the various parts of social welfare. More important, the major programs are placed in a broader analytical framework as they are related to historical, social, and economic developments in the larger society.

The Constitutional Framework

In the 19th century, social welfare was considered to be the responsibility of the individual and the family. When the family or relatives were unable to provide, the local parish, private charities, or voluntary agencies came to the help of the deserving poor. Those were the poor (for example, the orphans and widows) who became so through no fault of their own and hence were worthy of assistance. Since social welfare was a private and local matter at the time of Confederation, the British North America Act of 1867 assigned jurisdiction over social welfare to the provinces that were in turn given jurisdiction over local governments. According to Section 92 of the Act, the legislature in each province may exclusively make laws in such matters as:

(subsection 6)	public reformatory;
(subsection 7)	hospitals, asylums, charities, and ellemosynary institutions;
(subsection 8)	municipal institutions in the province;
(subsection 13)	property and civil rights; and
(subsection 16)	matters of a local and private nature.

Since the federal government has more revenue at its disposal than provincial governments, it has sought to expand from time to time its role in legitimizing the social order by promoting social justice and integration, and by providing the disadvantaged groups with minimum income security (Stevenson, 1977). Through the adoption of two constitutional amendments, the federal government has increased its powers in the area of social welfare policy. The 1940 amendment gave the Parliament of Canada exclusive legislative authority in unemployment insurance (Section 91 (2A) of the B.N.A. Act), and the 1951 amendment authorized it to make laws on old age pensions and supplementary benefits, including survivors' and disability benefits (Section 94A).

The federal government has not hesitated to use other powers provided in the constitution either. Thus, in 1945, it introduced Family Allowances without constitutional amendment because it had the right to make payments directly to individuals. Moreover, it has established extensive employment-related services on the basis of its powers over the economy and unemployment insurance; welfare services for veterans on the basis of its responsibility for the military service and the militia; social welfare for the native peoples because of its responsibility for the well-being of these peoples; and services to immigrants and citizenship services because of its responsibility for aliens and naturalization (Armitage, 1975, p. 61). Finally, the federal government has relied on conditional grants to the provinces to extend its influence in social policies. Medicare, public housing, postsecondary education and Canada Assistance Plan (CAP) are the most important examples of past or ongoing conditional grants.

Thus, it can be seen that power for social welfare (income security and social services) is largely divided between the two levels of government: federal and provincial. (The involvement of the municipal government is mainly in administration, as mentioned in the next chapter.) The virtual impossibility of matching the division of revenue sources with the division of government powers has led to serious constitutional controversies (Birch, 1955). But it would also be well to recall another observation made by Elizabeth Wallace in 1950 about the BNA Act:

> The Act did not impose any obligations to provide welfare services upon either the Dominion or the provinces, but simply allocated with less precision than its framers had hoped to achieve, the various spheres of jurisdiction, *any subsequent action being permissive, not mandatory* (Wallace, 1950, p. 384, emphasis added).

The fact that no mandatory obligations were imposed on either level of government has led to an extremely uneven development of social welfare policy in Canada. Consequently, the rights and needs of Canadians have been compromised, while "the federal government [wavers] between leading the nation and bargaining piecemeal with the provinces" (Bell & Tepperman, 1979, p. 181).

The post-Second World War development of income security

programs and social services must be seen within the context of federal-provincial relations because the Canadian state actually comprises 11 governments: one federal and ten provincial. The total Canadian social welfare institution can best be viewed as an outcome of a peculiar federal system with a weak and unpopular central government. The years between 1945 and 1962 are known as the era of joint federalism during which the federal and provincial governments, using the conditional grant cost-shared program device, jointly established no fewer than 56 programs (Guest, 1980). Particularly in the area of income security, the federal government's attempts at greater political centralization led to the creation of direct cash transfer payments from the federal government to individual Canadians (Banting, 1982). This move toward greater federal involvement and, in fact, leadership in social welfare was not simply due to the financial inability of the provinces to meet increasing demands. The main reasons that the federal government assumed more power in social welfare, while acknowledging paramount provincial power in the area, were the following:

1. Only the central government could effect a national income redistribution;
2. The federal government wished to be seen by citizens as conferring tangible cash benefits, such as Family Allowances and Old Age Security;
3. Only the federal government could ensure some common standard, such that there would be a measure of equity in social welfare provision from province to province;
4. The welfare programs had to be portable, so as not to impede the movement of Canadians across the country.
5. The federal government saw in the exercise of welfare powers the opportunity of stabilizing the economy by influencing Canadians' total demand for goods and services (Armitage, 1975).

The last consideration, that is, federal influence on national economic policy, was especially important in the expansion of public assistance. According to Drover and Gartner (1980), the development during the 1960s of growing domination by foreign-based multinational corporations over the Canadian economy, the creation of a branch-plant economy, and reliance on the resource sector as opposed to the manufacturing sector, combined to weaken the power and control of the federal government over economic decisions. As the federal government lost its grip on the economy, it turned steadily to the legitimization function of introducing social welfare programs to promote social harmony and of assuring an acceptable standard of living for the poor. This legitimization function was all the more urgent in the face of the increasing militancy among Quebec nationalists that threatened the country's unity itself. This legitimization function was carried out in the name of the war on poverty (Thatcher, 1982).

Meanwhile, since the end of the Second World War, the economies of the larger provinces, especially in the resource industries under their jurisdiction, rapidly developed. This not only brought more revenues from resource royalties, but it also led to the expansion of provincial government institutions and structures, as demands for their services increased. Provincial government spending also increased from 6.4 percent of the Gross National Product in 1955 to 16 percent in 1974. While sizeable amounts of the increase were due to health and welfare expenditures, most of the additional costs were related to the development of the physical infrastructure and education, as required by economic growth. Increasing provincial spending created frictions between the provinces and Ottawa, with growing pressures from the larger provinces for fiscal decentralization and more "tax points" (Stevenson, 1977).

Through conditional transfers, the federal govenrment was able to persuade some provinces to institute medicare and various social programs. However, the federal government's participation in policy decisions on social welfare was viewed as an invasion of a provincial jurisdiction. The provinces opposed the federal intervention for a number of reasons. People in different regions had different needs, and the provincial government was in the best position to assess these needs and provide for them. Moreover, different provinces had set precedents in introducing new programs, for example, medicare and the Family Income Plan had been set up in Saskatchewan; they did not have to wait for the federal initiative. The provinces also pointed out that divided jurisdiction over social welfare only added to the questions of responsibility and accountability. Finally, a high profile of the federal government in social welfare would necessarily mean more transfers from the richer provinces to the poorer ones. This was not always looked upon favourably by Ontario, British Columbia, and Alberta (Armitage, 1975).

Between 1968 and 1977 there was a series of federal-provincial negotiations over revenue collection, financial contributions, and distribution of monies and services. The issues have by no means been resolved, but the entire question of welfare policy has receded from the limelight in federal-provincial relations, preempted by the question of constitutional division of power over natural resources and severe economic problems in the early 1980s. There was, however, agreement on the Established Programs Financing (EPF) arrangement for funding health and postsecondary education programs by the end of the 1970s. Those programs would no longer be cost-shared. The federal government gave up a share of the income tax to the provinces, thus allowing the provinces a free hand in the operation of the programs. In the area of income security and other social services, no clear-cut resolution was achieved.

Income Security Programs

Income security programs may be classified into five broad categories (Table 9.1):

1. universal cash transfers;
2. selective cash transfers;
3. contributory social insurance programs;
4. tax credits; and
5. other related government measures.

Table 9.1 Programs of the Welfare State

Income Security Programs	*Social Services*
Universal Transfer Payments: Family Allowances Old Age Security	**Universal Services:** Health Care Primary Education Secondary Education
Selective Cash Transfers: Old Age Security-Guaranteed Income Supplement Canada Assistance Plan **Social Insurance Programs:** Workers' Compensation Unemployment Insurance Canada and Quebec Pension Plans **Tax Credits:** Refundable Child Tax Credit Other Nonrefundable Tax Credits	**Selective Services — Partial List:** Child Welfare Child Day Care Legal Aid Indian and Métis Friendship Centre Services Services for Victims of Violence Correctional Services Rehabilitation Services Employment-related Services Services for People with Special Needs Home Care Housing

Universal Transfer Payments

Universal cash transfers are also known as demogrant programs. Fixed rate grants are made to individuals or families with some given demographic characteristics. In Canada, the two demogrants, Family Allowances and Old Age Security, are both based on the criterion of age and provided by the federal government. In Quebec, the provincial government administers the Family Allowances. Demogrant payments are given with no regard to the needs or income levels of recipients. Since all people within certain age categories receive them, there is no stigma attached to the benefits. The take-up rate is, therefore, usually high. The programs are relatively simple and inexpensive to administer. Also, since demogrants are not income-tested prior to payment, a constant benefit is always present regardless of fluctuations in income. Because of their universality, the overall cost of demogrant programs is extremely high. Due to the overall high costs, benefits of these programs are usually low and, therefore, inadequate for those really in need.

Since the demogrants confer the same amounts of cash on high and low income citizens alike, they do not lessen the disparities in income distribution. Even though the two demogrant programs are made taxable so that the nonpoor will pay back at least some money in income tax, the tax exemptions work in such a way that the high income groups will always derive greater benefits from the tax and transfer systems.

Family Allowances. The universal Family Allowances program, legislated in 1944, was implemented in 1945. It was intended as an economic measure to stimulate consumer spending in the post-Second World War period. But from the start it has been viewed primarily as an income security program (Armitage, 1975, p. 126). Its introduction was greatly influenced by the 1943 Marsh report that strongly favoured children's allowances as the "key to consistence" in any social welfare system. It was Canada's first universal welfare program and signified the beginning of three decades of an active federal role in the welfare field.

Labour initially looked upon Family Allowance with disfavour. The organized segment of the working class opposed the program because it was seen as a substitute for adequate wages and a device to weaken the workers' bargaining power for higher wages. It perceived that the obligation of employers to pay adequate wages was shifted to the shoulders of all taxpayers. But by 1945, Canadian unions fully accepted the program "and saw that, far from weakening their bargaining position, it gave labour extra resources with which to withstand the financial pressures of a strike or lockout" (Guest, 1980, p. 130).

The position of labour is a classic example of how recipients often experience the contradictions of the welfare state. On the one hand, a welfare program clearly represents the attempts of the state to socialize the cost of labour-power reproduction and to maintain a certain level of economic activity and social peace. These attempts are efforts at social control. On the other hand, benefits are real and important to the subordinate classes. But the federal government openly acknowledges that the payment is inadequate and refers to it as a contribution to private or family earnings.

Originally, Family Allowances were provided for all children up to the age of 16. In 1961, Quebec pioneered a new program, called Youth Allowances. It extended the coverage up to the age of 18 provided the recipients attended school on a full-time basis or were prevented from doing so by disabilities. Canada legislated Youth Allowances for the entire country in 1964. The extension of this demogrant recognized that in an advanced industrial society, the dependency period of the young was lengthening (Guest, 1980, p. 150).

Old Age Security. The universal Old Age Security program was established in 1951, effective 1952, replacing the selective Old Age Pensions of 1927. Initially, only those aged 70 or older were eligible. The age levels have subsequently been lowered to 65, provided the recipient has lived at least ten years in Canada. The program is funded and administered by the federal government. Although no stigma is attached to the benefits because of the program's universality, the benefits are, nevertheless, inadequate. This weakness is partially compensated for by the Guaranteed Income Supplement to Old Age Security. Old Age Security is taken for granted in Canadian society today. But the original Old Age Pensions Act of 1927 was not passed without agitation by the working class and much public pressure (Guest, 1980, pp. 74–77).

Selective Cash Transfers

Selective programs are the descendants of the "dole" or "relief" traceable to the Elizabethan Poor Laws. In its present form, a selective program consists essentially of money transfer from the general revenue of any level of government to selected individuals or families. The selection is made according to established eligibility criteria, and is typically determined by a needs-test (assessing the applicant's needs), or means-test (assessing the income and other means the applicant has at his or her disposal), or both.

Old Age Security-Guaranteed Income Supplement. This program was established in 1964 to help the elderly whose sole or major source of income was the OAS. It is administered by the federal government to protect the elderly from poverty. Receipt of OAS-GIS benefits depends on application for and completion of an income declaration and eligibility for OAS. Although it is selective, OAS-GIS is not stigmatizing largely because the eligibility test is not highly visible, being in the form of an income declaration made when income tax returns are filed.

A new program called the Spouse Allowance was enacted under the OAS Act in 1975 to provide an income-tested allowance to people aged between 60 and 64, who are spouses of OAS recipients. This program is largely intended to help women.

Canada Assistance Plan. The Canada Assistance Plan of 1966 consolidated previous federal-provincial cost-shared programs, including unemployment assistance, old age assistance, blind and disabled persons assistance, child welfare, and administrative costs. Through the Plan, the federal government entered into agreements with the provinces to reimburse 50 percent of the approved costs incurred in provincial or municipal assistance to the needy. There would be no upper limit on the federal contribution provided that (a) there would be a needs-test, (b) residence would not be a condition of benefit, and (c) there would be a procedure for appeals by recipients against administrative decisions (Armitage, 1975; Guest, 1980).

The administration of social assistance is left to the provinces, and in seven provinces, some allowances are administered by the municipalities. The Canada Assistance Plan contains two important features. First, assistance is intended not only for persons in need, but also for those who are likely to be in need. The latter category is interpreted to include individuals and families of the wage-earning poor who could be given public assistance to supplement their income from employment. However, in practice, assistance to the wage-earning poor has been insignificant. Second, the plan provides services to help people, mainly social assistance recipients, find and maintain employment. The services include training, counselling, homemaker, and child care services.

The rates of assistance and criteria for eligibility are set by each province. The differences among the provinces are determined not so much by differential living costs as by differential provincial ability or willingness to spend on the poor (Armitage, 1975). Thus, the definition of a recipient's need and the way these needs are met are somewhat arbitrary. The eligibility test usually takes the form of an interview between the individual or family and a government welfare worker. The test is often demeaning or embarrassing to the applicant, who feels an unnecessary stigma. Besides, the process places considerable discretionary power in the hands of welfare authorities.

The rates established by all the provinces are below the poverty line, whether one uses the poverty line provided by Statistics Canada, the Canadian Council on Social Development, or the Senate Committee. Table 9.2 compares the social assistance benefits of one province,

Table 9.2 Comparison of Saskatchewan Social Service Benefits with Statistics Canada Poverty Line, December 1981

Family Size (One Wage Earner)	*1*	*2*	*3*	*4*	*5*	*6*	*7*
Poverty Lines (Statistics Canada)	$485	703	897	1067	1193	1309	1436
Saskatchewan Social Assistance Benefits*	$377	620	785	930	1050	1175	1295
S.S.A. Benefits as % of Poverty Line	78%	88%	88%	87%	88%	90%	90%

*Benefits include food, clothing, personal allowance, household expenses, shelter, utilities, special needs and medical expenses, and child tax credit.

SOURCE: Department of Social Services, Saskatchewan.

Saskatchewan, with the Statistics Canada poverty line incomes in December 1981.

The comparison shows the inadequacy of social assistance benefits. Nevertheless, from 1960 to 1975 the growth of public assistance was phenomenal: the number of persons assisted increased by 278 percent, while expenditures in constant dollars increased by 840 percent (compared to 254 percent and 246 percent in the United States respectively) (Drover & Gartner, 1980).

The three conditions on which federal reimbursement is based are symbolic of the national scope of the welfare state. But they do not detract from the expediency of assigning the control of social assistance to the lower levels of government: the coverage of social assistance is broad but discretionary. As Armitage (1975, p. 134) has noted:

> It is broad in that there are no exclusions from coverage in the way that social insurance programmes exclude persons who do not satisfy defined criteria. This leads to social assistance programmes supporting all those persons whose need is not met by other income security programmes (persons unemployed for more than one year, persons disabled but not severely disabled, elderly persons who are not yet 65 etc.). Coverage is discretionary because no person is assured a right to benefit. Instead, his or her circumstances are examined and assessed by the administering agency which then makes a judgement as to whether "need" exists. Subject to limited rights of appeal, the agency's judgement is final.

In the early 1970s, it became apparent that the exercise of discretionary power by welfare authorities could result in flagrant violations of civil liberties. The manner in which social assistance was administered exacted "a high price in civil liberties for the provision of subsistence income," a conclusion reached by the Canadian Civil Liberties Education Trust (1975, p. 107) after it conducted a survey of welfare practices across the nation. The survey researchers were dismayed at the departure from common law requirements of "due process" in welfare administration and the substantial unawareness of any appeal machinery on the part of recipients. The state, through the welfare program, seemed to intrude on the most intimate situations in the lives of recipients. It encroaches on the privacy of marriage, of cohabitation, of unwed mothers, and of the home. The welfare state, in providing subsistence to the poorest members of society, was holding them in deep distrust, while, in effect, exercising complete control over their lives. Welfare practices that embodied such orientations of the state naturally supported and encouraged the "welfare bum" stereotypes among the nonpoor members of society. By the 1980s, the most serious violations of civil liberties in the administration of social assistance had been reduced. Nevertheless, the contradictions between social control and social benefit in the welfare state still remain.

Besides the OAS-GIS and CAP, selective programs include provincial supplements to the elderly and the Saskatchewan Family Income Plan. The latter, introduced in 1974, makes payments to low income families who have children. Recipients submit quarterly statements on actual income. Benefits are adjusted to income every year (Canada, Government of, 1980, p. 43).

Social Insurance Programs

As has been discussed earlier, the three main proposals in Marsh's Report were children's allowance; a universal health insurance scheme; and social insurance against unemployment, sickness, disability, old age retirement, and premature death. In the 1973 *Working Paper on Social Security in Canada*, the Minister of Health and Welfare, Marc Lalonde, maintained that the first strategy in providing income security to Canadians must be employment. The government of Canada should continue to encourage people to save for the contingencies of life. The second strategy is that of social insurance. Social insurance plans would cover temporary loss of employment income due to short term unemployment, sickness, accident, or maternity. They would also provide for retirement (by reason of age or disability) and for survivors in the event of death. But the *Working Paper* emphasized that social insurance plans should always be supplemented by private pension and personal insurance arrangements (Canada, Health and Welfare, 1973: pp. 26–27).

Thus, in the view of the Canadian welfare state, social insurance occupies a central place in the total social welfare institution. Social insurance programs, based on contributions by employers and/or employees, would be forced savings schemes, to be activated when the need arises. In other words, coverage would be universal, but only particular persons faced with any contingencies would receive benefits.

Marsh in 1943 and Lalonde in 1973 emphasized the principles of insurance. But in practice, insurance programs have evolved quite differently. Current needs of the insured are such that they cannot be met according to the usual actuarial principles of granting benefits in accordance with contributions. In fact, social insurance programs are subsidized by government revenues or current contributions are used to pay current benefits. Consequently, these programs resemble private insurance schemes less than public transfer payments. Thus, increasingly the suggestion is made that social insurance programs "should be funded totally out of general revenue and any allusion to insurance or to contribution-related benefits should cease. This would acknowledge their evolving status as universal transfer payments" (Melchercik, 1981, p. 222). There are three social insurance programs for income security in Canada: (a) Workers' Compensation, (b) Unemployment Insurance, and (c) Canada/Quebec Pension Plans.

Workers' Compensation. As workers' compensation in Canada falls within the constitutional area of "property and civil rights", it is under the jurisdiction of the provinces. Thus, there are ten Workers' Compensation Commissions reporting to ten provincial ministers of labour, respectively (Armitage, 1975, p. 132; Guest, 1980, p. 39).

Workers' Compensation established in Ontario in 1914 was Canada's first social insurance scheme protecting workers against work-related sickness, disability, or death. Public concern over the mounting toll of death and injuries at the workplace was first expressed in the 1880s. The Ontario government's initial response was limited and ineffectual. Laws enacted in Ontario and later in other provinces generally gave workers the responsibility to prove negligence on the part of the employers. Later, when more adequate legislation was proposed, the employers first attacked the basic notion itself and then demanded that labour contribute to the cost of a compensation scheme. It was after much concerted effort that labour won protection under the law and also the demand that workers not contribute to the cost. Labour's argument was that "the pain, suffering, and loss of income suffered by the injured worker was more than a sufficient contribution" (Guest, 1980, p. 43).

Today, all employers beyond certain minimum sizes must insure all employees under Workers' Compensation, which means that injured employees are protected from income interruption. The benefits are paid in regular instalments while disability lasts, although in cases of permanent disability or death, a lump sum is usually paid. Provision also includes medical and rehabilitative services. But cash benefits may be denied to recipients who reject medical advice. Workers injured while working outside their usual line of duty may lose protection. Levels of benefit under workers' compensation vary widely from province to province.

The most frequent complaint against workers' compensation is that the procedure of eligibility and subsequent benefit determination is lengthy and contentious, especially in cases where injury is not readily observable. This is increasingly the problem in industries where health hazards are apparent only after long-term exposure, or where the injury is inflicted on the unborn, as shown by the growing evidence on birth defects in babies born to women who worked on video-display terminals during pregnancy.

Workers' Compensation actually brings considerable benefit to employers. The collective insurance system provides cheaper coverage than could be obtained from private insurance companies (Guest, 1980, p. 46). But the single most important benefit is that workers insured under Workers' Compensation lose their right to sue their employers for damages. Possibly because of this protection against liability for the employers, workplaces are not as safe as they should and could be. Industrial accidents still kill over 1000 workers per year in Canada. The Canadian Labour Congress argues that "accidents and diseases connected with work are the largest source of lost working time in the economy" (Rabinovich, 1982, p. 14). The basic right of Canadian workers to refuse hazardous work without risk of reprisal and to be informed of potential hazards is yet to be won.

In the above brief description, the contradictions of the welfare state—savings for the employers and some benefits for the employees—can again be seen in the development of Workers' Compensation. The struggles of the subordinate classes for better workplace, health, and safety protection in the 1980s also illustrate the dynamics of the welfare state.

Unemployment Insurance. Unemployment insurance was introduced in 1940 after the provinces agreed on a constitutional amendment allowing the federal government to establish this program. An earlier attempt in 1935 by the federal government to introduce unemployment insurance was challenged by Ontario; the courts and the Privy Council declared it unconstitutional, as welfare was interpreted to be a strictly provincial matter under the BNA Act.

Cuneo (1979) has made a detailed analysis showing how the interests of the capitalist and working classes, and those of the state were represented in the events that led to the passage of the act. The federal government sought to introduce Unemployment Insurance in order to control unrest among the unemployed during the Depression of the 1930s. Its success in doing so in 1940 coincided with the state's desire to accumulate its own capital in the context of the Second World War.

The capitalist class consistently opposed Unemployment Insurance between 1920 and 1940. Ontario's challenge to the constitutionality of the first attempt by the federal government to establish Unemployment Insurance in 1935 came as a result of lobbying efforts by the capitalist class. Employers feared that Unemployment Insurance would increase their labour costs, and they succeeded in persuading the government of Ontario to bring the matter to the courts on the grounds that social welfare should be a provincial matter and the federal government had no authority to propose legislation in this area. The Supreme Court of Canada ruled in favour of Ontario, a decision upheld by the Privy Council when it was appealed by the government of Canada.

In 1940, capitalists opposed the proposed legislation again because they saw that Unemployment Insurance would hinder their own process of capital accumulation under war conditions. First, they viewed Unemployment Insurance as a tax, an added burden on business. Second, since the workers were also to make contributions to Unemployment Insurance, they saw their workers paying such taxes and then demanding higher wages. Third, the increased taxes and higher wages caused by UI would be passed on to the consumer, resulting in higher commodity prices. This would bring about a reduction in consumer purchasing power, ultimately causing an adverse effect on business. Lastly, higher production costs because of UI would also make Canadian products less competitive on export markets.

Labour organizations consistently supported the UI program since the end of the First World War, and their radical demands reached a peak during the Depression. Labour had asked for a much broader occupational and industrial coverage. But the 1940 Act would protect only those workers who were in the advanced sectors of the capitalist economy, excluding those in the primary industries, service industries, the state sector, and industries with a high risk of unemployment (Cuneo, 1979, p. 167). In the first year of its operation, the UI program covered only 50 percent of the labour force. Trade unions accepted the state's restriction on UI, mainly because they represented workers with more stable employment than the unorganized workers. Workers with more stable employment typically would experience only temporary unemployment, and insurance benefits were supplements to incomes earned while employed. Unemployed workers were not involved in the debate leading to the establishment of UI. While UI was introduced supposedly to help the unemployed, it was ironic that they were excluded from the discussion on UI legislation. This illustrated how relatively powerless the unemployed were vis-a-vis the state, the capitalist class, and organized labour. And it was the intention of the state to foster such powerlessness. Unemployment Insurance was established to encourage peace among industrial organized labour and workers with more secure jobs, and it was designed to help them during periods of temporary unemployment and distress. The legislation was never meant to assist the chronically unemployed whose best recourse was the provincial or municipal "dole" and public work programs (Cuneo, 1979, p. 170).

Cuneo concludes that the Canadian state displayed relative autonomy from the capitalists, since it introduced Unemployment Insurance largely in spite of their objections, thereby accommodating some demands of the working class. The analysis also reveals the fragmentation within the working class—the cleavage between organized and unorganized labour—that weakens its struggles.

Unemployment Insurance has been revised many times since 1940, extending coverage to almost all employees and changing eligibility criteria and levels of benefits. In recent years, it has been the topic of much controversy in relation to work incentive. Like CAP, the program allows for limited amounts of part-time earnings but in principle a person cannot be employed while receiving benefits. Many people see this regulation as a penalty for those who work.

In the early 1980s, as the economy experienced its worst crisis since the Great Depression, plant shutdowns and massive layoffs turned some single-industry or single-company towns into ghost-towns virtually overnight. Other cities experienced high unemployment rates of 30 to 40 percent. Among the unemployed were former managers and professional staff members (the "new" middle class, discussed in chapter 6). The Unemployment Insurance program softened the harsh reality of being out of work, with all its economic, social, and psychological ramifications. Many of the unemployed, after their UI benefits ran out, eventually resorted to social assistance. Unofficial police statistics from some cities indicate that family conflicts and alcohol-related crimes increased as the rate of unemployment rose. Certainly, members of the working class were disgruntled and unhappy. Yet, remarkably, there were not many large-scale militant, protracted confrontations between the workers on the one hand and the state and/or corporations on the other. While the phenomenon was complex, it could in part be explained by the power of the ideology of consumerism and individualism, which some segments of the working class had internalized. Workers with mortgage and other consumer payments to make welcomed income from any source: employment (while it lasted), underemployment (as in the form of work-sharing programs), or Unemployment Insurance benefits. But, more fundamentally, many unemployed workers did not see their personal plight as rooted in the social structures of inequality and exploitation. Typically, they saw their unemployment or other employment problems as private and temporary troubles. Thus, they tend to blame themselves or to act out their aggression against those closest to them, their families and friends.

In sum, Unemployment Insurance is a social benefit, as well as a form of social control. But to be effective, a social control measure is best complemented by the appropriate ideological predisposition of the subordinate group (see Baldus, 1975). However, working class consciousness is dynamic. As the economic crisis prolongs and structural unemployment persists, it is likely that more workers will develop awareness of the class nature of their individual troubles. As more workers become politicized, their conflicts with the employers and/or the state could become more invidious and sharpened, and take on new forms.

Canada and Quebec Pension Plans (CPP/QPP). These two plans introduced in 1965 were intended to provide retirement, disability and survivors' pensions, and a lump sum death benefit in a single social insurance package (Guest, 1980, p. 150). The establishment of CPP occasioned another demonstration of the capital accumulation interests of the capitalist class and, more specifically, the financial capitalists in the life insurance industry. When the legislation for CPP was still in its planning stage, the industry lobbied in the national and provincial capitals for the abandonment of the plan. Although their efforts failed to prevent the enactment of CPP, the industry did win some concessions. The government's plan as it was passed was a less effective version of the original scheme. The public plan was set up to provide "a rather low level of benefit so that the interests of the private insurance industry would not be seriously hurt" (Armitage, 1975, p. 70). Moreover, the plan was established with the understanding that individuals' life insurance premiums would remain as tax exemptions, providing an incentive to buy private insurance.

In Quebec, the public pension plan is administered by the provincial government. In Canada as a whole, CPP/QPP cover almost all employed persons, including the self-employed. But it does not cover the unemployed or the unemployable, including housewives, who, being not employed, are excluded from coverage. Criticisms of the plan resulted in some changes in recent years. Equality of status between men and women in relation to survivors' benefits is now recognized and has been implemented. Some provision is made for spouses who work at home, that is, pension credits earned by the employed spouses during their marriage are to be divided equally upon the dissolution of the marriage. However, it remains that spouses who work at home do not have the opportunity to participate in the plan in their own right.

Although CPP/QPP are inadequate in coverage and benefit levels, they do protect the retired from poverty, in combination with other programs. As a social insurance program, it does not confer a stigma on the recipient as would have been the case in a selective transfer payment. But because of the manner in which it is financed in the 1980s, the insurance notion simply conceals a *de facto* transfer from the employed to the retired (Armitage, 1975, p. 131).

Tax Credits

The tax system's influence on income distribution has already been discussed in chapter 7. Under the present system, tax exemptions always negate the intent of progressive income taxes, an undesirable effect that can be redressed if tax exemptions are replaced by tax credits. A tax credit is a reduction in the amount of tax to be paid, whereas a tax exemption is a reduction in the amount of taxable income.

In 1978 the federal government introduced a new measure of using the refundable tax credit to give financial support to families with children. For the first time, the federal income tax system was used to deliver benefits to low and middle income families, including those living below the poverty line (NCW, 1978b).

The Refundable Child Tax Credit is intended to provide full benefits to the poorest families with the lowest incomes. As incomes rise above the national average, the benefits are gradually reduced and finally withdrawn. For example, in 1978, a family would be eligible for a basic $200 tax credit for each dependent child under the age of 18. If the family income was so low that the taxpayer's income tax was less than $200 or that no tax was owed at all, the refundability of the tax credit ensured that the taxpayer would receive a full $200 in benefit, to be paid by the government to the individual. If the total family income exceeded $18 000 in 1978, the basic credit would be reduced by 5¢ for each dollar of family income over $18 000. It was estimated that the Refundable Child Tax Credit would increase benefits for 1.9 million low income families and decrease benefits for 1.7 million families with incomes above the national average.

The effect of a tax credit is always progressive in that it reduces the size of tax and lessens the tax burden of the low income earners. Aside from the Child Tax Credit, other tax credits now in existence are not refundable. The federal government provides an employment tax credit for employees who have improved their employment situation over that of the previous year (Ross, 1981, p. 93). The Quebec provincial tax system administers the Quebec Work Income Supplement, which pays benefits, up to a ceiling, when there is earned income. Ontario has property tax credit for pensioners, and sales tax credits. Ontario and all Western provinces operate some form of housing-related tax credit (Ross, 1981, pp. 69–70).

Other Income Security Related Measures

The main income security programs have been discussed above. It would be inaccurate to say that they collectively make up a system. A system presupposes co-ordination among parts in pursuit of some common goal(s). But interactions among the various income security programs are characterized by confusion in planning and co-ordination, and inefficiency in administration (Canada, Government of, 1980, p. 113). For example, there is no provision for integrating or co-ordinating benefits for widows and children under Workers' Compensation and CPP/QPP.

While income security programs may have the overall objective of alleviating poverty, the benefit levels of most programs fall below the poverty line. Despite these various programs, numerous Canadians were still living in poverty in 1976 (Caskie, 1979, p. 26):

Poverty Line	*Number in Poverty*
Statistics Canada	2 831 000
Canadian Council on Social Development	4 423 000
Senate Committee	5 372 000

Furthermore, money provided for the needy through income security programs is often taken back in taxes. The result is that little income redistribution takes place: the pattern of income distribution has remained unchanged since the Second World War.

In addition to income security programs, other government policies also affect people's incomes. Three such public policies will be briefly examined here: (a) minimum wage legislation, (b) employment strategy, and (c) job creation.

Minimum Wages

Canada has 13 minimum wages: ten provincial, two territorial, and one federal. Minimum wage rates are set in labour standards legislation that regulate general conditions of employment, such as hours of work and work safety. In most jurisdictions, students and young persons are paid at a lower minimum wage rate. However, in most jurisdictions, even some adult workers are not covered by adult minimum wages: domestic, farm, seasonal, disabled workers, and some restaurant workers. In all provinces except Quebec, disabled workers can be paid below the minimum wages, and often they are paid at ridiculously low rates (NCW, 1981, p. 102).

It has been estimated that between ten and 15 percent of the labour force work at the minimum wage level or lower. However, whereas only ten percent of male workers are paid at the minimum wage rate or less, 50 percent of all female workers receive the minimum wage or less. Surveys conducted in four different provinces also show that more than half of minimum wage workers of both sexes were under the age of 25. About two-thirds of minimum wage workers are in clerical, sales, and service occupations; only in Quebec are more than one-third of the minimum wage earners in manufacturing industries. In other words, people who work for minimum wages are those in the marginal labour market. The typical low-wage employers are small firms in the competitive sector (Ross, 1981, p. 73).

As an income security policy, minimum wage legislation is a topic of debate. Opponents argue that minimum wages destroy marginal employment opportunities (Ross, 1981, p. 92). The defenders, on the other hand, point out that, without legislation, wages of many low-wage workers would fall further behind those of the average-wage workers, and those workers would be exploited by unscrupulous employers. Nevertheless, minimum wages alone do not and cannot eliminate poverty.

The poverty gap, that is, the number of dollars above or below the Statistics Canada poverty line, for single-parent and two-parent families is shown in Table 9.3. It can be seen that only the single workers who work full time and year-round at minimum wage rates can rise above the poverty line. Yet this category of workers includes many under the age of 25 whose unemployment rate is typically higher than that of the general labour force. Only single parents working for minimum wages and supporting one child in Saskatchewan and Quebec are able to rise above the poverty line, not because of minimum wages, but because of government income supplements in these two provinces. In all other provinces no single- or two-parent families could live above the poverty line by relying on earnings of one worker employed full time and year-round at the minimum wage rate. The larger the family, the greater is the poverty gap. The reason is simply that minimum wages do not adjust for family size: the same wage is paid to the single person as to a worker with dependents.

Another controversial aspect of the minimum wage rate is its relationship to Social Assistance. Critics are concerned about the erosion of the work incentive, arguing that the minimum wage rate must be higher than the Social Assistance level to provide an individual the incentive to find employment. However, the problem with this reasoning is that most recipients of long-term assistance are elderly, disabled, or otherwise unemployable. Income from minimum wages is compared to that from Social Assistance for families of different sizes in Table 9.4. Figures over 100 percent indicate that minimum wages would provide greater income to an individual or family, while figures below 100 percent would indicate the opposite. The NCW reports that single persons and, in most provinces, childless couples receive more income by working at minimum wage rates rather than being on assistance. In half the provinces, single-parent families with one child are slightly better off working at minimum wage rates than receiving assistance. Except in Quebec, all other single- and two-parent families are better off receiving Social Assistance than with one earner working at minimum wage rate. Quebec's Work Income Supplement tax credit puts the working family ahead of those on assistance (NCW, 1981, p. 100).

Finally, in Table 9.5, minimum wage earnings are compared with average earnings. By and large, the gap between minimum wages and average wages narrowed up to the mid-1970s, whereas trends in the late 1970s show that minimum wages as a percentage of average earnings declined in all jurisdictions.

In summary, minimum wage legislation does give some protection to marginal single workers. But the rates are too low to provide adequate support for families. Like the income security programs, it has not appreciably improved the income position of the poor, but has barely managed to prevent the poor from falling further behind.

The Employment Strategy

As presented in Marc Lalonde's Orange Paper, the first strategy in providing income security to Canadians is to provide people with jobs rather than income through Social Assistance. This employment strategy is intended to help people "who cannot readily find jobs in the general labour market" (Canada, Health and Welfare, 1973, p. 23). It involves providing these individuals with (a) incentives to stop receiving public assistance; (b) services (rehabilitation, training, and counselling) that will help them obtain employment; and (c) employment opportuni-

Table 9.3 Poverty Gap for Families with only One Earner Working at the Minimum Wage, 1980

	For families with two adults but only one wage-earner				*For families headed by a single wage-earner*			
	childless couple	*couple, 1 child*	*couple, 2 children*	*couple, 3 children*	*1 adult*	*single parent, 1 child*	*single parent, 2 children*	*single parent, 3 children*
Vancouver	−$1591	−$3434	−$4990	−$6015	+$ 989	−$1115	−$2947	−$4506
Edmonton	− 1308	− 3151	− 4756	− 5713	+ 1269	− 844	− 2730	− 4209
Regina	− 300	− 1706	− 2533	− 2862	+ 2151	+ 476	− 627	− 1453
Winnipeg	− 1375	− 3201	− 4742	− 5750	+ 1124	− 899	− 2712	− 4256
Toronto	− 1911	− 3747	− 5296	− 6314	+ 612	− 1431	− 3268	− 4816
Montreal	− 254	− 1877	− 3156	− 3713	+ 1678	+ 450	− 1117	− 2204
Saint John, N.B.	− 1815	− 3517	− 4944	− 5873	+ 636	− 1335	− 3038	− 4464
Halifax	− 2049	− 3751	− 5178	− 6107	+ 402	− 1569	− 3272	− 4698
Charlottetown	− 1074	− 2544	− 3767	− 4552	+ 1114	− 594	− 2065	− 3287
St. John's, Nfld.	− 1711	− 3413	− 4840	− 5769	+ 740	− 1231	− 2934	− 4360

SOURCE: National Council of Welfare, *The Working Poor: People and Programs*, 1981, Tables 57 and 59.

Table 9.4 Net Minimum Wage Income as a Percentage of Social Assistance Income, by Province and Family Size, 1980*

	Nfld.	*P.E.I.*	*N.S.*	*N.B.*	*Que.*	*Ont.*	*Man.*	*Sask.*	*Alta.*	*B.C.*
One adult	143%	125%	120%	152%	177%	174%	153%	164%	155%	145%
Two adults	93	98	91	101	128	109	112	119	102	101
One parent, one child	88	91	88	95	132	102	105	104	103	89
One parent, two children	83	79	74	91	121	90	89	87	86	76
One parent, three children	80	72	67	88	116	81	79	83	78	68
Couple, one child	89	85	77	95	120	97	94	98	87	85
Couple, two children	85	78	70	92	114	88	84	92	79	76
Couple, three children	83	71	64	89	111	81	76	87	74	71

*Minimum wage incomes are net employment-related expenses and, for single-parent families, child care costs to allow a more realistic comparison than if gross minimum wage incomes were used.

SOURCE: National Council of Welfare, *The Working Poor: People and Programs*, 1981, Table 61.

Table 9.5 Minimum Wage Earnings as a Percentage of Average Earnings by Jurisdiction, Selected Years

	1965	*1967*	*1970*	*1972*	*1974*	*1975*	*1976*	*1977*	*1978*	*1979*	*1980*
Federal	54.9	48.6	46.0	47.6	47.7	46.6	49.6	46.4	43.7	40.2	36.9
Newfoundland	34.9	30.5	40.0	39.8	45.1	44.8	45.1	41.2	40.3	39.4	41.1
Prince Edward Island	64.0	62.2	59.7	49.5	53.6	56.4	56.2	55.4	55.0	52.4	50.9
Nova Scotia	57.2	53.2	48.0	47.1	47.3	52.0	51.8	51.9	49.2	44.9	42.4
New Brunswick	42.8	37.5	44.2	44.0	47.2	48.8	49.2	50.1	48.1	43.7	41.1
Quebec	38.4	41.0	41.7	42.7	47.5	50.0	51.0	50.2	50.1	48.5	45.8
Ontario	42.4	37.8	41.0	42.6	45.5	45.9	44.3	42.5	41.4	42.0	38.6
Manitoba	41.3	43.9	47.9	49.4	49.8	51.0	52.2	52.1	49.2	46.3	44.4
Saskatchewan	44.8	41.8	43.5	51.8	52.8	51.8	52.1	50.9	50.9	48.0	47.2
Alberta	44.5	42.2	43.8	41.3	44.2	45.8	45.8	45.2	43.4	39.1	38.9
British Columbia	39.7	38.2	41.1	37.3	47.8	43.9	44.7	42.2	39.8	36.7	35.4

SOURCE: National Council of Welfare, *The Working Poor: People and Programs*, 1981, Table 63.

ties. The first two objectives will be examined in this section and the last in the next section.

Work incentive is a controversial issue. It is true that two major income security programs, Social Assistance and Unemployment Insurance, have built-in features that discourage work. Under existing regulation, recipients of benefits from either program are allowed very small amounts of part-time earnings. Earnings beyond these limits would lead to reduction in benefits or even disqualification. Given the insecurity of job opportunities faced by the recipients and the tedious bureaucratic procedures and delays in discontinuing and requalifying for benefits, many recipients would tend to avoid looking for employment in order to retain the relative security of Social Assistance or Unemployment Insurance (Ross, 1981, p. 85).

Despite the disincentives associated with Social Assistance and Unemployment Insurance, many recipients usually leave these programs before long, partly because of the stigma attached to transfer payments. One-third of the recipients of UI benefits return to work before one month and two-thirds, before three months (Ross, 1981, p. 85). Canadian and American studies have shown that dependence on public welfare may be a regular occurrence for some people, but for most recipients who are employable, their time on assistance lasts only a few months and terminates when they find employment (Butler and Buckley, 1978). The obvious exceptions are the elderly, the disabled, the infirm, and single parents with small dependent children. Jobs that are usually available to recipients are low-paid, unskilled, insecure, and have poor working conditions.

Thus, the problem of work incentive could be seen in an entirely different light. Despite the fact that the programs discourage intermittent employment and despite the undesirable and dehumanizing jobs in which they often find themselves, the vast majority of recipients of Social Assistance and Unemployment Insurance benefits have proven to be highly work-oriented. The two programs have often been used to channel recipients to seek jobs in the marginal labour market. So if unemployed Canadians continue to rely on these two programs, it may be the result of inadequate employment services and/or job opportunities.

Historically, the federal government's employment services (for example, job placement and adult training programs) are intended more to stimulate economic growth and to meet the demands of employers than to help the job-seeker. Even after the Orange Paper and the subsequent federal-provincial joint review of social welfare in Canada, the situation has not improved significantly. Job placement is not seen by counsellors as their primary duty. But it is in the area of training that the capital accumulation function of the state is best seen. In advanced capitalism, a skilled work force is vital to competition. In providing training and retraining programs, the state socializes the costs of producing and reproducing labour-power. The *raison d'être* of the welfare state is summarized in the government's informational literature on industrial training programs: "Although training is primarily a company responsibility, the government of Canada offers financial and consultative assistance to help employers initiate training or expand their training capability" (Canada, Employment and Immigration, 1981a, p. 1).

There are two types of training programs: institution-based and on-the-job. In the former, financial assistance is provided to the trainee while he or she acquires useful skills. But in times of high levels of unemployment, fewer resources are allocated to institutional training.

In on-the-job training programs, the government reimburses the employer for direct training costs incurred and subsidizes trainees' wages up to 100 percent. But a training program may merely be an employment creation project. Once the wage subsidy is discontinued, it is questionable whether the workers would have learned useful skills to help them earn an adequate living. In other words, on-the-job training may not improve the trainees' employability and raise them above poverty line or minimum wage levels. Companies are not required to retain the trainees afterward. In fact, then, the government is "subsidizing low-wage employers, and creating a new pool of workers willing to take low-paying and menial jobs under the guise of training" (Canadian Council on Social Development [CCSD], 1973, p. 54).

Furthermore, the employment strategy has a "creaming" effect, that is, it trains the "cream of the crop" and provides it with employment opportunities, while leaving behind the less competitive and older people who have the greatest need for training. Even the individuals who are singled out for training and/or employment may not necessarily receive higher incomes. The point is that in the competitive sector, wages are fixed for given jobs and the better trained workers get the jobs. Workers compete for jobs, not wages. Thus, it would seem that Canada Employment Centre's training and employment programs may provide a subsidy to employers and industries, but they are ineffective in ensuring that individuals have income security (Armitage, 1975, p. 123).

In more recent years, training and employment programs for women in nontraditional occupations and for other disadvantaged groups, such as native people and the disabled, have been added to the employment strategy. This is the result of public pressure, particularly from the various disadvantaged groups themselves. It is still too early to assess the impact of such programs, but the fact that the disadvantaged groups, traditionally excluded from meaningful participation in the paid labour force, have gained even a small part of recognition is significant in itself. It shows how it is possible for the subordinate classes to influence the welfare state in their own interest.

Canada's employment and immigration policies are closely related;

this can be seen simply from the fact that employment and immigration are administered in the same federal department. The number and kind of immigrants allowed into Canada have always been based on economic considerations. More specifically, immigration follows fluctuations in the labour market and responds to specific demands for labour by industries. Historically, Canada has tended to import the required labour for economic growth rather than plan its own educational and industrial training programs in anticipation of changing demands for labour. This strategy of meeting labour force requirements could have undermined the effectiveness of training programs.

Aside from skilled labourers, who, with their dependents, usually immigrate to become permanent residents in Canada, the immigration department deals with temporary workers, who come to Canada on special work permits to work for a limited period of time. Their dependents are not allowed to accompany them to Canada and they themselves must return to their place of origin when the contract expires. Temporary labourers usually work in menial or seasonal jobs, such as domestics and agricultural workers during harvest time. Their jobs are often not regulated by labour laws on minimum wages, working hours, and working conditions. By relying on temporary workers, Canada benefits from having some unpleasant jobs done at very low cost. It entails tremendous savings for employers who would have to pay higher wages if those jobs were treated as regular jobs, and Canadians were employed to fill them. It also leads to savings for the government, whose expenditures in social capital and social expenses would otherwise be greater (see chapter 8). Most of the temporary workers in Canada are nonwhites from Third World countries. The history of Canadian immigration is a record of institutional racism and sexism, and while this issue will not be dealt with in this book, some of the functions of discrimination will be discussed in chapter 11.

Job Creation

The third part of the federal employment strategy is that of providing people with job opportunities. The federal government has tried to accomplish this by (a) offering incentives to private companies to move to depressed areas, and (b) establishing programs to increase employment opportunities directly.

Incentive programs for employers in general have not had any significant impact on the alleviation of poverty in Canada (CCSD, 1973, p. 62). Plants established in designated regions are scattered and on a limited scale. They do not form an industrial base from which economic development can be sustained. But there are other contradictions in the scheme. Incentive programs exist in the form of capital grants that participating firms have sometimes used to update and expand their capital equipment. Consequently, the grants not only fail to foster labour-intensive production processes, but also contribute to reductions in jobs because of automation, retooling, and so on. Moreover, job creation in one part of the country may mean loss of jobs in another part in the case of a company move. The net gain may be little or nil.

Companies moving to depressed areas are not required to hire local people. In fact, senior level and skilled jobs are often advertised in major cities across the country or even abroad. Thus, the local job-seekers are again left with low-paying and relatively unskilled jobs that have few prospects for the future. Local inhabitants have often been dissatisfied with the treatment they have received under these programs. They have no input into the programs; they are not consulted about what type of industry or activity will be established in their area (CCSD, 1973, pp. 61–66). The powerlessness of the local people is accentuated when there is competition among the federal, provincial, and municipal governments. Each government may want the potential employer to set up operations in a different locale. Governments at all three levels will then vie with each other to offer "the best deal", often without regard for the long-term effects of the project. The governments seem to be more concerned with the interests of private companies and economic growth than with the needs and problems of the people.

In attempting to create job opportunities directly, the federal government, with involvement from different departments, has offered an impressive array of programs: Local Initiatives Program (LIP), Opportunities for Youth (OFY), Local Employment Assistance Program (LEAP), Canada Works, Young Canada Works, and Local Economic Development Assistance (LEDA). Provincial governments have similar programs.

The impact of these programs on income security has not been significant either. Although wages from some programs may raise some income units above the poverty line, all of the projects funded by these programs are temporary. There is no employment security; many, however, do last long enough to qualify the workers for unemployment insurance benefits.

The most serious shortcoming in most of these employment creation programs is that they fail to reach the Social Assistance recipients and those more or less permanently unemployed. These are people not likely to possess the necessary educational and social skills with which to develop projects, fill in the necessary applications, face bureaucracies without being intimidated, and then carry on the project (CCSD, 1973, p. 69). Quite certainly, the "creaming" function operates in these programs, too, so that only the most competitive benefit from them.

A large proportion of the projects funded by these programs were expressive (theatre, music, dance), recreational (trail cutting and maintenance in parks), or community-oriented (work in residences for the elderly) (Armitage, 1975, p. 123). At a time when the prospects for full employment are poor and when automation continues to eliminate jobs, the nature of these projects raises the question whether the concept of work should be redefined. In advanced capitalist societies, work is limited to activities that are income earning. But, conceivably, work could include voluntary activities, such as child raising, artistic accomplishments, and community service. In a society where work is redefined, the major issue will then be one of income distribution. "Will the process continue to be based primarily on rewards from employment, or will distribution become more dissociated from paid-work and be seen more as the result of a process of guaranteeing transfer payments?" (Ross, 1981, p. 91). The question inevitably raises the issues of value preferences, and capitalist and alternative ideologies. At the moment, there is little critical public awareness of the related issues of job opportunity, work incentive, and income distribution. But as economic conditions in the 1980s continue to deteriorate, critical awareness and questioning will undoubtedly increase.

Social Welfare Review: Guaranteed Annual Income

In 1970, John Munro, then minister of Health and Welfare, published *Income Security for Canadians*. According to this White Paper, while demogrants, social insurance, and social assistance were to be retained as instruments of income security policy, the main thrust of the government's proposed policy for the coming years was "developing the guaranteed income technique as a major antipoverty policy" (Canada Health and Welfare, 1970, p. 2).

The Guaranteed Annual Income (GAI) is not a special method of income security. Rather, it represents a social goal. In public discussion so far, the basic components of GAI include an income support program to assist those not in the labour force and an income supplement program to assist the working poor. These programs would be administered according to demonstrated need and would have built-in incentives to encourage recipients to earn additional income. GAI would cover many more of the working poor than presently covered by the CAP. Assistance received in this way would be less stigmatizing, as a simpler income test for eligibility could be integrated into the income tax system. However, the differential reduction rates in the two-tier program would reaffirm the "less eligibility" principle, that is, "total financial rewards to those who work would always exceed benefits to those who do not work" (Guest, 1980, p. 193).

There was a great deal of interest in the GAI in the early seventies although only Manitoba took up the federal offer of assuming 75 percent of the costs in launching a GAI experiment. Meanwhile, in 1973, the new minister of National Health and Welfare, Marc Lalonde, initiated a comprehensive review of social welfare with his Orange Paper, *Working Paper on Social Security in Canada*. As mentioned in chapter 1, the term "social security" is used in this paper, in the sense of the term "social welfare" that has been used in this book. The joint federal-provincial review of Canada's total social welfare system was called for in the January 1973 Speech from the Throne. Between 1973 and 1976, periodic meetings were held by the ministers and deputy ministers of welfare of Canada and the provinces, and their staff and other experts in social security. The Mincome Manitoba experiment staff worked closely with the Federal-Provincial Working Party on Income Maintenance, one of three major components of this social welfare review. (The other two were Working Parties on employment, and employment and social services).

In 1977, as a result of the social welfare review, the federal government tried to persuade the provinces to accept some form of GAI. There was some urgency in the view of the federal authorities in light of the new constitutional crisis posed by the election of the Parti Québécois in 1976. However, the interest in GAI had waned. The provinces, led by Ontario, opposed the scheme. Inflationary pressures following the 1974 oil pricing crisis, increasing unemployment, and a general economic downturn did not augur well for a new thrust in income security endeavours. The GAI was shelved. However, the technical reports of the Mincome Manitoba experiment published in 1979 provide valuable data on technical and policy questions, such as the integration of the GAI into the tax system and existing social insurance programs. Should some form of nationwide GAI be reconsidered at a later date to replace the stigma-conferring social assistance plan, useful information and experience could be gleaned from the Mincome Manitoba reports (Splane, 1980).

There were changes in other income security programs in the seventies. In 1974, the amount of Family Allowances was increased. While Ottawa continues to provide all the funds for Family Allowances, the provinces could vary payments according to the age and/or number of children in the family. This change was proposed in an attempt to reach some measure of jurisdictional harmony between and federal and provincial governments.

As a result of the social welfare review, the benefits of both Old Age Security (OAS) and Old Age Security Guaranteed Income Supplement (OAS–GIS) were increased and indexed to the consumer price index on a quarterly basis. On the other hand, in the late 1970s, unemployment insurance regulations were tightened to limit eligibility. Economic projects, such as Opportunities for Youth and the Company of Young Canadians, were abolished and the Local Initiatives Programs were curtailed. These changes all took place in the income security field traditionally handled by the federal government and were instituted as part of the budgetary restraint policy. But this decreased responsibility for welfare programs also took place at a time when the provinces were asserting their jurisdictional rights and prerogatives with renewed vigour. As will be demonstrated in the next chapter, personal and community social services became an even greater casualty in government cutbacks and increased tensions in federal-provincial relations.

10

Welfare Institution II: Social Services

Social services refer to the broad range of nonincome security measures that are intended to enhance the well-being of individuals and communities. Some are centred around personal needs, such as adoption, day care for children and the elderly, and crisis intervention. Others are more community-oriented, such as community health clinics and recreational facilities involving social planning and community development. The lines between personal and community services are not rigid, just as administrative responsibilities for different services by various government departments are not always easy to define. In Canada, the issues are further complicated by the constitutional problem of jurisdiction. But like the income security programs, social services are not just "welfare" services, that is, services used by or associated with social assistance recipients, such as subsidized day care or legal aid. Just as everyone in Canada, rich or poor, receives cash transfer payments at some point, in the form of family allowances, tax expenditures, or old age security, everyone needs social services at some stage, in the areas of education, health care, or referrals (see Table 9.1 in the previous chapter). As indicated in chapter 1, this book focuses on the welfare state. Thus, the personal and community services discussed in this chapter are mostly government programs or largely funded by the government.

Personal and Community Services

Most of the personal and community social services established in the first half of the century were operated by philanthropic organizations in the private, voluntary sector. Until 1966, the provinces alone were responsible for state-provided social services, except for vocational rehabilitation services for the disabled for which federal cost-sharing had existed since 1952 (Guest, 1980). Through the cost-sharing arrangements agreed upon in the Canada Assistance Plan (1966), the federal government began to exert influence on the development of social welfare service across the country. The broad objectives of the CAP social services were "the lessening, removal or prevention of the causes and effects of poverty, child neglect, or dependence on public assistance" (quoted in Armitage, 1975, p. 149). Services include casework, counselling, homemaker and day care services, and community development. It should be noted that preventive services are part of the express purpose of the Plan, although in practice access to services is limited to those who are already deemed to be "in need," that is, social assistance recipients. Thus, social services provided by the provincial departments of social welfare are labelled and they, along with social assistance payments, confer a stigma on the recipient.

Although the provision that the federal government has to pay 50 percent of the costs of the welfare services has been instrumental and even decisive in establishing many services badly needed in some communities, the provinces have also resented the priorities set by the central government, often without due regard for the particular needs and conditions of different regions.

What follows is a discussion of some of the most commonly used social services. The list is by no means exhaustive. Moreover, each of the services examined merits a book in itself. The services also differ from each other in terms of comprehensiveness, levels of development, and importance to the state. The more comprehensive and developed services and those services having a more direct social control value (such as health care, education, and corrections) are governed by special legislation. Others continue to be associated with Social Assistance. Still others have barely moved beyond the self-help group stage (such as shelters for battered women).

The rationale for choosing these social services is simply that they are the most frequently used and, in that sense, the most important services in Western societies. However, this apparent random selection in fact illustrates the impact of modified individualism, the dominant ideology that has guided the development of the welfare state in the West. Modified individualism does not claim any collective goals for society or specific outcomes for the individual as the objectives of the welfare state. The central idea in modified individualism is that the state intervenes to ensure each individual enough well-being to pursue her or his own self-interest. Given this, there is no coherent rationale in the choice of services provided by the state, except an *ad hoc* response to public pressure as a need arises. There is, therefore, inevitably an arbitrary element in the pattern of existing services. The choice of services for discussion here reflects this.

Health Care

Universal health care covering hospital and physician's services has been established in every province, an aspect of the social welfare institution in which citizens and governments alike have taken great pride. Undoubtedly, universal health care has been beneficial to the general public. There are, however, several features in the existing health care system that deserve attention and improvement.

First, as mentioned above, health care programs are no longer cost-shared between the federal and provincial governments; they now fall under the Established Programs Financing Arrangement, whereby the provinces have greater autonomy in their operation. In Ontario, Alberta, and British Columbia, the provinces also levy flat-rate premiums on individuals and families. It is common in those three provinces for employers to pay for the premiums in part or in full as fringe benefits. But those so benefited usually have jobs in the primary labour market. Moreover, as we have discussed in chapter 7, flat rate taxes such as the health care premium are always regressive. Health insurance premiums are not only unfair to low income people, but also act as a deterrent. They affect the wage-earning poor particularly as in most provinces people on Social Assistance are entitled to free coverage.

Second, in the existing health care system, the concept of health needs is ignored. Instead, the economic concepts of supply and demand are employed. The notion of health needs is qualitative and depends on the recognition by self or by a physician whether or not one is in a state of physical well-being. The notion of demands, on the other hand, pertains to the actual uses of services regardless of one's health status. The existing health care system ensures that services are universally accessible but does not ensure that Canadians are as healthy as they could be. Evidence shows that there are still extensive unmet health needs, chief among which are those of low income families and native peoples. These groups are more often and more severely afflicted with illnesses than those in average or above-average income groups. In principle, they indeed have as ready access to health services as the rest of the population, in fact, those who live in isolated areas are at a disadvantage. More important is the consideration that disadvantaged groups have a greater need for special programs in disease prevention and health promotion efforts, (Badgley and Charles, 1978, p. 75), and these needs are not being met.

Third, as mentioned above in relation to the distributional effects of health and education benefits (chapter 7), there is unequal use of health care services by different income groups, with the exception of hospital services. In general, all Canadians have gained from universal health care, but the high income groups have gained the most in terms of using services (Badgley & Charles, 1978).

Fourth, in recent years, extra billing by doctors, especially specialists, tends to undermine the very foundation of universal free medicare. Given the strong lobby launched by the national and provincial medical associations, the practice of extra billing will be entrenched and will only bring further inequities to health care.

Fifth, most provincial health care plans do not cover drugs or dental care.

Education

Free primary and secondary education is provided for every child by the provincial government and is compulsory for children under the age of 16. Postsecondary education is subsidized by the federal government under the Established Programs Financing Arrangement.

It is a well-established fact that education is linked to family income in terms of access to opportunity and educational achievement. Because of the conventional wisdom that more education raises a person above poverty, the entire relationship between education and social inequality will be analyzed in greater detail in the next chapter's discussion of education.

Housing

Housing in Canada is mostly commonly obtained through the market, by buying or renting. It is assumed that as long as there are annual increases in housing starts and as long as average housing standards are rising, people are generally better housed. Yet there are gross inequalities in the use and distribution of housing stock (Moscovitch, 1981). Relatively large numbers of low income family units who live in buildings constructed before 1940, are without a bath or flush toilet, and rent, rather than own, their homes. For the relatively high price they pay, their housing is the smallest and in the poorest condition. The National Housing Act administered by the Canada Mortgage and Housing Corporation (CMHC) is in part intended to provide suitable accommodation to low income families and individuals. So, although there is legislation pertaining specifically to housing, its intention and operation definitely fall within the residual conception of welfare. The CMHC independently, or in conjuction with the province, the municipality, or a public housing authority, provides housing for those with low income in several ways.

First, there are housing projects directly owned and operated by public authorities. Public housing programs are selective and means-tested. As Armitage puts it, "public housing looks like poverty on exhibit" (1975, p. 125). It is characterized by high density, minimum room sizes, inconvenient locations in terms of services and potential employment, and drab exterior finishes. Residents are often stigmatized and socially segregated from the surrounding neighbourhoods. While the quality of public housing is unsatisfactory, so is the quantity, as the number of public housing units is vastly inadequate. Moreover, rents in public housing projects are adjusted to income. An increase in income either from employment earnings or from cash transfer payments leads to an increase in rent. This rent-to-income scheme has its counterpart in private sector housing. For example, landlords have been known to increase rents following increases in universal Old Age Security benefits (CCSD, 1973, p. 83).

Second, the public housing authorities guarantee and supply mortgage funds at reduced interest rates to families with incomes below a certain level. However, the amount of funding provided is inadequate. Furthermore, people in the bottom or even second quintile are not likely to have enough savings for down payments. This kind of home ownership program is therefore less helpful to the lowest income groups than to the lower middle income groups, who have incomes low enough to qualify but high enough to allow savings for down payments.

Third, CMHC offers several forms of financial assistance designed to encourage public and private efforts to provide low-rental housing accommodation. Under Section 15 of the National Housing Act, up to 100 percent loans are available to nonprofit organizations and up to 95 percent loans to any organization, corporation, or individual wanting to undertake low-rental housing projects either through new construction or through the purchase and improvement of existing buildings. In the case of companies and individuals undertaking low-rental projects as business ventures, the question arises as to whether the state is investing in housing or working to promote private profit (Moscovitch, 1981). Developers (corporations and individuals) typically construct commercial complexes downtown and industrial buildings or single residential units in the suburbs because these undertakings carry fewer risks and lead to greater profit margins. By making loans to the commercial developers for low-rental housing projects the state, through CMHC, is in effect assuming risks and guaranteeing profits. The state also offers tax shelters as incentives to achieve the same results. Instead of providing assistance to developers in the form of tax relief, socialization of risks, and guaranteed profits (thus fulfilling its capital accumulation function), the state could be producing more housing and protecting consumers (Moscovitch, 1981).

Lastly, public housing authorities also make up to 95 percent loans to families with low or moderate incomes for co-operative housing. There is growing interest in this type of housing provision. However, the lowest income groups are not given much assistance through this program.

Despite the problems associated with public housing, it is still better in terms of cost and standard than the slum dwellings owned by members of the private sector. In that sense, public housing, assisted home-ownership plans, nonprofit housing corporations, and co-operative housing together constitute a form of social wage to low and lower-middle income Canadians. Given the shortage of serviced lands and quality housing, direct provision of housing by the public sector is urgently needed if consumers are to be protected from unscrupulous landlords and real estate speculators. In addition, a system of rent control or rent review should be broadly institutionalized (CCSD, 1973, p. 84).

Correctional Services

Correctional services are part of the criminal justice system, the other main functions of which are apprehension (policing) and adjudication (court functions). Separate legislation pertains to adult and juvenile corrections. Services are intended to rehabilitate offenders at various stages, including probation, incarceration, parole, and release. There is a general tendency, in theoretical thinking at least, to place less value on incarceration than on more community-based programs, as empirical evidence shows that imprisonment is positively correlated with recidivism. This means that increasingly larger proportions of offenders are on probation or parole. Innovative programs such as the following have also been set up: providing a wider range of academic and vocational education in correctional institutions; giving day passes or allowing temporary absence from prisons; family visiting privileges in institutions; and establishing community residential centres from which offenders serving sentences may go into the community for employment or education every day. However, in the only federal prison for women in Kingston, Ontario, the facilities are inadequate for educational/vocational/cultural program development as well as basic living accommodation, as compared to the male institutions. Because of the lack of rehabilitation and other opportunities for women in the federal penitentiary, a complaint has been lodged with the Canadian Human Rights Commission that women inmates are being discriminated against on the basis of sex.

In order to appreciate the proper function of correctional services in the criminal justice system, one must examine the relationship between social class and crime. The laws of any capitalist society are overwhelmingly in favour of the capitalist class. "The definition of some behaviours as criminal while other socially harmful acts are not so defined is, in large part, if not totally, a function of class domination" (Greenaway, 1980, p. 262). The overrepresentation by the poor from the working class and members of the underclass among the offenders is, therefore, partly by definition. Moreover, experiences of poverty and frustration of the subordinate classes are often so demeaning and devastating that resorting to crime appears to be reasonable or desirable. "Crime and delinquency are social products and, given the nature of Canadian political and economic organization, it should surprise no one that the status of criminal or delinquent is one which is, with few exceptions, reserved for those at the bottom of the social order" (Greenaway, 1980, p. 262).

There is no doubt that some of the existing correctional services help to enhance the psychological functioning of some offenders. But greater effectiveness can be achieved by also relating correctional service programming to a politico-economic analysis of crime and the justice system.

Child Welfare

The underlying principle of child welfare services is inherently contradictory. On the one hand, parents are expected to raise and care for their children. Implicit in this view is that children are the property of their parents. The state, therefore, has the primary obligation of protecting parental rights. On the other hand, children are citizens in their own right. The state, therefore, has the obligation to protect the interests of the child (Melichercik, 1981, pp. 129–32). The latter view is congruent with the capitalist state's function of ensuring the generational reproduction of labour power. But the proper socialization of the young, which includes their learning the norms, ideology, values, and behaviour appropriate to their future role in a capitalist economy is more efficiently accomplished within the nuclear family. Thus, in an advanced capitalist society such as Canada, parents have the primary responsibilities in child raising. State child welfare services exist to assist parents or to provide alternative care when parents are unable to care for their children adequately. Such a scheme leads to a residual, problem-centred view of child welfare services.

While child welfare services should include all services related to children, legislation pertaining to child welfare in each province is more narrowly defined so as to allow intervention only "to correct a series of specific problems, including child abuse, child neglect, child behaviour problems, and unmarried motherhood" (Armitage, 1975, p. 151). In the narrower legal definition, child welfare services are those provided to children whose parents are unable or unwilling to fulfill their child-raising responsibility (Melichercik, 1981, p. 125). The provinces legislate and monitor the provision of child welfare services, but the actual services may be delivered by provincial departments of social welfare or private organizations such as the Children's Aid Society. Child welfare programs are often integrated with the provinces' social assistance programs, and are cost-shared by the federal government under the CAP.

Substitute care for children can be permanent or temporary. The most common form of permanent substitute care is adoption of children who are legally free, that is, whose natural parents have voluntarily given up their guardianship rights through a formal legal procedure. Adoptions are generally regulated by provincial law and those arranged by child welfare agencies are preceded by screenings of potential adoptive parents. However, some adoption policies and practices leave much to be desired. The disproportionately large number of native children adopted by nonnative parents and the typically slim chance of adoption by unmarried individuals are two examples of problematic situations caused, at least in part, by regulation. Temporary substitute care takes the form of foster home, group home, or residential care, although the same facilities may be used by those who are made permanent wards of the state.

It is sometimes necessary to place children under substitute care because of repeated sexual or physical abuse, abandonment, parental death, or parental incapacity because of mental or physical illness. However, in other cases, removing a child from the family may not be necessary at all if the family has certain resources such as better housing, more income, home care services, and day care. The lack of these resources is an economic matter, and not primarily a cause for the stigma-conferring child welfare services provided under the existing legislation. In a report by the National Council of Welfare (1979b), it is pointed out that poor families are more likely than those with high incomes to use child welfare services. First, low income families typically experience problems related to poverty that affect the care they can provide for their children. Second, families with higher incomes may "buy" supportive services in the private sector to prevent or relieve stress in child care. Such services include domestic help, marriage counselling, recreation, and vacations. In low income families, untreated problems accumulate and develop into more serious ones. Then the child welfare system is the only source of help available to the poor. The report summarizes the situation as follows:

> On the face of it, of course, parental inability is the reason underlying any decision to place a child in care. Whether the problem lies with the parent, the child, or both and whether or not the initiative to remove the child is taken by the parents or by the child welfare authorities, the state can only intervene when it judges parents unable or unwilling to care properly for their children. What is often forgotten, however, is that the term "unable or unwilling to provide care" is nothing more than a convenient administrative label lumping together a wide variety of family problems, many of which stem from inadequate income, unemployment and other factors that cannot fairly be blamed on their victims (NCW, 1979b, p. 11).

The child welfare authorities and the family court have a great deal of power in dealing with "problem" families. "The grounds for declaring a child 'in need of protection' are expressed in general terms that permit widely varying interpretation according to the inclinations and biases of a particular judge or caseworker. Vaguely worded references to a child 'living in unfit or in improper circumstances', 'beyond the control of the person caring for him' and 'in the care of a person whose conduct endangers his life, health, or emotional well-being' are commonplace clauses in Canadian child welfare statutes" (NCW, 1979b, p. 13).

Discretionary power by the authorities is probably an element that cannot be eliminated in child welfare services.

> . . .But those who disagree with a particular decision, especially if they are the parents of a child in care, may regard "judgment" as bias or even prejudice. Some argue that the middle-class values of judges and child care workers sometimes influence their view of families from different ethnic and income groups who follow different standards and practices of child rearing. The fact that children from low-income families, particularly native kids and those with single parents, are overrepresented among those in substitute care likely results in part from discrimination against such "problem" families by some child care authorities (NCW, 1979b, pp. 13-14).

The NCW report (1979) notes that today one in every one hundred children in this country lives "in care". Costs of child welfare services provided by the federal, provincial, and municipal governments run into three-quarters of a billion dollars a year. Child welfare is an industry providing employment for a host of experts, such as social workers, lawyers, and psychiatrists. But the greatest human cost is borne by the children themselves. Most of them feel stigmatized. They also feel bewildered, abandoned, and unwanted. Those put "in care" temporarily average four different sets of foster parents, while permanent wards of the state are likely to live in eight different foster homes. The longer a child is "in care", the more likely the child will spend the rest of his or her childhood and adolescence apart from the natural family. A study in British Columbia showed that 80 percent of children in care for six months or longer have little chance of returning to their parents (McParland, 1978, p. 35). The longer children remain "in care", the less also is the chance of their being adopted. Children in care learn to hold their feelings back and to distrust adults, since too many broken relationships with initially sympathetic people leave them numbed and scarred. The same children perform less well in school and are disadvantaged as they begin adult life. The NCW report concludes that solutions to problems in child welfare services lie in better income security programs so that a lack of income would no longer be the primary cause of increased child welfare caseloads. Child welfare services can then move from the residual, problem-centred approach to a comprehensive system of support and services for all families.

Under the present CAP, family counselling, day care, and visiting homemakers' services are available to parents on social assistance to help them in caring for their children. Because of their association with CAP, these services are often regarded as "welfare" services. Yet there is clear evidence that *all* families experience difficulty in fulfilling their child raising responsibilities. All families therefore need family life education, day care, homemakers' services, and family counselling services at some time or other (Armitage, 1975, p. 151). The need is the most acute among low income families that are not on social assistance. If some services were made available to these families now, it would help to prevent many of the problems that might otherwise lead them to the doors of child welfare agencies.

In recent years, the Unified Family Court has been established in Saskatoon, Hamilton, Fredericton, and St. John's. It provides for the legal resolution of all family related problems in a single court. Family matters include divorce, custody and access, maintenance and support, marital property, child protection, family assaults, juvenile delinquencies, and adoption. The Unified Family Court is designed to deal with traumatic matters in a humane and sensitive fashion. Within this system, the needs and rights of children are formally recognized. Counselling and information services are available prior to, during, and after legal proceedings.

Child Day Care

While both parents are expected to raise their children, in Canada and other advanced capitalist countries, it is usually the mother who acts as the principal care-giver, especially when the children are young. During the Second World War, when women were drawn into wartime production, many nurseries and day care centres were set up to provide substitute care. However, most were closed at the end of the war and for the next two decades most women with preschool children remained at home.

Since the late 1960s, more mothers with preschool children have entered the labour market or taken up full-time studies. This trend together with the growing women's liberation movement advocating greater equality between the sexes, has led to increasing public pressure on governments to provide and to supervise day care facilities for children. Day care services not only allow mothers to seek full-time employment, which is a necessity in many families, but could also provide the children with a safe and stimulating environment and an opportunity to interact with many people outside the nuclear family.

A day care facility could be a licensed day care centre for groups of children or a government-approved private home that provides care for children outside their own home for eight to ten hours a day. The pattern of growth in day care facilities in the past decade has not been consistent, an indication that the right of every child to quality day care service is far from recognized and accepted. Increases in day care services occurred in the early 1970s, and reached a peak in 1974. The growth then slowed down. During 1977 and 1978, however, there were actual decreases in day care spaces. The trend was reversed in 1979, but in the 1980s the pattern has been one of growth.

In spite of these growth trends, the availability of day care services varies according to the age of the children. Table 10.1 gives the age of children in day care centres and family day care homes for 1980.

It can be seen that the greatest proportion of spaces (nearly 80 percent in licensed centres and 48 percent in approved homes) are occupied by children between the ages of two and six. About 15 percent of the spaces in centres and 21 percent in homes are occupied by children aged six and over, who usually go to the day care facility during school lunch hour and after school. The smallest proportion of combined centre and home spaces are for children under the age of two: 7.9 percent, totalling 8704

Table 10.1 Ages of Children Registered in Day Care Centres and Family Day Care Homes, 1980

	Centres		*Family Day Care*	
Ages	*No.*	*%*	*No.*	*%*
Under 2	5 288	5.38	3 416	31.33
2 - 6	78 534	79.94	5 185	47.56
6 and over	14 416	14.68	2 302	21.11
Total	98 238	100.00	10 903	100.0

SOURCE: Health and Welfare Canada, *Status of Day Care in Canada*, 1980, Table 2. Reproduced by permission of the Minister of Supply and Services Canada.

spaces. This actually represents a loss of 147 spaces from 1979 and a loss of 3276 spaces from 1978 for children under the age of two (Canada, Health and Welfare, 1980, p. 7). Infant care is therefore in a critical stage. Reports suggest that it is easier to recruit family day care homes to provide care for children over the age of two than for infants. Although many day care centres do not accept infants, the greatest percentage of mothers entering the labour market are mothers with infants.

It is estimated that in 1980, 3.8 percent of infants (children under the age of two) whose mothers were working outside the home were in regulated day care, that is, receiving care in licensed centres or approved family day care homes. It is also estimated that 15.8 percent of children aged two to six with mothers in the labour force and 0.68 percent of children between the ages of six and 16 of working mothers were enrolled in day care facilities. Since older children require less supervision, the 0.68 percent figure has less relevance than do the corresponding figures for the other age groups (Canada, Health and Welfare, 1980, p. 8). The percentages mean that most working mothers with small children resort to relatives, neighbours, babysitters, or other similar types of private arrangements between the parent and the caregiver that are not under the supervision and regulation of the province or authorized agencies. Or, where older school-age children are involved, the "latch-key child" phenomenon is prevalent. The lack of regulated day care spaces discriminates against women who are then denied the choice of full-time paid employment or studies.

This dearth of good day care reflects a public attitude of indifference to child welfare. But above all, it reflects the pervasive sexism of a capitalist society. Women are treated as the reserve labour supply. When their participation in the labour force is required by economic growth, they are called upon to work outside the home. At such times, public child day care is more readily available, as during the Second World War. When women's participation is not required, as during an economic slump when the unemployment rate is high, women as the marginal workers are among the first to be dismissed. During such times, public child day care services also tend to decline in quantity and quality. Thus availability of day care, or the lack of it, follows the dictates of the economy, rather than the needs of the women themselves.

Sponsorship of day care centres differs from case to case. Each province has its own pattern of delivering services (Table 10.2). Only Ontario and Alberta have privately owned day care centres. In Saskatchewan, only nonprofit parent co-operatives are licensed. In most other provinces, nonprofit community board centres or parent co-operatives form the majority. In Alberta, the ratio of commercial to nonprofit centres is 2:1 (Canada, Health and Welfare, 1980, pp. 10-12).

Legal Aid

The usual method of obtaining legal service in Canada is through the market mechanism: a client buys expertise that a lawyer has to offer. Legal aid is the assistance given to those who cannot afford to buy legal services on their own. Since criteria regarding financial eligibility exist in all provinces (Table 10.3), residualism is built into legal aid.

There are two broad types of legal aid: the public defender system and judicare. In the former instance, the provincial government or its authorized agency (such as the provincial legal aid commission or law society) maintains a staff of salaried lawyers who deal with all legal aid work. In the judicare plan, legal aid cases are farmed out to private lawyers who are paid by the provincial government or its authorized agency according to law society tariff schedules. In Canada, there is a strong aversion to the public defender system and a strong protection of the private bar (*Globe and Mail*, 18 January 1982, p. 9), ostensibly to protect the client's freedom to choose a lawyer. Yet, how meaningful is the concept of choice when applicants are shown only a list of names and asked to pick one, or where the client is unlikely to be in a position to assess the skill of the chosen lawyer? Existing evidence indicates that

Table 10.2 Interprovincial Comparison of Day Care Spaces

	Public Centre Spaces		*Community Board Spaces**		*Parent* Cooperative Spaces*		*Commercial Centre Spaces*		*Family Day Care Spaces*	
Provinces	*Number*	%	*No.*	%	*No.*	%	*No.*	%	*No.*	%
British Columbia			1 560	3.7	4 678	57.4	2 530	6.4	4 500	44.3
Alberta	921	10.8	4 863	11.6	67	0.8	9 972	25.2	581	5.3
Saskatchewan			90	0.2	2 317	28.4	89	0.2	999	9.2
Manitoba			2 871	6.8	255	3.1	1 334	3.4	481	4.4
Ontario	7 574	89.2	10 127	24.1	587	7.2	17 995	45.5	4 262	39.1
Quebec			18 665	44.3	245	3.1	4 823	12.2	60	0.6
New Brunswick			1 300	3.1			1 349	3.4		
Nova Scotia			2 080	4.9			595	1.5		
Prince Edward Island			150	0.4			450	1.2	20	0.1
Newfoundland			136	0.3			355	1.0		
Northwest Territories			100	0.2						
Yukon			137	0.4			23			
National Totals	8 495	100	42 079	100	8 149	100	39 515	100	10 903	100

**Community Board Centre* — A licensed day care centre that is established as a nonprofit organization and is governed by a community board of directors.

Cooperative Day Care — A licensed day care centre set up as a nonprofit association and governed by a board of directors of which at least 50% are parents of children in the centre.

SOURCE: Health and Welfare Canada, *Status of Day Care in Canada*, 1980, Table 5. Reproduced by permission of the Minister of Supply and Services Canada.

Table 10.3 Legal Aid in Ten Provinces

Province	*Total Expenditures Cost/Capita 1979-80*	*Total Population of Province 1979-80*	*Total Applications; % Rejected 1979-80*	*Lawyers' Tariff for Preparation of Murder Case + 1st Day of Trial (Maxim.)*	*% of Work Done by Staff Legal Aid Lawyers*
Ontario Legal Aid Plan	$36.6 million $4.28/capita	8 558 200	118 007 29% rejected	$1 620	4%
British Columbia Legal Services Society	$11.6 million $4.42/capita	2 626 400	37 375 24.1% rejected	$500	5%
Legal Aid Society of Alberta	$4.5 million $2.20/capita	2 068 800	17 387 31.6% rejected	$330	0
Legal Aid Services Society of Manitoba	$3.5 million $3.42/capita	1 027 100	14 105 18.8% rejected	$1 750	24%
Saskatchewan Community Legal Services Commission	$3.9 million $4.06/capita	947 400	16 250 no statistics on rejections	$2 800	98%

(Continued)

Quebec Legal Services Commission	$35.9 million $5.72/capita	6 298 000	216 306 11.2% rejected	$725	70%
Legal Aid New Brunswick	$744 787 $1.06/capita	705 700	1 523 11.1% rejected	$2 355	0
Nova Scotia Legal Aid Commission	$1.99 million $2.34/capita	851 600	13 267 no statistics on rejections	$1 750	98%
Newfoundland Legal Aid Commission	$698 942 $1.21/capita	578 200	(1980-81) 4 657 44% rejected	$1 740	54%
Prince Edward Island Office of the Public Defender	$86 898 70 cents/capita	124 000	approx. 450 16% rejected	$1 975	98%

(Continued)

Table 10.3 (cont'd.)

Province	*Coverage Restrictions (Civil)*
Ontario Legal Aid Plan	Subject to discretion of local director in juvenile or family court, small claims court, before a quasi-judicial or administrative board or for drawing documents, negotiating settlement
British Columbia Legal Services Society	Exclusions include small claims court matters, breach of promise, proceedings under Election Act, defamation actions, private prosecutions
Legal Aid Society of Alberta	Exclusions include divorce matters, unless "urgent need"
Legal Aid Services Society of Manitoba	Excludes breach of promise
Saskatchewan Community Legal Services Commission	Excludes fee-generating matters

(Continued)

Quebec Legal Services Commission	Excludes plaintiff in defamation and libels, contesting an election, plaintiffs in breach of promise of marriage, parking violations
Legal Aid New Brunswick	Civil coverage started Oct. 1, 1981
Nova Scotia Legal Aid Commission	
Newfoundland Legal Aid Commission	Exclusions include defamation, breach of promise of marriage, loss of services of female as result of rape or seduction, election proceedings
Prince Edward Island Office of the Public Defender	Only civil coverage is family law

(Continued)

Table 10.3 (cont'd.)

	Eligibility
Ontario Legal Aid Plan	Calculated on maximum amounts allowed for basic needs: single person — $5 832/yr. (maxim.) family of 4 — $12 960/yr.
British Columbia Legal Services Society	Test to see if paying legal bill would hurt person's ability to live decently: single person — $9 600/yr. or less family of 4 — $16 000/yr.

Province	*Eligibility*
Legal Aid Society of Alberta	Income Guidelines single person — $9 600/yr. family of 4 — $13 200/yr.
Legal Aid Services Society of Manitoba	Income Guidelines single person — $8 500/yr. family of 4 — $12 000/yr.
Saskatchewan Community Legal Services Commission	Tied to social assistance levels: Net Income Guidelines single person — $6 200/yr. family of 4 — $11 000/yr.

(Continued)

Quebec Legal Services Commission	Income Guidelines Test single person — $8 840/yr. family of 4 — $11 960/yr.
Legal Aid New Brunswick	Based on disposable income; decision left to discretion of area directors
Nova Scotia Legal Aid Commission	Tied to social assistance levels: Income Guidelines single person — $4 716 to $7 488/yr. family of 4 — $8 292 to $13 452/yr.
Newfoundland Legal Aid Commission	Flexible Guidelines of approx. single person — $1 200/yr. family of 4 — $4 800/yr.
Prince Edward Island Office of the Public Defender	Take-home pay Guidelines $6 240/yr. (single person)

SOURCE: *The Globe and Mail*, Toronto, 18 January 1982.

the poorer a person is, the less likely she is even to know a lawyer (Taman, 1971, p. 40).

In Saskatchewan, Nova Scotia, and Prince Edward Island, virtually all legal aid is done by salaried lawyers in the public defender system; in Quebec about 70 percent and in Newfoundland 54 percent of legal aid work is done by salaried lawyers. In these five provinces, if the case involves a serious criminal charge, the client can choose between a staff lawyer or a private lawyer. The remaining provinces all operate their legal aid on the judicare basis (*Globe and Mail*, 1982).

All provinces provide legal aid to eligible clients involved in criminal cases; there are restrictions on civil cases in all provinces (Table 10.3). In some provinces, civil matters taken up in legal aid are those that private lawyers find unprofitable as, for example, welfare, unemployment insurance, and immigration appeals. By and large, the public defender system costs considerably less to operate.

In the United States in the 1960s, some experimentation in legal aid took the form of Neighbourhood Legal Services (NLS) programs. Whereas there was no single standard NLS program, there is sufficient evidence to indicate that not only were NLS cheaper but they possibly also offered aid of better quality. Clients were less intimidated by lawyers in these circumstances, and as the NLS staff came to know poor people's problems better, efforts at law reform were launched as part of a broader strategy in the war on poverty.

In some provinces such as Saskatchewan, Nova Scotia, and Quebec, the existing public defender system is modelled after the American NLS to varying degrees. In Saskatchewan, for example, legal aid clinics are established in the neighbourhoods of potential legal aid clients. In addition, these programs have a long-term objective of educating the poor to use the law to their advantage and showing them preventive measures in order to escape legal troubles. However, staff lawyers are so overworked that the burn-out rate is high. There is not much evidence that the advocacy role envisioned in the American NLS program is seriously pursued in any province, due to the lack or resources.

Services for People with Special Needs

This section deals with an array of services for apparently disparate populations. The fact is that when a person is incapacitated in some way, permanently or temporarily, he or she will likely require several broad types of services. The mentally retarded, the physically disabled, the mentally ill, the elderly, and the chronically or acutely sick may face different problems. But the routes they take to meet their special needs are quite similar. The common features in these types of services are discussed here. To some extent, the same features also characterize services for alcohol and drug addicts.

First of all, the disabled, the sick, and the elderly usually require some medical attention in the form of medication, checkups, hospitalization, or therapy. Health care is therefore an important component of the services required. Second, some of them may require residential care, be it in the setting of a hospital, nursing home, or community-based institution. Residential care is usually expensive, and residents could be easily demoralized because of segregation from community activities. So whenever feasible, people requiring assistance are encouraged to live in their own communities while additional care is provided. This is the third type of services: home care.

Home care is by and large funded by the provinces and the municipalities and, to a lesser degree, by private sources. Services are administered by a provincial government department, the municipality, a private agency, or a combination of the three. Services include the following:

1. *Visiting Homemaker's Services*: assistance with general physical care and household tasks; supervision of those who cannot be left alone.
2. *Home Maintenance Services*: assistance with yard maintenance, snow removal, interior and exterior house repairs, and renovations where necessary to enable independent mobility.
3. *Transportation*: provided for those unable to use public transit, such as those in wheelchairs.
4. *Meals on Wheels*: volunteers delivering hot meals prepared by an organization such as a city hospital.
5. Friendly visits by volunteers.

Finally, service delivery to the disabled, the infirm, and the elderly, usually involves national or local associations that act to advance their interests. Among these are the Canadian Mental Retardation Association, the Canadian Mental Health Association, human rights associations, the Injured Workers' Union, the Canadian Paraplegic Association, and the Senior Citizens Council. These organizations are consulted in setting up and delivering specialized services. They also lobby for funding and changes in law and other areas affecting the mobility or independence of their constituents, and they provide counselling and referral services. Above all, they form the basis of a network of contacts so that people with special needs are not isolated or alienated.

Quite often, services for people with special needs are not coordinated; considerable fragmentation and sometimes duplication of services exists. In most locales, there is a shortage of services, especially home care services on a long-term basis. Under the terms of CAP, federal funding for certain services is available only for social assistance cases. Universality is still elusive.

Indian and Métis Friendship Centre

Indians and Métis in Canada have suffered severe institutional and personal racial discrimination (see also chapter 11). In the last century and the early part of this century, they were half forgotten by the general population and certainly shunted out of sight onto reserves and isolated rural areas. In the last 20 years, increasing numbers of Indians and Métis have been migrating to urban centres where their disadvantaged position is worsened by their difficulty in adjusting to city life. The friendship centre is a drop-in place for urban native people. Its basic objective is to provide support, and to ease the transition between rural and urban life. There are altogether 80 friendship centres across the country, each of which has a board of directors and salaried staff. Centres are funded by both federal and provincial governments and have a central organization called the National Association of Friendship Centres in Ottawa.

The Indian and Métis Friendship Centre is chosen for discussion in this book not merely because of the unique status and special problems of the native people, but also because the friendship centre represents an integrated approach to providing services. Moreover, the accent in these centres is on education and on prevention of personal and social problems.

In a typical friendship centre, there are family workers who provide counselling and information, and deal with social assistance cases. Native courtworkers who are paralegal professionals provide information regarding the law, legal aid, and court proceedings. The Fine Options Program is often administered through the friendship centre. The centre also provides information services for housing and employment, two areas in which newcomers to the city encounter a great deal of discrimination. In some friendship centres, there are also day care services. Finally, there are a variety of recreational, athletic, educational, and social programs organized at the friendship centre.

The friendship centre is generally appreciated by the urban native population and is also frequented by nonnative people. The major problem encountered is funding for new programs and expansion of existing programs.

Services for Victims of Violence

This section concentrates on (a) shelter for battered women with children and (b) rape crisis and sexual assault information centres. The latter are receiving an increasing number of calls involving incest and sexual assault of children. They have also provided assistance to a few male victims of sexual assault. But it is mostly women who make use of these two kinds of services.

Shelters for battered women exist in all the major cities in Canada and there are about 40 sexual assault crisis centres across the country. Since the late 1960s, the growth of both services has been closely linked with the feminist movement. As feminist analysis has revealed, sexual inequality at the workplace and in society in general has been rationalized and reinforced by the subordination of the female in domestic relations. This domestic subordination also influences situations in which rape occurs. Contrary to the general misconception that rape takes place in dark alleys and deserted parks, the rapist or the sexual assailant is in most cases known to the victim; many are family members. In those domestic situations, the victims are vulnerable and in a subordinate position, as is usually the case with the battered woman. So the problems dealt with by both services are to be seen as acts of violence and aggression against women whose position in society is structurally dependent, and who are socialized to be and perceived as weak and submissive. Wife battering is also found to be closely related to the economic dependence of women, to the prevalent social acceptance of the man's authority over his "property" (his wife), and to the immunity of the family from many of the laws regarding assault in the larger society (Canadian Advisory Council on the Status of Women, 1980, p. 28). In the case of sexual assault, the assailant seeks to establish his masculine dominance, a quality extolled in the society.

On the face of it, shelters for battered women and rape crisis centres appear to be gaining acceptance by the public, and have become part of the established services in most Canadian cities. However, this is far from the truth. Although such centres may be accepted on principle, major funding problems prevent them from being established in sufficient numbers. Monies from all three levels of government plus private sources such as the United Way have been involved, but none of the sources are stable. In fact, in times of economic hardship and government cutbacks, these centres are in crisis (Kostash, 1982, pp. 8–13). A more fundamental issue is that of sexism, as increasing evidence of a backlash against feminism emerges. The male-dominated institutions in society—police, legal profession, courts, church, and family—are still reluctant to view violence against women from the woman's viewpoint. Self-help and social action groups acting in the interest of women victims are seen as threats to male dominance and labelled as undermining the family structure. Some groups have been forced to "tone down" their approach. For example, one women's shelter in a metropolitan area is teaching battered women such domestic skills as canning; similar shelters elsewhere run self-defence courses. When the rape crisis centre in Saskatoon and several women's groups in Toronto applied to the Department of National Revenue for charitable organization status, their application was delayed for considerable lengths of time. Some were eventually told to reword their objectives in order to conform with the provision of law (Chapin, 1977, pp. 42–43).

In the struggle for progressive and humane services, women victims are not alone in encountering obstacles. The gay community, for example, faces tremendous difficulties in even establishing support services for its members. It would seem that the state is willing to fund certain services for various minority groups. However, when the basic structures of inequality are challenged, the state is quick to withdraw resources in defence of the status quo.

Nongovernment Agencies

In the above discussion of social services, it is quite clear that in the provision and delivery of services, the welfare state relies to a great extent on voluntary organizations, volunteers, and commercial enterprises. In the next two sections, we shall discuss how the commercial and the voluntary sectors supplement and complement the services directly provided by governments.

The Commercial Sector

Commercial enterprises are active in child day care; residential care for children with special problems, psychiatric patients, and the elderly; and some home care services. In recent years, there has also been a growing trend in the private practice of social work. Services sold by social workers range from marriage and family counselling to consultancy to governments, corporations and voluntary organizations on community planning, neighbourhood development, and program evaluation. These commercial services may be paid for by the consumers directly. Alternatively, the government (federal, provincial, or municipal) "buys" these services and then makes them available to the consumers, or the government may subsidize the consumers up to a ceiling. In any case, the profit motive is present in those who produce the services.

Generally speaking, people do not like the commercial provision of social services as in their view they have paid for the services through taxes and donations and, therefore, should not be charged again. Moreover, the profit motive of commercial enterprises may conflict with government requirements for certain standards. Nevertheless, the participation of the commercial sector in social services is perfectly consistent with the free enterprise philosophy of capitalism. Commercial operators claim that the competition they inject into the system, be it day care or home care, poses a challenge to the quality and standards of public services. It is on the basis of this kind of argument that the commercial sector has become fairly large and strong in provinces with conservative governments, such as in Ontario and Alberta. Yet commercial sector social services constitute an inherent denial of people's universal right to needed social services.

Purchase of services from the commercial sector frees governments from the irksome task of having to provide the services themselves. This practice contradicts the responsibility of governments to maintain and supervise standards (Hepworth, 1975, pp. 15–16), and the state resorts to this practice predominantly because the services provided by the commercial sector are not deemed to be high priorities. Most of the services provided are in the area of maintaining the nonworking population.

The Voluntary Sector

The voluntary sector in social services is a complex phenomenon, and is linked to two ideological notions. The first is that of humanitarianism, a notion first demonstrated by well-born ladies in the first waves of the industrial revolution. The founding of the Charity Organization Society in mid-19th century England represented one of the first attempts to systematize volunteer work. Today, the altruistic appeal is still strong. Caring for one's fellow human beings to counteract the dehumanizing effects of industrialization and urbanization is still a rallying cry in the helping services.

The second notion is based on de Tocqueville's theory that voluntary action and pluralism are the very foundations of liberal democracy. Voluntary associations mediate between the state and the mass of citizenry. Thus they prevent authoritarianism of the central state, protect individual initiative and freedom, and stabilize democracy (Oommen, 1975, pp. 163–80).

Thus, the origins of voluntary activities can be traced to the ideology of individualism that has always guided the development of the welfare state. In Western capitalist societies, there is an acclaimed tradition of responding to social needs with a combination of government and voluntary efforts. The state and the voluntary sector are sometimes described as partners in dealing with social problems. Before we analyze the exact nature of this partnership, some definitions and classifications of voluntary action are in order.

The following definitions may clarify unnecessary semantic confusion (Chapin, 1977, p. 6):

> *Volunteerism*: The involvement of volunteers in providing services in governmental or voluntary agencies, organizations, and institutions as well as in self-help and social action groups.
>
> *Voluntarism*: The role, function, and composition of voluntary organizations.
>
> *Voluntary Action*: Action(s) undertaken by individual volunteers and voluntary organizations to promote their views, policies, and programs.

Generally speaking, voluntary organizations may be divided into two broad types:

1. Voluntary organizations that provide some services to the public
   These organizations can be quasi nongovernmental agencies that are privately incorporated but predominantly funded by the government(s) (such as the Children's Aid Society), or they can be private service agencies not answerable to a membership but to a paid professional staff and a self-perpetuating board of directors (such as the Y.W.C.A. or a family service agency) (Armitage, 1975, pp. 211–12). All these agencies are voluntary in the sense that they are nongovernmental and nonprofit organizations. But they are also voluntary in the additional sense that in varying degrees they rely on volunteers for resources and/or services. In this setting, volunteer services are those performed more or less on a regular and permanent basis, usually through the established institution and usually benefiting people who are not relatives or friends (Hawrylyshyn, 1978).
2. Organizations that are truly voluntary
   In this case, private citizens on their own initiative form a self-help group or association (such as welfare mothers' groups, Alcoholics Anonymous). Self-help organizations may also be funded by the government(s). These groups are typically involved in issue advocacy in areas such as women's rights, pollution, poverty, and racism.

Advocacy/social action is more common with the second type of voluntary association. But service-providing voluntary agencies could also be involved in public campaign or political activities, such as lobbying for some particular social reform.

In line with the above two types of voluntary organizations, Hawrylyshyn (1978) has pointed out a dichotomy of volunteer action. Corresponding to the self-help voluntary association is self-benefit action, which does not generally yield a benefit to people other than the participants. One may argue that issue advocacy by self-help groups may have a ripple effect that benefits people not associated with or directly involved in the action. But such indirect outside effect is usually not a main purpose of the self-benefit action. Corresponding to the service-providing voluntary organizations is social-benefit action that yields a benefit to third parties, although it may at the same time yield a benefit to the volunteer in the form of satisfaction. Hawrylyshyn further distinguishes two kinds of social-benefit action: charitable donations that merely transfer existing economic value from one party to another, and economic volunteer services (EVS), which create or produce new economic value. Economic volunteer services are defined as

> those activities which were done by a person outside the market but may have been accomplished by hiring a third-person from the economic market; they are distinguished from household work by the fact that the benefits accrue to someone other than the volunteer or the volunteer's immediate family (Hawrylyshyn, 1978, p. 4).

The point being made here is that volunteers working for service-providing voluntary organizations are productive members of the society, although the economic value of their work is not recognized as such by the agencies that use them or by the larger society. Moreover, since EVS are not paid for, they are not measured by the Gross National Product (GNP). Using the third-person market criterion, Hawrylyshyn has focused attention on EVS. Excluding such volunteer action as youth work, church/synagogue work, fund raising committee work, and self-help or citizen group work, he estimates the value of volunteer work to be $800 per annum per volunteer in 1971, or as much as $1000 to $1200 at 1976 inflated price levels. "A conservative estimate of the numbers of volunteers doing EVS places this value in the aggregate at one percent of GNP; an upper bound estimate for volunteer involvement makes the aggregate three percent" (Hawrylyshyn, 1978, p. 1). The enormity of the economic value of volunteer services stands in stark contrast to the fact that financial resources raised by the voluntary sector for social services (such as the United Way appeal) comprise less than one percent of state expenditures on social welfare (Armitage, 1975, p. 54).

In a national survey, it was estimated that more than half of the population aged 14 and over were involved in some form of volunteer activity or charitable giving (Carter, 1975). But not all of the activities counted as volunteer work in the survey were of the kind that generated an economic value. Contrary to the myth that volunteers are predominantly affluent women with spare time, volunteers actually come from all walks of life and, according to the survey, about 44 percent are men (Carter, 1975). People become volunteers for a variety of reasons. Altruism is frequently expressed as a motive. But reasons based on self-interest are also acknowledged: to gain satisfaction, to develop self, and to learn some skills and experience that may eventually be useful for career or employment.

That there is a great deal of demand for volunteers is reflected in the fact that there are about 60 volunteer centres or bureaus across Canada that act as clearing houses for associations or agencies requiring volunteers. Although some agencies recruit, screen, and train their own volunteers, the volunteer centres are extensively involved in recruiting and directing volunteers to social service agencies. While volunteers are quite aware of the fact that their services reduce agency costs, the agencies seem to prefer to emphasize the human touch and special skills as reasons why volunteer services are sought (Carter, 1975). Given the considerable economic benefits to the agencies, this difference in perception is probably one source of friction between the agency staff and volunteers. Some volunteers feel that they are asked to do unpaid "dirty" work that is a "nuisance" for the paid staff. On the other hand, in times of government cutbacks in funding to the agencies, some volunteers have begun to fill positions previously occupied by paid staff (Chapin, 1977, pp. 10–11). This kind of managerial practice on the part of the government or the voluntary agency has predictably caused the ire of staff unions. The sometimes less than cordial relationships between the volunteers and the staff are also traceable to the fact that many professionally trained human service workers are unfamiliar with volunteerism: little in their education or training has prepared them to work with and to respect volunteers.

In light of the above discussion, the partnership between statutory effort and voluntary effort in the social services has certain unmistakable features. First, the state gains a tremendous economic advantage by having volunteers work with voluntary agencies or directly with the government. Predominantly in the delivery of services, but also in administration and public education, the volunteers' contribution is vital to the continuing operations of many programs. Should the services of the volunteers be withdrawn, the state would be faced with ever greater costs of welfare programs.

Second, volunteerism and voluntarism are ideological tools useful to the state. The involvement of volunteers and the function of voluntary agencies, to the extent that they emphasize altruism and are the genuine expression of concern for others, reinforce the basic values of capitalism: individual initiative and freedom. While the state recognizes that it must provide certain levels of social welfare in fulfilling its legitimization function, private responsibility is never completely denied. Volunteerism and voluntarism buttress the concept of private responsibility. More important, the response of the state to some initial voluntary effort and the subsequent co-operation between the state and volunteers/voluntary associations also promote the view that the state is neutral, cares for all segments of society, and is not the agent of the dominant capitalist class (Loney, 1977).

Third, through volunteerism and voluntarism, the state can identify groups inclined toward dissidence. By providing funding and perhaps later withdrawing funding, the state monitors, contains, and often defuses the potentially disruptive forces of dissident and critical groups. This is particularly true in the case of self-help groups. Youth programs, welfare rights groups, associations of racial minorities (especially of the native peoples) in the 1960s and early 1970s all had a strong citizen participation orientation. The state's funding of and involvement with these groups generally had a conservative effect in the sense that it blunted their social criticisms and neutralized their objectives of social change. "In most cases political activity which falls outside the conservative paradigm will not be funded" (Loney, 1977, p. 454).

Finally, some programs in health care and personal social services have become statutory as a result of voluntary efforts. A few public programs have indeed become "humanized" and services have been offered with greater sensitivity to the needs of clients because of pressure from volunteers and public campaigns. These are the positive aspects of volunteerism and voluntarism. In fact, voluntary efforts have contributed greatly to both the quality and quantity of social services in Canada. They have provided direction for the development of social policy at various times. Nevertheless, the danger of voluntary services becoming merely a legitimizing tool for the state does exist.

Municipal Governments

While the provinces have jurisdiction over the entire social welfare field, social assistance and services from the time of Confederation to the Great Depression were largely provided at the municipal level. This practice still prevails in some locales, to a greater extent in the Eastern provinces than in the West. However, "in most places local government traditionally had a bad name" (Hepworth, 1975, p. 10). Municipal governments were thought to be "parochial and regressive" (Armitage, 1975, p. 174) by social welfare professionals who looked to senior levels of government for support and resources in order to raise standards of programs in their districts. By now, all provinces have centralized some programs that were previously run by local governments.

The reluctance of the social welfare professionals and administrators to include municipal governments in the jurisdiction of their field also springs from other sources. Municipalities vary greatly in size, making standardization and comparison difficult. More important, city hall politics "is dominated by issues of physical development and it is feared that social service issues will not get the attention they warrant" (Armitage, 1975, p. 174). Yet greater involvement of the municipal government structure would provide a stability and viability in local participation that social services could not achieve on their own. In recent years, it has been recognized that certain programs, especially services such as shelters for battered women, cannot be sustained without the active support of the local government, or at least its police force. Consequently, input in municipal policy making by citizen groups supporting various social services seems to be growing. This is especially notable as it entails, at times, the difficult task of challenging the interests of developers who have a preponderant influence on the municipal government in most cities.

Social Welfare Review: Social Services

By the early 1970s, inadequacy in both quality and quantity of publicly provided social services became increasingly apparent (Canada Special Senate Committee on Poverty, 1971; Quebec Commission of Inquiry on Health and Social Welfare, 1971). The thinking on social services in Marc Lalonde's Orange Paper (1973), however, did not indicate any significant departure from the orientation already embodied in the CAP. The paper focused narrowly on those services related to income security and the entry or reentry of those on assistance into the labour force. Job counselling, training, placement, rehabilitation, homemaker, and child care services were among the services emphasized. Despite the limited vision of the Orange Paper, new perspectives on social services were soon introduced by the Federal-Provincial Working Party on Social and Employment Services. The Working Party rejected the "case" approach in providing social services heretofore relied upon by government social workers. Instead, members of the Working Party argued for community development and social change goals for social services. Among the recommendations were that eligibility for services should be separated from financial assistance. "Certain public social services should be available to anyone upon demand, without needs-testing or payment of fees. . ., other services upon the basis of diagnosed need ("case services"). User charges should apply to some services. . ." (Kelly, 1977). Citizen participation in planning and provision of social services was also recommended.

As a result of Marc Lalonde's social welfare review and negotiations, the federal and provincial ministers of welfare acknowledged in a communiqué, 4 February 1976, that there is

> a recognition of the importance of social services for ensuring the opportunity for personal development of all Canadians and preventing and alleviating the social and economic problems of individuals and communities. It is intended that the new legislation assist the provinces in responding to the changing social and personal needs of Canadians. To that end, the scope of cost-sharing of a number of services will be extended and a number of new services will become eligible for cost-sharing (Canada, Federal-Provincial Ministers of Welfare, 1976).

The Social Services Act (Bill C-57) introduced in the Commons in June 1977 sought to meet this promise. Under Bill C-57, some services would be cost-shareable when provided on the basis of identified need. User charges related to a person's income would apply to certain services (such as day care, meals on wheels, and counselling of all types) Other cost-shareable services would be made available free upon demand, without any needs- or means-test. This arrangement was proposed for information and referral, crisis intervention, family planning, and preventive services such as family life and prenatal education.

Bill C-57 was intended to provide an impetus toward and a financial incentive for developing a system of universal and less stigmatizing social services by the provinces. It signified a strong federal commitment to the development of personal and community social services. The provinces, on the other hand, would waive residency as a criterion of eligibility and establish appeal boards independent of the provincial department of social services (Riches, 1977).

Despite the approval accorded to the proposed legislation by all the provinces in prior negotiations, during the summer of 1977 there was opposition by Quebec and two other provinces. The federal categorization scheme of certain services as universal, limited access, or fee chargeable was perceived to be inflexible and to indicate undue federal control. Demanding more tax points to finance and run its own programs, Quebec denounced the Bill as "an unwarranted intrusion by the federal government into an area of exclusive provincial jurisdiction" (NCW, 1978c, p. 11).

In September 1977, three months after Bill C-57 was introduced, Marc Lalonde withdrew it from Parliament. He announced that the income security programs under the CAP would continue to operate on the current 50:50 cost-sharing arrangement, while social services would be financed by block funding. The block funding would consist partly of a "basic cash contribution" (a lump sum grant of equal per capita amounts to each province) and partly of a "levelling payment" (Boadway, 1980).

The block funding proposal differed significantly from Bill C-57 on a number of points. It was intended to give the provinces complete flexibility and autonomy in designing and administering their social service programs. "At least it will put an end to the use of jurisdictional limitations and cost-sharing restrictions as excuses for rejecting proposals for expanding or improving services. Decisions on social services will rest clearly and undeniably with the provinces" (National Council of Welfare, 1978, p. 14). However, several progressive features in social policy would be lost:

1. There was no guarantee that any of the transferred money would be used for social services;
2. provinces were not required to establish independently administered appeal procedures or to abolish residence requirements;
3. there was no guarantee that all provinces would separate eligibility for services from eligibility for financial assistance;
4. there was no guarantee of designation of certain services as universal and free; and
5. no assurance was given of national standards in service provision.

Critics of the block funding proposal pointed out that it represented the federal government's abandonment of its leadership role in the development of social services in favour of a principle of decentralization (Kelly, 1977).

A bill (C-55) proposing the block funding formula was given first reading on 12 May 1978, but died on the order paper. So legislation is still at the stage of the CAP 50:50 cost-sharing arrangement for both income maintenance programs and social services. Nor have there been any remarkable changes in the kinds of programs offered.

The inability of the federal and provincial governments to devise a concerted strategy for improving social services has serious consequences, not just for the poor, but also for many other minority groups, such as women, the native peoples, the elderly, the disabled, and the mentally retarded, regardless of socio-economic background. All these categories of people share the experience of having to cope with a bureaucracy that makes it difficult to discover which level of government offers a given service or funding program.

Prospects for the Future: Income Security and Social Services

The above review of federal-provincial disagreements on social welfare shows that the present jurisdictional division of powers in this area, even with amendments to the constitution and periodic federal-provincial negotiations, has not resolved the contradictions of split responsibilities. The conditional grant as a method of financing social welfare has its supporters and opponents. However, the question is more than just that of the best method of federal financing: conditional grants, tax abatements, or unconditional equalization payments. The question is also more than one of jurisdiction. As has been noted, there was very little discussion of income redistribution in Canada during the entire period of the social welfare review, although that problem was "central to the articulation of an equitable social security plan" (Bergeron, 1979, p. 3). This silence on a very crucial point in social welfare is all the more distressing when one recalls the stated goal of the social welfare review by Marc Lalonde in his 1973 *Working Paper*. While assuring the provinces some degree of flexibility in determining the levels of income guarantees and supplementation within joint federal-provincial programs in their own provinces, Lalonde reiterates that the Parliament of Canada must continue to play a role in the total income security system. The reason is that the Parliament "has a responsibility to promote national unity through preventing extremes in income disparities across the country" (Canada, Health and Welfare, 1973, p. 38).

If social welfare, including both income security programs and social services, is considered in the light of redistribution of income, commitments and obligations are at issue. Obviously only the federal government can redistribute income on a national scope, but there are also disparities within provinces for which redistribution by the provincial government is needed. Thus, shared responsibility as a principle should be recognized as such, the presence of the federal government in social policy should be ensured, and the duties of the federal government in social welfare, especially in the income security programs, should be more clearly stated. Similarly, the acknowledgement of provincial authority in the provision of social welfare is not enough. Rather, obligations to provide social welfare should be imposed on specific levels of the government, be they federal, provincial, or even municipal.

During those times when the federal government tried to expand its role in social welfare policy, it used arguments such as "strengthening national interest", or "achieving some degree of uniformity in standards". Yet we have seen that during periods of economic decline, it has not hesitated to back away from these goals or diminish its support for social equality in Canada (Carrier, 1981, p. 8). On the other hand, provincial governments have typically argued that they are in the best position to judge local needs and, hence, to provide the appropriate social services. On the basis of this argument, they have vehemently opposed federal intervention in areas of provincial jurisdiction. However, there is no convincing evidence that the provinces on their own have the will or resources to provide a social services minimum paralleling the income security minimum. Perhaps the case of Saskatchewan, where a social democratic government with an avowed social conscience was in power for 11 years, 1971–82, may illustrate the point.

Saskatchewan's average annual growth rate of real spending on the Departments of Health, Education, and Social Services declined from 4.5 percent from 1971–76 to 1.3 percent for 1976–81 (Harding and Riches, 1982). Yet by 1977, 77 percent of provincial spending on social services was designated for institutional care (mostly operated by commercial agencies), and 50 percent was spent on "privatised" welfare, or services provided by nonprofit, commercial, and voluntary agencies. This pattern of spending left little resource for initiating and developing preventive services, or more generally, for developing a comprehensive social welfare system aimed at an equitable distribution of social and economic benefits from Saskatchewan's growing wealth. The government was "primarily concerned with (natural) resources, such as oil, potash, and uranium, and with the capital requirements of two major Crown corporations—Saskpower and Sasktel" (Riches, 1980, p. 14). It would appear that in ideology, policy orientation, and practice in the area of social welfare Saskatchewan, like other provinces, was throwing back the responsibility for citizens' welfare to the individual, the family, private organizations, and the forces of the marketplace.

The new Canadian constitution does not resolve the dilemmas ensuing from split responsibilities between the federal and provincial governments. Section 92 of the Constitution remains unchanged. The *Canadian Charter of Rights and Freedoms* also falls short of expectations. Although it is said in Part III of the Charter, "Equalization and Regional Disparities," that "Parliament and the legislatures, together with the government of Canada and the provincial governments are committed to. . .promoting equal opportunities for the well-being of Canadians" (Canada, Government of, 1981, p. 12), there is no guarantee that every person has social and economic rights, that is, the rights to work, to equal economic opportunity, and to social welfare.[1] In many European countries it is generally accepted that rights of citizenship include social and economic rights (Wolfe, 1980). It is recognized that the nature of social rights is neither self-evident nor given. The content of social rights, moreover, is relative to the prevailing standard of living in a particular society at a particular time. However, in this regard, we can refer to the *United Nations Universal Declaration of Human Rights* (Canada, incidentally, played a key role in bringing about its proclamation in 1948). The *U.N. Universal Declaration* includes economic, social, and cultural, as well as political and civil, rights. Article 25 (1) reads:

> Everyone has the right to a standard of living adequate for the health and well-being of himself and his family, including food, clothing, housing and medical care and necessary social services, and the right to security in the event of unemployment, sickness, disability, widowhood, old age or other lack of livelihood in circumstances beyond his control;

and Article 24 reads:

> Everyone has the right to rest and leisure, including reasonable limitation of working hours and periodic holidays with pay (United Nations, 1978, p. 1).

The *U.N. Declaration* not only recognizes that social services to human needs are a human right, but also that economic rights include the right to an adequate standard of living. One can argue that the latter could embrace the right to a guaranteed income. In Canada, we are in a good position today to venture into this type of income security program. Not only do we have the technological capabilities for the data processing and computation necessary for such a program, but experience gained in recent years has provided answers to some important questions about it. The refundable child tax credit program established in 1979 has demonstrated that the personal income tax system can be integrated with the social welfare system in the form of an equitable, nonstigmatizing income security program. The simple income test employed in the Guaranteed Income supplement to Old Age Security has also proven to be workable. Moreover, the Mincome Manitoba reports have provided solutions to some technical problems in implementing the GAI.

Whether or not GAI will become a reality in the 1980s will be "related more to political and constitutional factors than to the availability of answers to technical problems of social security" (Splane, 1980, p. 87).

Some of the wording in the *U.N. Universal Declaration* may be subject to discussion and modification. Nevertheless, the general principles proclaimed are sound guidelines for a constitutional framework that seeks to ensure the well-being of citizens in a modern industrial society. The right to equality of economic opportunity, which has been advocated by some women's groups, would have been a good example of attempts to delineate social and economic rights.

---

1. I follow the definition of "rights" given by Baines (1980, p. 1): A right is any claim protected by law. The phrase "human rights" will be used to designate those claims that people make against the state by virtue of their membership in the state. There are other terms, such as "civil liberties" or "fundamental freedoms and rights", that might be used interchangeably with "human rights". Generally speaking, these terms focus on the distinction between what a citizen is entitled to do or not do and what a government can do or not do. If the normal function of government is to make and enforce rules, then a human or citizen's right imposes limitations on that rule-making ability. There is nevertheless a wide variety of expectations about what those limitations should be.

11

Cultural Dimensions of Social Inequality and Welfare

As discussed in chapter 7, the capitalist mode of production generates social inequality. Here we shall briefly recapitulate this process and, in addition, identify the ways in which secondary social inequality (inequality within the subordinate classes) is linked to the conditions of poverty and disadvantage experienced by the poor members of the working class and the underclass. The chapter concludes with an analysis of the implications of social welfare.

Inequality and Discrimination

Ownership of capital allows capitalists to buy productive property and the labour-power of workers. They then reap the greater part of the profits from the sale of products. Owning no means of production, members of the subordinate classes (the working class and the underclass) must sell their labour-power and thus enable the capitalists to accumulate more capital, but receive in return only wages. When the capitalist has no further need of the worker's labour-power, the worker is dismissed and no further wages are paid. The relationship between the capitalist and the worker is known as the cash nexus; this means that the worker is always subordinate to the capitalist. Because it owns its productive property, the capitalist class not only has the right to the profits realized, but also determines employment conditions and, therefore, the extent of unemployment. The essence of the capitalist system is unequal exchange between capital and labour.

The differential distribution of rewards within the subordinate classes (that is, secondary inequality) is also an inherent feature of the capitalist system, since the sale of labour-power depends on the operations of the capitalist labour market. To succeed in selling labour-power, a worker must have marketable skills; this means that the ability to work must include those skills that are in demand on the market. Supply and demand, the forces that operate on the labour market, are essentially determined by the capitalist class. The position of child day care workers illustrates the point. As has been mentioned in chapter 7, workers with skills directly of use to the capitalist class are usually employed through the normal labour market. In the capitalist mode of production, mothers are usually assigned the responsibilities of child raising and domestic work, and women and children are expected to be economically dependent on men. Under the normal circumstances of capitalism, there is no place for the child day care worker. Child care and nurturant skills are not directly useful to or in great demand by the capitalist class, although the acquisition of these skills requires training and experience. Thus, in general, child day care workers are not highly paid; in fact, they are among the lowest paid workers in our society. An exception occurred during the Second World War when women were employed in production related to the war effort. Day care centres were established and workers' pay in those centres was reasonable.

While supply and demand are the basic market mechanisms in capitalist society, other factors, such as social conventions, customs, prejudices and biases, also enter into the labour market to modify the forces of supply and demand. These factors do not negate supply and demand, but rather channel them in such a way as to maximize economic return to the capitalist class (Johnson, 1979, p. 154). They do this by exploiting racism, sexism, or any other social bias or pressure. For example, there are certain prevailing racist and sexist assumptions, attitudes, and practices in society that focus on the attributes of individuals or groups. These attributes and characteristics affect people's chances of success in the marketplace when used as criteria for secondary social inequality among the subordinate classes. In Canadian society, it is commonly assumed that white males are more competent in positions of authority. Colour and sex are consciously or unconsciously built into the reward system and career development paths.

What are the consequences when differences in race and sex become bases for reward? Obviously, those who possess these attributes can "move ahead", while those without those attributes are disadvantaged. But racist and sexist assumptions, attitudes, and practices also benefit the capitalist class, in that it emphasizes the differences among people of the subordinate classes, and thus obscures their common interests. Consequently, the capitalist class can and does lower wage rates, affecting most adversely the low income groups of the working class and the underclass.

This is not to say that social customs and biases that discriminate against some individuals or groups are all established or instigated by the capitalist class. Sometimes the capitalist does encourage racial hatred and introduces discriminatory practices that cause strife and dissent within the subordinate classes. A past example from Canadian history was the use of Chinese labourers in the construction of the Canadian Pacific Railway. The railway company openly or tacitly condoned prejudices and discriminatory practices by the white workers against the

Chinese: segregation, verbal derision, assigning the Chinese to the most dangerous and strenuous tasks. The white workers genuinely hated the Chinese workers because the latter were seen as driving down wage rates, the average wage for the Chinese being about half that of the whites. The savings in labour costs were, of course, the main reason for importing Chinese workers in the first place. Racism, as it was practised by both the company and white workers, made the savings possible.

Today, discrimination works in a somewhat different way. Instead of encouraging or relying upon overt discrimination, capitalist employers simply use unexamined assumptions and "unconscious" discriminatory practices to their advantage. The earmark of an "unconscious" discriminatory act does not lie in the intention of the person(s) practising discrimination, but in the effect of the act. In other words, the motive of prejudice and the intention to discriminate may or may not be present. Prejudices and intention to discriminate are probably present in many cases involving people of minority status,[1] although they may not be overt. In any case, it is difficult, if not impossible, to prove motive or intent. Recent studies of discrimination have recognized that

> the most damaging discrimination does not result from isolated individual acts motivated by prejudice, but rather from historical assumptions and traditions which have become embedded, even unintentionally, in the normal operations of our employment, education, and social institutions (Day, 1980a, p. 1).

These traditions and assumptions are experienced by members of minority groups not simply as individuals, but also because of their membership in particular groups or categories—for example, being a woman, being a native, being a homosexual, and so forth. The problems of minorities are thus group problems, not individual problems. In light of this fact, discrimination is not defined simply as individual, identified by intent, but as a systemic phenomenon, identified by impact. In Canada, it has been discovered that "many employment and education systems, through their normal operations, have inadvertent discriminatory effects, and they therefore perpetuate historical patterns of disadvantage for people of native ancestry, women, and people with physical disabilities" (Day, 1980b, p. 1). A few examples of "systemic barriers" will show how seemingly neutral practices do prevent the disadvantaged groups of the subordinate classes from gaining access to better employment. When certain jobs in particular fields are held predominantly by white males, a word-of-mouth recruitment procedure will keep knowledge of vacancies among white males, thus effectively excluding native people and women from even knowing about those job opportunities, let alone competing for them. Sometimes nonessential and nonjob-related requirements, such as a Grade 12 education for janitors, or certain height and weight standards, will have the effect of preventing some ethnic groups and women from jobs they could well perform. Similarly, workplaces that are inaccessible to the physically disabled will bar that group from jobs that they could otherwise perform (Day, 1980b, pp. 1–2).

What are the consequences of systemic discrimination in employment? For members of the minority group personally, they are denied the better opportunities in the primary labour market. Instead, they are shunted into the low-paying jobs found in the marginal labour market. The result is familiar: certain jobs in some industries are predominantly filled by women and ethnic minorities. Systemic discrimination thus structures labour market segregation. For the capitalist class, systemic discrimination, like overt discrimination, brings the benefits of lower wage costs and a working class divided along sex, race, ethnic, or religious lines. A fragmented working class is weak and unable to defend itself against intensification of exploitation, such as a general lowering of wage rates or the withdrawal of social wage.

Blaming the Victim Ideology

Secondary social inequality also has an ideological function for the capitalist system. The differential distribution of income, social prestige, information, and influence within the working class helps to reinforce the basic primary structure of inequality. Members of the working class who strive and manage to move upward through any dimension of the formal or informal rank differences in their own class may inadvertently come to approve and trust the established social order, including the basic inequality structure. Members of the working class with higher socio-economic status may come to view the social system as open to social mobility, upward or downward, and regard those who fail to move upward as necessarily inadequate, unmotivated, or lazy. Consequently, they come to view both primary and secondary inequalities as being caused by individual effort, not by structural arrangements of the community or of the society. In the process, the underclass and the poorer members of the working class are made the scapegoats of an economic system more concerned with profits than with the needs of people. This ideological process is called "blaming the victim".

The ideology of "blaming the victim" has an earlier version called "social pathology". It is also expressed in terms of the ideology of "culture of poverty" and, in the field of education, "cultural deprivation". What these various versions refer to is the same: an ideology that claims to explain problems caused by a social structure as being the result of the attributes and characteristics of the individuals who are experiencing these problems. An excellent analysis of the ideology of "blaming the victim" has been undertaken by William Ryan (1976). Following Karl Mannheim's notion of ideology, he defines this ideology as a set of ideas that systematically distorts reality with the specific function of maintaining the status quo in the interest of a particular class or group. Ryan (1976, p. 11) emphasizes that the ideological process, that is the systematic distortion of reality, is unintentional. However, as was discussed in the previous section on discrimination, intention is hard to prove. Even if those who formulate the ideologies have not intended to create distortion, it can certainly be said that many who use them in defense of the status quo are aware of or have intended the distortions. But the question of intentions is not a fruitful area of debate; as with discrimination, attention should be focussed on the impact of the ideology on the victims.

Victim blaming is a subtle process. It is "cloaked in kindness and concern . . . obscured by a perfumed haze of humanitarianism" (Ryan, 1976, p. 6). It sounds scientific, and is championed by "sympathetic social scientists with social consciences in good working order and liberal politicians with a genuine commitment to reform" (Ryan, 1976, p. 7). The whole process is quite different from the crude and vulgar assaying of rugged individualism and social Darwinism. Outdated conservative and "blaming the victim" ideologies differ considerably in that the former defined victims as genetically defective, morally unfit, psychologically weak, and, in general, inferior, with emphasis on the hereditary and inherent factors. The "blaming the victim" ideology, on the other hand, traces the problem to poverty, ghetto life, social injustices, and racial discrimination. The stigma that victimizes a person is said to be acquired from social rather than genetic origins. "But the stigma, the defect, the fatal difference—though derived in the past from environmental forces—is still located *within* the victim, inside his skin" (Ryan, 1976, p. 7, emphasis in the original).

The important point is that in the ideology of "blaming the victim", although there is on the surface an identification of environmental causation, the real causation is seen to be "located within the victim, inside his skin." According to the reasoning of the humanitarian ideology, the environmental conditions that produced the defect were unfortunate but they happened *in the past*. What is ignored is the continuing impact of the same victimizing social force right now. "It is a brilliant ideology for justifying a perverse form of social action designed to change, not society, as one might expect, but rather society's victim" (Ryan, 1976, p. 8).

Ryan (1976, pp. 8–9) summarizes the process of "blaming the victim" in four simple steps:

1. Identify the problem.
2. Study those affected by the problem and discover how they are different from the rest of the society.
3. Define the differences (which are in fact the effects of injustice and discrimination) as the causes of the social problem.
4. Assign a government bureaucrat to invent a humanitarian action program to correct the differences by changing the people affected by the problem.

What happens in this ideological process is a game of semantic substitution. The old-fashioned, reactionary, individualistic terms of social Darwinism (for example, unfitness, idleness, immorality, hereditary/character flaw) are replaced by new progressive, humanitarian, individualistic terms (for instance, cultural deprivation, unstable family organization, weak ego structure) (Ryan, 1976, p. 26). The best example of the semantic game is in the individualist explanation of poverty. According to the outmoded ideology of rugged individualism, people are poor because they lack initiative, ability, motivation, or discipline. But in the new ideology of "blaming the victim", poverty is explained by the so-called "theory" of the "culture of poverty". Although the concept of individualistic causation is less apparent, it does exist, expecially in the way that it is applied to education.

The "Culture of Poverty" Fallacy

The term "culture of poverty" was first coined by the anthropologist Oscar Lewis in 1959 in his case studies of five Mexican families. In the 1960s, with the "discovery" of poverty in affluent America, the concept became popular and was widely used by other social scientists under such names as "dregs-culture" or "culture deprivation" (Leacock, 1971, pp. 7–37).

Oscar Lewis elaborates on the "culture of poverty" in his book *La Vida* (1965, pp. xi–lv). According to Lewis, one crucial characteristic of the "culture of poverty" is the lack of effective participation and integration of the poor in the major institutions of society. For example, the lack of effective participation in the economic system of the larger society is explained in this way: "Low wages, chronic unemployment and underemployment lead to low income, lack of property ownership, absence of savings, absence of food reserves in the home, and a chronic shortage of cash" (1965, p. xlvi). On the level of the local community, the "culture of poverty" is manifested in "poor housing conditions, crowding, gregariousness, but above all a minimum of organization beyond the level of the nuclear and extended family" (1965, p. xlvi). On the level of the family, the major characteristics of the "culture of poverty" are the absence of childhood, early initiation into sex, consensual unions, sibling rivalry, mother-centredness, tendency toward authoritarianism. On the level of the individual, the major traits are feelings of inferiority, marginality, and dependence. People have weak ego structure and confused sexual identification. They exhibit a sense of resignation and fatalism, a widespread belief in male superiority, and a high tolerance for psychological pathology of all sorts. They cannot control impulses, are present-oriented "with relatively little ability to defer gratification and plan for the future" (1965, p. xlviii).

The traits of the "culture of poverty" listed by Lewis may describe the situation of some poor people some of the time. But in Lewis's view, the "culture of poverty" is more than a collection of loosely related traits. He actually views it as the definitive explanation of a broad range of phenomena. "The concept of the culture of poverty provides a high level of generalization which, hopefully, will unify and *explain* a number of phenomena viewed as distinctive characteristics of racial, national or regional groups" (1965, p. lii, emphasis added). He cites the example of matrifocality, formerly thought to be prevalent in Caribbean and American black family organization, as a "culture of poverty" trait found among diverse peoples in different parts of the world. The reasoning is circular: matrifocality, a trait of the "culture of poverty", is explained only in terms of the "culture of poverty".

Lewis's explanation rests in more than simply the universality of traits of the "culture of poverty". Most social scientists would agree that these traits represent both a reaction and an adjustment of the poor to their poverty and to their subordinate class position in a capitalist society. The traits considered to be typical of the "culture of poverty" result from attempts to cope with the feelings of utter despair and futility that develop from the poor person's inability to meet his or her needs through the usual channels operating in society. Thus, for example, the poor, unable to obtain credit from banks, must work out local solutions, such as organizing informal credit lines without interest (Lewis, 1965, p. xliv).

The more critical social scientists object to Lewis's assertion that the "culture of poverty" is a positive way of life handed down from generation to generation along family lines. According to him, the "culture of poverty" is not simply an adaptation to social conditions of the larger society; it is a value that is passed on. He claims that "by the time slum children are age six or seven, they have usually absorbed the basic values and attitudes of the subculture and are not psychologically geared to take full advantage of changing conditions or increased opportunities which may occur in their lifetime" (Lewis, 1965, p. xlv).

In this interpretation, the "culture of poverty" has been elevated from a concept that refers to a collection of traits, to a full-blown "thesis", ascribing people's poverty to the fact that they have worked out a design for living, "a ready made set of solutions for human problems so that individuals don't have to begin all over again each generation" (Lewis, 1965, p. li). According to Lewis, because the "culture of poverty" has a *positive* adaptive function, children are socialized with those traits. In other words, adults teach their young to desire poverty and to remain poor. Lewis concludes that "the elimination of physical poverty *per se* may not be enough to eliminate the culture of poverty which is a whole way of life" (1965, p. lii). The individualistic causation of poverty is now made abundantly clear. Herein also lies the fallacy. This ostensible explanation is merely a description of the problem, based on the assumption that the causes are located *within* the poor. No question is raised about structural arrangements of inequality in society that constrain the poor to exhibit various traits of the culture of poverty as adaptive mechanisms. Instead it is argued that since the poor want poverty to be their way of life, there is little that others can do to help. Poverty is the poor people's own problem.

Cultural Deprivation and Education

In recent years, the ideology of blaming the victim has undergone two changes. First, there has been a resurgence of the ideology that links individual achievement and advancement to genetic factors. Jensen, Herrstein, Eysenck, and others have reintroduced the notion that intellectual merit is an inherited characteristic (Ryan, 1976, p. 304). Such views have been cited as a justification for social inequality, and represent a return to the more blatant kind of individualism and victim blaming. This has, in turn, led to some strong intellectual and scientific debates, which at least have provided a forum for the critics of the "blaming the victim" ideology. The second change is, however, more disturbing. This ideology has become conventional wisdom. Catch phrases, such as "the cycle of poverty" and "cultural deprivation", have become "real entities in the minds of many educated persons" (1976, p. 301). This is to say that the ideology has not disappeared or become less popular. It has, in fact, become more legitimate and respectable. The "blaming the victim" ideology is presented in social policies and in textbooks as a bona fide scientific theory, and is accepted by policy makers, educators, social service workers, and lay people alike as a sound explanation for social inequality. It is for this reason that one variant of the general ideology of victim blaming—that is, the "culture of poverty"—has been discussed in some detail here. Although it was first suggested in the 1960s, the "blaming the victim" ideology embodied ideas that were widely used in the 1980s, albeit under different names. It is, therefore, especially necessary and socially relevant to expose the "culture of poverty" fallacy today (Djao, 1979).

The "culture of poverty" fallacy has been used to explain problems experienced by children of native people and of low income families, such as doing less well in school and having higher drop-out rates than children from white, high income, or middle income families. The "culture of poverty" fallacy would explain the phenomenon thus: from an early age children from native and low income families have been imbued with the traits of the culture of poverty. Among the most damaging traits with which the children have been socialized is low educational motivation. So the first reason for their low educational achievement is a lack of motivation that is buttressed by other undesirable traits, such as present-time orientation, fatalism, and dependency.

A second reason offered by the "culture of poverty" fallacy is that native and low income children are culturally deprived. The traits found in the "culture of poverty" are simply inadequate to prepare these children for the dominant educational system. It is alleged that native and low income parents do not read to their children or accompany them to school on the first day. There are no magazines or encyclopaedias in the home. These families do not take vacations abroad, which means that the children's mental horizons are more limited than those of children from white or higher income families. The home environment is dull and not conducive to developing intellectual curiosity. All in all, these children are assumed to be unstimulated and less developed because their background is materially poorer. Proponents of this fallacy would claim that the native person's background fits the culture of poverty definition in a double sense. Most native families have low incomes. But more important, native culture is seen as lacking in the values and traits of the dominant white society. Thus, regardless of their family income, native children are seen by the "culture of poverty" advocates as poor in the ways of the white people. A background of poverty therefore refers to both material poverty and cultural poverty.

It is a well established fact that children of native ancestry and low socio-economic status perform less well in school than other children. However, it is by no means clear that native ancestry and low socio-economic status by themselves cause low educational achievement. The relationship between native ancestry and low socio-economic status, on the one hand, and low educational achievement, on the other, is in fact very complex. For one thing, schools in native communities and low income neighbourhoods possess fewer modern facilities and teaching resources. Their teachers are often less qualified and less experienced than those teaching in schools in nonnative, higher socio-economic neighbourhoods. These inadequacies are the direct effects of economic inequalities and have an undesirable influence on the learning experience of children. The differences in academic achievement are, therefore, the effects of affluence and poverty. The low achievement and supposed lack of educational motivation characteristic of native and low income children cannot be viewed as effects of the "culture of poverty". Even the supposed lack of educational motivation, whether on the part of the poor parents or that of poor children, cannot be the result of the "culture of poverty". Studies in the United States have indicated that parents of the so-called disadvantaged children and the children themselves show more motivation and desire for education than the more affluent (Ryan, 1976, p. 52; Wax and Wax, 1971, pp. 127–39).

If the native or poor background does not dampen the desire for education, then how does it happen that the native and low income children do in fact acquire so much less education? The answer lies in *the educators' conceptualization* of the "culture of poverty". There is no doubt that low income and native children suffer from poverty, and may even exhibit some of the cultural traits delineated by Lewis. But they do not live in a "culture of poverty" as hypothesized. Rather they are *assumed* to live in that culture by the school system and by the teachers. These children have a different subcultural background, that of a particular social class, of a particular income group, and of a particular racial group. But they are not deprived of culture. They have deeply held values, meaningful relationships, personal and social philosophies, and rich linguistic expressions. But because these traits are not shared by the larger society, they are ruled as irrelevant and, worse still, nonexistent. Thus they are labelled by the proponents of the "culture of poverty" as "culturally deprived".

At this point, it is well to stress the conceptual inadequacies of the term "culture of poverty". Lewis (1965, p. xliii) mentions in a footnote that the term "subculture of poverty" is technically more accurate, but he has chosen to use "culture of poverty" as a shorter form. Unfortunately, this apparently innocuous modification has caused confusion in the perception and logic that some social scientists apply to socially and economically disadvantaged people. It has eventually led to social policy formulations based on erroneous assumptions and faulty reasonings that have done enormous harm to the disadvantaged. There is a need, therefore, to reiterate two basic concepts in sociology: "culture" is the entire way of life followed by a whole society, while "subcultures" refer to lifeways of subgroups or subunits within the society. To speak of a subculture, there must be first of all some notion of the structural relationships between the subunit and the rest of the society. "Subculture" holds elements common to the society as a whole and it shares common attributes with other subunits (other classes or other ethnic groups, for instance). The subunits, such as the native people and low income people, are by definition "distinct from the total system only in the same logical sense that any part is differentiated from the whole in which it is embedded" (Valentine, 1968, p. 106). From this, it can be seen that the patterns of life of any racial minority group or a social class in Canada, no matter how distinctive, cannot constitute anything but a racial or class subculture. The reason is fairly obvious. Members of the ethnic minority group or of a particular income group are first members of the larger society. They must all conform to national laws, will potentially acquire many behavioural patterns from the national inventory, and are influenced by national institutions (Steward, 1967). Disadvantaged people share in the culture of the larger society but, at the same time, develop adaptive mechanisms in order to cope with conditions of poverty and discrimination. The "culture of poverty" fallacy, however, assumes that they live in and perpetuate an entirely different and irrelevant culture.

Once disadvantaged children are labelled as "culturally deprived" simply because they are materially poor, a subordinate and inferior status is forced upon them. This is the real effect of the fallacy of the culture of poverty: children of poor background are expected to fail and they do. In her study of classroom situations in black and white schools, in both middle and low income neighbourhoods, Leacock observed that the projection of a white, middle income orientation to life in general was not the major problem for poor and black children. "It was rather that *a middle class attitude toward them and their inferior status as poor and black was being foisted upon them*" (Leacock, 1971, p. 29, emphasis in the original). Expectations for the future subordinate status of children from racial minority and low income backgrounds were expressed in explicit and subtle ways. Minimal goals for these children were communicated by teachers in interviews and in the classroom. Although the children indicated their readiness to assume formal responsibilities, teachers often failed to structure classroom interaction in ways that would have encouraged such behaviour. Teachers often responded in negative ways to the disadvantaged children's academic performance and class participation (see also Dickeman, 1971, pp. 140–48).

Canadian studies on education and socio-economic backgrounds rarely go beyond describing the superficial aspects of the problem: low status children do less well in school, and so forth (Martin and Macdonell, 1982, p. 274–77). Although they have examined family structures, these studies rarely look at the educational system itself: the organization and the atmosphere of the school and the classroom. They do not investigate the attitudes, biases, and expectations of teachers and administrators but focus on parental attitudes and expectations, nor do they examine classroom dynamics, consisting of interactions and relationships between teachers and pupils.

The few studies that have focussed on the structure of the education system, the school, and classroom interactions, have revealed that the hierarchical and authoritarian relations of the larger society are reproduced in the classroom and the school. Conversely, children of low status (racially, socially, and economically) are socialized to accept their subordinate place (Harp, 1980, pp. 219–46). For example, boys and girls are streamed into disciplines and eventually occupations that are traditional to their sex. The streaming effect is often the result of indirect and covert practices: stereotyping of gender roles including occupational roles, assumptions of teachers, and lack of nontraditional roles. Similarly, low income children are predictably "counselled" into taking vocational or industrial courses rather than academic courses. Native children are further disadvantaged insofar as native language, history, culture, and values are absent from school curricula. Where native people are mentioned, as in history classes, they are most often cast as being savage or stupid. These are the "systemic barriers" for the native children's achievement; worst still, they tend to drive the children out of the educational system.

Ryan (1976, pp. 54–55) summarizes the impact of social and racial background on educational achievement as follows. First, the effect of poverty, race and family background is observed to a small extent in the minds of the children, but to a much greater extent in the interactions in the classroom, and this eventually produces a decline in academic performance. Second, poverty, race, and family background has less effect on the children than on the teacher, who accordingly expects poorer performance from children from racial minority groups or low income families. When such children make up the majority of the classroom population, the teachers' expectations are even more pessimistic and debilitating. Lastly, expectations of the teacher are a major determinant of the children's performance—evidence of the now-famous self-fulfilling prophecy syndrome.

So the problem is not one of the cultural deprivation of ghetto children, but rather of culturally depriving schools (Ryan, 1976, p. 61). According to the cultural deprivation version of the victim blaming ideology, the formula for action is: change, amend, and repair the victim. But if it is the educational system that is deficient, then the strategy for change is to transform the structures and processes of the educational system and the schools.

Implications for Social Welfare

We have analyzed two cultural processes—systemic discrimination and the blaming the victim ideology—through which social inequality is legitimized and reinforced. It is through these and similar processes that inequality impinges upon the subordinate classes and produces the host of problems that social welfare is called upon to redress and, at times, in rhetorics at least, to prevent. The operation of victim blaming in the educational system has been discussed at length because education is usually seen as the vehicle by which people can raise themselves out of a low income or disadvantaged position. Yet education has not provided such a service for native children or for children of low income parents. In fact, education has often been the means by which relations of inequality are reproduced in the next generation. Perpetuation of social inequality is done in two ways. First, through the double track system, the high educational achievers are separated from the low achievers. The latter will repeatedly find throughout their lives opportunities leading to high social and economic rewards closed to them. Second, the socialization process in school is subtly but most certainly political in nature and content. The cultural and ideological norms favourable to the capitalist class are passed on to children of all socio-economic status groups. One very crucial component of the socialization process is the acquisition of the ideology that legitimizes inequality. Children learn to see inequality as natural and to want to be of high status (Baldus and Tribe, 1978, pp. 50–60). A further consequence of this kind of ideological socialization is that children of low income or minority background who are victimized to the extent that they become low educational achievers also come to accept their inferior position as natural, because they see themselves as individuals who have failed. In other words, children learn to blame themselves.

There is a lack of systematic research into the delivery of other services. Existing evidence, however, does seem to indicate that the health care system treats high and low status people differentially. Employment and adult training programs also have such built-in mechanisms of processing people so that immigrant groups from Third World countries are typically classified among the "unskilled". It has also been mentioned earlier that the "welfare" services connected with CAP confer a stigma and give a subordinate status to clients. Viewed in this way, the various social services are useful for the perpetuation of social inequality. They also have a function of social control in that they keep low income and some racial minority people in their low status positions. The processes operating in education can be seen to operate, with some variations, in other social services as well.

Social Control or Social Development

The issue of social control is a controversial one in the institution of social welfare, as even the term "social control" sounds cynical and vicious in a welfare state and voluntary sector that have an ideological basis of altruism. Most of the workers engaged in social welfare activities (providing income security and social services), be they teachers, nurses, social workers or volunteers, are motivated by the desire to serve and to help, among other factors. The social welfare workers are discussed in the next chapter. But here it is necessary to point out that to explain the social control function of social welfare is by no means an indictment or even a criticism of workers. The issue here is that inherent in social welfare is the contradiction that, on the one hand, social welfare has the potential of enhancing the quality of life for people, while, on the other, it also supports and reinforces those values, institutions, and processes that are profit-centred and dehumanizing (Galper, 1975). Insofar as social welfare promotes these dehumanizing and antisocial principles, values and institutions, which are shaped by the profit motive of the capitalist class, it is maintaining the status quo for that class. This is the meaning of social control.

Pointing to the good impulses underlying numerous social welfare efforts without recognizing the social control that comes as a consequence only deepens the contradictions. In the end, such an unrealistic stance will worsen the situation of those whom social welfare is supposed to serve, and add to the frustration of those who want to help. To recognize the social control function of the welfare state is not to deny the real benefits that many social welfare programs bring to the subordinate classes. On the contrary, one useful consequence of a critical analysis of the welfare state is that once the basic contradictions are acknowledged, strategies and actions can be undertaken to raise the beneficial potential. At the same time, based on that knowledge, concerted efforts can be launched to minimize or even to eliminate the social control function of welfare.

In order to do this, the functionalist and pluralist explanations of social welfare first must be seen as they are, merely ideological formulations in defence of the capitalist society. True explanations of the welfare state must be able to locate individual and community problems in their proper larger context. The context is a national society based on class inequalities within a larger system of international capitalism. Second, overcoming the social control function of social welfare means advocacy or struggle on the part of the social welfare (income support and social services) recipients as well as those who help to shape the policies and others who deliver the programs.

No longer would the lack of funding or resources be an adequate reason for the failure of particular programs. The social problems and the meagre welfare programs that are meant to be solutions must be seen as structural failures of capitalism. Consequently, casework and community organization, while useful in restoring or increasing the functioning capacity of individuals or groups, must be seen as inadequate in themselves. The aim is to transform dehumanizing and discriminatory social structures through these procedures into egalitarian relationships responsive to human needs. There is no blueprint for such a transformation. The process will probably be gradual and, in some important respects, may not be drastically different from social reforms. However, there is one crucial difference between fundamental social change and reform. In the former, the goal of transforming social structures is always kept in sight. Because that goal is kept in view, class conflicts will be as much a part of social welfare as cash transfer payments, counselling, and referrals. This is the meaning of social development.

---

1. Minority status does not refer to numerical minority but to the fact of being deprived of power and occupying a subordinate position.

12

Participants in Social Welfare

A common assumption about people working in social welfare is that they are social workers. Rightly or wrongly, social workers are sometimes targets of criticism. Because of their dependence on the meagre and often inadequate provisions of the welfare state, recipients of financial assistance and clients of social services see social workers as the cause of their frustration. Social workers are the only human contacts they have in dealing with a mammoth, immovable, unresponsive, bureaucratic structure. In addition, the public is often outraged at the failings of various welfare programs, and their anger tends to focus on social workers. The political left criticizes social workers for being lackeys of the state, whose main task is controlling the welfare recipients in order to preserve social harmony. The attack from the right is even stronger: taxpayers feel that they are paying all the bills of the welfare state, and yet social workers cannot cure all social ills. Social workers are thus often placed in a situation that seems to please no one.

The analysis of the social welfare institution presented in this book shows that not only is the institution enormous and multifaceted, but it is inextricably linked to other major societal institutions. The entire institution is vast, encompassing much more than program delivery by social workers to recipients. A host of people directly or indirectly structure, shape, and influence social welfare in various ways. Social workers are merely the most visible; even then nurses, teachers, day care workers, homemakers, and many others also deliver social services. This chapter discusses four broad categories of participants in the welfare institution: (a) policy makers, (b) social scientists, (c) social workers, and (d) recipients and clients. They differ from each other in the amounts of power and resources they command and in their input into the institution. Variations in power and input also exist among individuals within each broad category.

Policy Makers

Throughout this book, the welfare state has been presented as the major provider of welfare programs; that it exercises state power is implicitly assumed or explicitly discussed. It has also been mentioned in chapter 8 that the state is more than the government and that state power lies in a complex of organizations (that is, the government, the civil administration, the representative assemblies, the judiciary, the military and the police, and the subcentral governments). The state also has many employees. However, power is not evenly distributed throughout the state sector. Rather, power "is wielded in its different manifestations by the people who occupy the leading positions in each of these institutions" (Miliband, 1969, p. 54). In other words, the reins of state power are held by the state elite that comprises identifiable individuals: prime ministers, ministers in the cabinet, top level civil servants, and administrators of other state bodies (such as central banks and Crown corporations), top military personnel, judges of the higher courts, some of the leading members of parliamentary assemblies (though these are often the same people as the senior members of the political executive), and political and administrative leaders of subcentral units of the state.

In light of the above, the power of the welfare state ultimately resides in the federal and provincial senior political executives and the top level administrators in charge of income security and social service programs. They are responsible for government departments or other state bodies of finance, employment and immigration, health, social welfare, justice, education, housing, Indian Affairs, veteran affairs, citizenship, and multiculturalism.

The inclusion of top administrators of relevant government departments, Crown corporations, and regulatory commissions among the welfare state decision makers merits some clarification. The extension of government bureaucracy into every aspect of life is a familiar contemporary phenomenon. In theory, officialdom is an obedient tool of the political executive. In actual fact, "the administrative process is also part of the political process" (Miliband, 1969, p. 50). At least in the upper reaches of administrative life where policy decisions are made, administration is always political as well as executive. This is so despite the wishes of some administrators to avoid politics and to depoliticize the public service apparatus. This subjective attitude toward turning all problems of politics into an administrative matter merely illustrates that political considerations and assumptions "are incorporated, consciously or not, into the 'problems of administration' " (Miliband, 1969, p. 51). Senior officials cannot free themselves entirely from ideological thinking and the impact of political realities when they advise ministers or make independent decisions. In administrative advice or action, they are not merely acting the role of instruments of policy; they are exercising state power. This is particularly true when there is rapid government or ministerial turnover.

The ministers, the deputy ministers, and senior administrators in control of the welfare state may not be involved in determining the details of any particular social policy. However, they do decide on the general thrust of any legislation concerning social matters. Kravitz describes the process of development of major American federal social legislation as usually originating from within "the anonymous middle levels of the bureaucracy" (1973, p. 37). The description may be appropriately applied to the processes in Canada, at both federal and provincial levels. Middle level bureaucrats, who are usually trained in one of the social sciences, work out the design of a new or expanded program. If the state elite finds it to be desirable or politically useful, it is presented as a legislative proposal in Parliament or in the provincial legislature. Then it is further examined by anonymous bureaucrats who serve as staff members on legislative committees. They improve the basic design and suggest the practical means of implementation. After some debate and sometimes public exposure, through a public hearing process, for instance, the proposal eventually becomes law.

It should be noted that throughout the process, the decision is political, made by senior political leaders. The maze of bureaucratic procedures entailing committees, subcommittees, consultations, public hearings, and so forth, only makes the power centre more obscure to the general public.

Furthermore, consumers of social welfare usually make few contributions to the entire process of social legislation. Only the views of a few key special interest groups are really considered. These groups are more likely to come from the capitalist class rather than the working class, the unions, or welfare rights groups, partly because the state elite is made up overwhelmingly of individuals with business background or interests. More important, the main function of the state in capitalist society is to serve the capitalist class (see chapter 8). The discussion of the Unemployment Insurance Act and the Canada Pension Plan in chapter 9 illustrates how lobbying efforts from the capitalist class have been successful in shaping welfare programs. Nevertheless, the state does have some degree of autonomy, especially in regard to maintaining social harmony or preventing civil disturbance, as was demonstrated in the development of unemployment insurance in Canada.

Finally, with regard to social policy makers, the role of provincial ministers and their senior administrators must be re-emphasized. Health, education, and welfare are under provincial jurisdiction although there has been and still is federal participation in initiatives and funding. In provincial as well federal programs, social policy flows from the top down. In whatever manner the social policy may be presented—alleviation of human suffering, development of human resources, and so forth—it is essentially based on a political decision.

Social Scientists in Social Policy

Social scientists are the host of professionally trained people whose expertise has been used in the formulation, analysis, and evaluation of social policy. Among them are sociologists, economists, political scientists, anthropologists, and psychologists. Included also are the urban planners, lawyers, statisticians, and experts in scientific management. Conventional wisdom about the role of the social scientists is that they propose a policy and its methods of implementation to political leaders in a neutral and objective way. In addition, they may offer a number of alternative policies with a fair assessment of the outcome of each. It is then up to the senior political executives to reject or to adopt any of the proposals, in a similarly neutral manner, guided only by the ethos of responsibility and service. In such a course of action, the social scientists are truly consultants, usurping no policy-making power (Warham, 1970, pp. 74–75; Piven, 1974, p. 212).

The role of the social scientists could be expanded forward to include diagnosis of the problem. In other words, they could not only offer a remedy to social ills, but also actively participate in analyzing the etiology of social problems. This would lead to social policies that would be determined, to a large degree, by how they perceive and address the problem. The influence of social scientists on social policies in such a setting would of course be greater than is presently the case (Warham, 1970, p. 75).

In any case, according to conventional wisdom, the role of social scientists in the development of social policy is a useful one and is constructively used by the political leaders. Ignored in conventional wisdom is the fact that "scientifically based" knowledge and policies are consistently abused or misused by the political leaders or the state elite. More specifically, most social scientists involved in the social policy process rarely play an important role in the overall design of programs; they seldom provide the scientific basis for the formulation of policies. Instead, the important role played by social scientists is in facilitating and rationalizing government programs by providing the scientific authority that the state elite could borrow to justify these policies (Piven, 1974, p. 215).

At present, the social scientists involved in social policy formulation also sometimes work in anonymous middle-level government bureaucracies. They are also sometimes found in universities or in private practice, acting as consultants to the state. The legitimizing function is most likely performed by those social scientists who deny or ignore that conflicting values underlie different paradigms used in scientific inquiries. In cases like this, these values are therefore also at the basis of social policies suggested for the amelioration or eradication of those social problems. When the question of value premises is disregarded, it is the implicit and hidden values of the social scientists that actually inform social research and policy formulation. The social scientists whose "expertise" is used by the state are most likely to have the basic value orientations and the general outlook congenial to the state approach, and it is in this manner that the participation of social scientists in policy formulation is to facilitate and justify programs. More important, they also directly or indirectly rationalize and perpetuate social inequalities, since their diagnosis of social problems typically lays the blame on inadequacies of the individuals or the malfunctioning of local institutional arrangements. Their "analysis" invariably fails to identify the unjust capitalist system as the primary cause of social and individual "pathology".

In a sense, the social sciences have never been seriously applied to social policy formulation. The state has merely used ideological formulae, rather than scientific knowledge: rationalization, mystification, and enhancement of state power have been put forward in the place of explanations and useful solutions (Piven, 1974, p. 216).

This criticism is by no means an implication that the social sciences are futile. On the contrary, social scientists who employ a value-critical approach can play a useful and badly needed role. A value-critical approach calls for the need to debate about basic assumptions and values underlying the various perspectives on social welfare (chapters 2–5). Social scientists are needed to bring into the open the dilemmas inherent in social policies (Rein, 1976, pp. 249–67). Only then will social scientists be able to effectively use their expertise in social research and policy formulation in a demystified way. Only then, too, would the social sciences be freed from their servile role in relation to the state and become truly critical and constructive in their function. At the moment, some social scientists do, in fact, undertake critical evaluations of Canadian social policies and comparative studies of welfare issues in different societies. But their number is small. Because of the critical analytical nature of these studies, they are rejected or ignored by the state. All the same, the need for such studies is growing. As the usefulness of such perceptive analysis of social policies becomes more apparent, the consumers of social welfare, if not the state, may come to apreciate and rely on the social scientists who employ a value-critical approach.

Social Workers

The analysis of the welfare state presented in this book should have by now dispelled the common erroneous view that social workers make up the entire personnel in social welfare. On the contrary, the welfare state is hierarchical and decisions are made by the state elite. In the process of decision making, "scientifically based" justifications and, less often, scientific knowledge, are used. The consequences of these decisions then affect decisions farther down the bureaucratic ladder; the administrators and more social scientists work out the finer details, and social workers actually implement these decisions. Social workers and other service personnel deliver services to the consumer and are therefore the most visible authority figures in the welfare state, but while they do wield a certain amount of power over the recipients, this power is limited. By virtue of the hierarchical nature of the welfare state, the power of social workers extends downward toward those who are dependent on social welfare. But social workers are usually constrained in their position to change or modify social policies determined in the higher echelons.

Social work has its origins in the philanthropic activities of private charitable organizations of the 19th century. At this time, good intentions and humanitarianism were the most important, if not the only, qualities required in a social worker. The analysis of the welfare state in this book shows that such qualities, while necessary in an understanding social worker, are clearly inadequate if he or she is to function effectively. As the problems of advanced capitalist societies are complex and interrelated and the processes of the welfare state equally perplexing to the general public, the social worker's role requires more than personal virtue and stamina.

Social work training requires a thorough and flexible working knowledge in economics, sociology, psychology, political science, and law, to name just a few disciplines on which social work is, in theory, based. The bureaucratic structures of most welfare programs make it important for students of social work to study business administration principles. Such would be the preparation and training that would best prepare social workers to help their clients in a constructive way. Helping the clients in this sense entails enhancing the level of their individual functioning (if they have been malfunctioning previously) *and also* addressing the social structural factors that contribute to the clients' personal and social problems. At the moment, both the training and practice of social workers are overwhelmingly concentrated on the psychosocial functioning of individual clients, to the neglect of the social and economic conditions of the larger society. This tendency is reflected in the professionalization of social work in the 20th century, three aspects of which will be discussed below. These are (a) the relationship between social work and the academic disciplines, (b) social work education, and (c) bureaucratism vs. social action.

The Relationship between Social Work and Academic Disciplines

Attempts to establish a professional status for social work began after the First World War when demobilized and returned soldiers required more systematic provision of psychological, social, and material support than private charities were able to provide. Therefore, a need arose for some organizing principles and a theoretical framework for the delivery of services. In the 1920s and 1930s, social work was under the impact of psychoanalysis. During this "psychological phase", interest was in individual pathology, and the clinical model was adopted in social work.

At the same time, sociology was preoccupied with its own endeavours to become a "pure science". Although there was some development in sociological studies of the family, crime and delinquency, and the city in the United States, the impact of sociology on social work was slight (Leonard, 1966, p. 10).

After the Second World War, the limitations of psychoanalytic theory became evident in social work. Social scientists, especially sociologists working in social work education, began to recognize the importance of the institution of social welfare in the total structures of the society. Some social workers sought theoretical guidance in the dominant branch of sociology: structural-functionalism based on consensus, developed principally by Talcott Parsons (Corrigan and Leonard, 1978, p. xii). Beginning in the 1950s, social work also came to rely on other developments in psychology. Social learning and behaviour modification theories, emphasizing the relationship between the individual and the immediate environment, began to influence social work. Initially, Parsonian structural-functionalist explanations coincided well with the work of the post-Freudian social psychologists, and together, these two schools of thought provided fertile ground for the germination of such ideas as "transmitted deprivation" and "the cycle of poverty".

Structural-functionalism and behaviourism did not prove to be entirely useful to social workers, for they failed to address the main problem of the relationships among the economy, social inequality, and the experiences of social workers and their clients. Indeed, although some social deviants, delinquents, drug addicts, and disabled persons could be rehabilitated through behaviour modification and alteration of local institutional arrangements, others could not. Worse still, new generations of delinquents, addicts, criminals, and the mentally ill continued to arrive on the scene. The theories in social work textbooks hardly reflected the desperate pressures of the day-to-day practice of social work, such as "the lack of resources, the bureaucratic oppression, the despair and fatalism which often come from struggling against problems which are totally unresponsive to social work intervention" (Corrigan and Leonard, 1978, p. ix).

In the mid- to late-1960s, sociologists from mixed backgrounds—vulgar undialectical Marxism, ethnomethodology, phenomenology, and the labelling theory of deviance—sent shock waves through the social work field by questioning its individualistic foundations. These sociologists, joined sometimes by political scientists and economists, denounced social work "as entirely oppressive, and social workers as exclusively agents of social control" (Corrigan and Leonard, 1978, p. xiii). These critics, as noted by Corrigan and Leonard, failed to recognize that they themselves were part of the ideological state apparatus of education. Their criticisms, while true in some cases, were largely unconstructive.

However, these criticisms jolted at least some workers inclined toward social action into reassessing their work. They began to grapple with theories that would let them engage in social action and at the same time meet the emotional, social, and material needs of the clients. However, for the time being, social workers who have social and political commitments are breaking new ground. They realize that the conventional disciplines of psychology, sociology, economics, political science, and public administration can make contributions to social work. But by themselves these disciplines are not enough. Inspiration lies in the Marxist critique of the capitalist mode of production. In employing the dialectical approach, which states that structures and processes embody contradictions, Marxism is also a method of analysis. Moreover, Marxism constitutes political action that attempts to resolve the contradictions in capitalism by replacing it with an alternative social order. However, to be useful or helpful, it must be a Marxism that is contemporary and adaptable to social work in the late 20th century. At the moment, leftist social workers are seeking "to develop a Marxist political economy, a Marxist theory of the welfare state and, most difficult of all, a Marxist theory of interpersonal relations" (Corrigan and Leonard, 1978, p. xiii). Whether they will succeed only time will tell. But for the moment, Marxist analysis has at least broken the monopoly of individualistic explanation in the field of social work.

Social Work Education

In attempting to attain professional status, social work initially made graduate education a basic requirement. It was so decided despite the fact that the majority of social workers did not have a Master of Social Work degree (MSW). Today, the professionally trained social worker is one with a Bachelor of Social Work degree (BSW). Those who have Certificates of Social Work (CSW) are considered paraprofessionals.

In spite of this, cleavage still exists among social workers. University graduates are on guard against nonprofessional encroachment upon their professional status; those without college training are resentful and suspicious of the academically trained. Professionally trained social workers eventually become supervisors and administrators, which means that they take positions far removed from service areas that deal with clients face to face. Not only does the training they had received in working with clients go unutilized, but also service provision is assumed by agency staff members who do not have the required training. This situation prevails more in some areas, such as financial assistance and corrections, and less in others, such as child welfare and medical social work.

This state of affairs requires some reconsideration on the part of social work educators regarding adequate and useful training for social workers at different levels and different areas of social work practice.

Moreover, since social welfare programs as they exist today are largely structured according to the residual conception, they are intended for society's dependent and poor members. Those able to train in the universities are not likely to come from low income backgrounds. How the students of social work can come to understand the experiences and viewpoint of the underprivileged and the disadvantaged, let alone deal with their problems effectively, is an important educational matter (see Midgley, 1982). Again the conventional social sciences would not be enough. As knowledge is perspectival, knowledge about social, economic, and political realities from the standpoints of minority groups, such as women, native peoples, and the disabled, is absolutely essential. Presently, this area is lacking, since knowledge in the social sciences is developed and provided mostly by white, middle to high income, able-bodied males. Finally, although social work education programs in Canada are of high quality, they still have room for improvement. To view the predicament of the clients with empathy is not enough. Students should help the clients to locate their problems and frustrations within the total social structure. Only then will concerted social action involving both social workers and clients be possible.

Bureaucratism vs. Social Action

In its quest for professional status, social work has in the main opted for the clinical approach to clients' problems. The focus has been unequivocally on the individual. As shown in the previous chapter, even when the causes of social ills are traced to local institutional arrangements as in the "culture of poverty" hypothesis, the onus is on the individual, or individuals in the local community, to change and to adapt. The most highly regarded methodology in social work is, unsurprisingly, casework. Even when social work deals with a group (such as the family) or community, the emphasis is on therapy and on helping groups of individuals to adjust, more often than not, to their disadvantaged position in society.

Such a tendency reflects the desire of the leaders in social work in the early days to establish a generic and unitary profession. In actual fact, social workers with different political and ideological persuasions have been engaged in a variety of methods of practice, including organizing clients and advocating radical change. While these different methods have persisted, the process of professionalization has increasingly and quite effectively discredited and dislodged social action from the range of actions undertaken by social workers, and this virtual elimination of social action as a work strategy option has been facilitated by state bureaucracies. As many social workers are state employees, negative sanctions against participation in political lobbying have been built into the reward system. Career advancement and promotion, signifying economic benefits and social recognition, are denied those engaged in social controversies. Some have even been dismissed as a result of political activity.

Social work has developed into a profession largely bounded by the confines of state bureaucracies. Such may not be the institutional goal of social work as a profession, or the personal objective of leaders in social work. Hence, the dilemma facing social workers is not that of the clinical approach vs. the social action approach (with a myriad combinations in between). To be sure, the clinical approach has its uses and limits. People who have been psychologically abused need help to regain their bearings and return to an optimal level of functioning. Criticisms against the clinical or casework approach are only valid if the approach is taken to be the sole or predominant mode of operation, based on assumptions found in the "blaming the victim" ideology. The dilemma that is posed is rather that of bureaucratism vs. social action. One of the basic qualities of a profession is its autonomy, the ability to set its own standards, and to regulate its practices. The very fact that the state bureaucracy has control over the practice of social work reduces the autonomy of social work. Thus, the observed phenomenon is the simultaneous development of bureaucratization and professionalization in social work, although in principle the two processes could be separate. It is within such a context that the social action approach to social work has more or less become extinct.

Theoretically speaking, social action is compatible with social work; in fact, the lobbying efforts of the early reformers as well as their humanitarianism helped to establish the profession. The challenge that now lies before social workers is that of reincorporating social action into their practice. It would be an arduous task in view of the solidity of bureaucratism and the widespread prevalence of individualistic ideologies. But it would not be impossible. Social workers in Britain and the United States have already embarked on such an endeavour (see Bailey and Brake, 1975; Corrigan and Leonard, 1978; Mandell, 1975; Gough, 1979). Galper (1975; 1980), in particular, has written at length about the gradual, nonviolent transformation of the dehumanizing social structures of capitalism and their organizing principles through social work practice. It begins with collective action at the grassroots level. Galper does not offer a blueprint, but he argues convincingly for the possibility of meaningful social action. Putting that possibility into operation requires, above all, efforts to transcend the bureaucratic barriers beteen worker and supervisor, worker and worker, worker and client, and client and client.

Although the professionalization of social work has led to numerous inadequacies such as this, it also contains potential for progressive action. Social workers can be either agents of social control (they certainly have enough power over their clients) or agents of social change, who would help to resolve the contradictions of the welfare state. Seen in this light, the responsibility of social workers is indeed enormous.

Consumers of Social Welfare

In the hierarchy outlined above, recipients of income support payments and clients in social services have little, if any, input into programming, let alone the total structure of the welfare state. Given the lack of involvement of recipients and clients in policy making and policy implementation, it is not surprising that client apathy and cynicism exist. Recipients and clients feel controlled because they are dependent on social workers and social welfare programs for whatever money or services they receive. But existing programs meet their needs only partially. The result is an adjustment tinged with resentment.

Low income social welfare recipients and clients are victims of an unjust economic system and, moreover, are blamed for their victimization. The processes surrounding their victimization have been identified in the previous chapters. It cannot be emphasized too strongly that they are at the bottom of the social hierarchy, both in the broader society and in the workings of the welfare state. Nevertheless, one cannot lose sight of the contradictions of the welfare state. Just as these recipients and clients are the object of social control, they are also the subject of social change. They have not allowed exploitative social structures and discriminatory practices to overrun their lives totally. Various self-help voluntary groups are ever appearing and making assertions. They publicize the plight of the particular groups, make demands on the political system, and organize their members for concerted action.

To say that the formation of self-help groups represents a phase of class conflict is not to subscribe to the logic of the pluralist theory of social policy. This theory claims that political decisions in liberal democratic states result from the interplay of power among various pressure groups. Although some social welfare self-help groups are interest and pressure groups, they do not all compete or struggle on an equal footing. Most self-help groups lack resources; a sizeable proportion of them depends on state funding. Their lobbying voice is weak and very often ignored by politicians and the public. Many have suffered ridicule and setbacks. The fate of the welfare rights movement is a familiar one. In the late 1960s, the Department of National Health and Welfare funded a few welfare rights groups in major urban centres across the country. The rationale was that if transfer payment recipients could exercise their right to services, their alienation would be reduced. The welfare rights groups organized protests and "sit-ins" in government offices. They raised the level of awareness among their members and received publicity in the press. They also came into confrontation with government officials. The situation became threatening to the "welfare establishment", which was able to gain the support of local politicians and, through them, to pressure the minister of National Health and Welfare. Eventually funding was reduced, stringent conditions were attached to grants, and no overall program to sustain such groups was ever created (Armitage, 1975, p. 70). This kind of situation also illustrates another type of contradiction in the welfare state: the contradictions between those who design and deliver social welfare on the one hand, and the consumers of welfare on the other.

Defeat of this nature is not uncommon. Yet the very fact that self-help groups are always being formed means that the contradictions in the welfare state are ever coming to the fore and cannot be contained. This is part of the dialectic that people seeking meaningful social change cannot overlook.

A case in point is the rape crisis centre. In the 1980s, rape crisis and sexual assault information centres across Canada are in danger of closing down. Funding has been cut and women's issues such as this are coming to be considered low priorities, as is typical in times of economic restraint (Kostash, 1982). Despite the ominous signs, the activities connected with these centres must be recognized as beneficial. They have provided assistance and support to victims; the research conducted by the centres has contributed appreciably to the sociology and psychology of violence; and the centres have provided opportunities for public education. Above all, their continuing struggle for survival attests to the will of victims and potential victims to alter structures that are founded upon inequality and to transform the institutions that foster violence.

13

Conclusion: Dilemmas of the Welfare State

The nature of the capitalist social system requires state intervention in social affairs. The many existing state and private welfare programs make up what is known as the institution of social welfare. The present analysis of the Canadian welfare state has relied upon the Marxist theory of the state and the dialectical method of analysis, in an attempt to explain the contradictions in social welfare.

As discussed in Part I, social welfare models and theories such as rugged individualism and welfare economics prescribe what welfare should do, and even what a society should be. Others (modified individualism and convergence theory) claim to explain why the welfare state exists and what its consequences are, but these theories tend to mystify the phenomenon or merely justify the existing social order. One major conclusion reached in this book is that while many of these views have been considered as theories, they are, for the most part, ideologies. The distinction is therefore made between ideology and theory. The latter seeks to explain social reality, which is not to deny that a theory has value assumptions and can be inspired by a vision of how things ought to be. In that sense, it could be said that a theory may also be ideologically motivated. However, the final test of a theory is whether it is supported by evidence and found to be capable of explaining reality. Moreover, a theory of the welfare state must also be capable of explaining the common features of the welfare state as well as the diversity in programming found in all advanced capitalist societies.

The Marxist theory of the welfare state is found to be most capable of meeting this dual demand. On the one hand, Marxist theory argues that the state in a capitalist society must fulfill the legitimization function, as constrained by the requirements of the capitalist system. On the other hand, with its emphasis on historical conditions, Marxist theory also posits that the shape and structure of the welfare state in any particular capitalist society is influenced by its traditions, cultural legacy, external relations, and the social action engaged in by members of the subordinate classes. In analyzing the welfare state in Canada, this book shows how the Canadian welfare state in fact fulfills its legitimization function as required by capitalism. But in tracing the development of the welfare state and publicly endorsed private welfare, we have also seen how historical conditions and the struggles of the Canadian people have left their mark on the institution of social welfare in Canada, such that it has distinctive features. That the total Canadian institution reflects federal-provincial tensions is one such feature.

This brings us to a second major conclusion. This book has consistently stressed the dialectical reality as conceptualized in Marxist theory. Social welfare is indeed a mechanism of social control used by the state to maintain peace and harmony in capitalist society, which is the most typical conclusion derived from undialectical Marxist analysis. However, vulgar Marxists tend to ignore the fact that social welfare also represents class conflicts. It involves the struggles of the subordinate classes to change class structures and to redefine social relations. That the subordinate classes have not been successful in transforming the overall makeup of society does not mean that they have not made advances; they have won some benefits and, more important, resisted further inequality. The book also places particular emphasis on the importance of looking at the fact that the subordinate classes are capable of shaping their own conditions. This capability does not diminish, even though the efforts of the subordinate classes are circumscribed by dominant social forces, and in spite of meagre gains. Social welfare is one arena in which social change can take place. Clients, social workers, and social scientists must be reminded of the constructive and progressive aspects of social welfare.

It is in this regard that conscientization for social action should be emphasized in social work. Conscientization is a method of adult education developed by Paulo Freire (1972a and 1972b), a former professor of education at the University of Recife. It developed from Freire's experience in literacy training among the poor peasants of North East Brazil. Freire rejected the conventional method of teaching that was based on rote learning and paternalistic in approach. Instead, he based his pedagogy on a dynamic dialogue between the students and the instructor. Through this process the former came to acquire a wider consciousness of their position in society and the broad social factors that had caused their oppression. Almost invariably, conscientization led to greater awareness of social and political issues, political organization, and political involvement. In the early 1970s, the approach was taught as a method of social work intervention in the Catholic University of Chile. It was also widely adopted by social workers in other Latin American countries. As a result, social work was reconceptualized as a horizontal (as opposed to hierarchical), dynamic communication between social workers and the people, a process that would dialectically feed back into social action (Midgley, 1981, pp. 144–45; Leonard, 1975, pp. 53–55).

As Midgley (1981) notes, the techniques used in conscientization are essentially similar to those in conventional social work. However, there is one significant difference. Conventional social work is introspective, often motivating people to change their behaviour, thereby adjusting to their circumstances. Conscientization, on the other hand, encourages people to gain insights into their circumstances with a view to changing those circumstances. Conscientization is, therefore, oriented toward social action.

Conscientization in social work is not a practice or method apart from casework, group work, or community development. While it is probably most effective in the setting of group or community work, it is also feasible in casework. The unique and important feature of conscientization is its dual objective of making a critical analysis of reality and undertaking appropriate action for social change. By bearing this in mind, some erroneous notions about social action can be dispelled. Social action consists of efforts to reduce social inequalities and to transform the exploitative conditions in society into more people-oriented, liberating ones. Yet sometimes social workers with a conventional approach and those with a social action orientation mistakenly believe that action for change can emanate only from social work involving collectivities, such as promoting the welfare rights movement. On the other hand, social workers from both groups may think that casework necessarily leads to the adjustment of clients to the status quo. But group work and community development, no less than casework, could be supportive of existing inequalities and used as measures of social control (see Loney, 1977). Conversely, individual work, as well as work with collectivities, could include efforts at meaningful social change. It must be emphasized that conscientization for social action in casework, group work, or community work, does not abandon the humanitarian concern that is central to conventional social work. For this reason, direct intervention is still seen as the basic *modus operandi* in social work. What social work with a social action orientation seeks to accomplish is this: without compromising the commitment to improving the well-being of individuals and groups *here and now*, it aims to bring about long-term changes opposed to inequality and exploitation. The tactics adopted will almost certainly be gradual, small-scale, and nonviolent, but they will always be based on a critical analysis of the present reality shared by social workers and the people they are trying to help (Galper, 1975 and 1980).

Conscientization for social action is not systematically adopted in social work education or practice in Canada. However, this is not to say that individual social workers or social work educators might not have used the approach on various occasions. In the late 1960s and early 1970s, welfare rights groups and welfare recipients' self-help councils were established in large cities across Canada. In some cases, social workers led or supported welfare recipients who were opposed to government social policies. For example, in 1974, Winnipeg welfare recipients supported by social workers, professional associations, and community agencies succeeded in convincing the city council to reject a proposal that would have reduced the city's welfare allowances by the amount of increase applied to federal family allowances. In 1974–75, natural parents, foster parents, and social workers in Quebec formed a coalition that succeeded in winning significant changes in the provincial government's proposal of requiring low-income natural parents with children in foster care to pay a large portion of the cost of foster care (NCW, 1975).

It can be inferred from these examples that social workers as well as clients run the risk of negative sanctions from government when they engage in social action. Restive welfare recipients are subject to greater scrutiny by welfare authorities, and social workers, insofar as many of them are employed by the government, would be seen as opposing their present or potential employers. The whole weight of bureaucratism could therefore be brought down against them. Thus, before social action advocacy can become the norm in social work, realistic methods of dealing with the structural conditions of recrimination and control of clients and social workers must be developed.

Most instances of raising clients' critical consciousness, especially in the casework setting, are probably never recorded. Moreover, measuring the politicization process of people is a difficult feat, and not a particularly fruitful or useful endeavour at this point. But ways and means of effective conscientization in the Canadian context should be broached, at least informally, by those social workers committed to the approach. More research is needed to develop techniques of applying conscientization to casework, group work, and community development.

In sum, effective social action has occurred in Canada. The extent of the practice of conscientization is more difficult to discern. The process of gaining open acceptance of the conscientization approach in social work education and practice will be a difficult one. Yet conscientization for social action represents the only meaningful alternative to "retreatism" and cynicism experienced by many social workers who have a humanitarian conscience. While it is true that most policy decisions are ultimately made by the state elite, social scientists should not cease to provide the general public with constant critical analysis of social policies and their implications. In order to produce such useful analysis, a means by which social workers and clients can transmit information about their day-to-day experiences must be established.

Finally, further sociological analyses of social welfare are needed. For too long, social welfare as a societal institution has been neglected by sociologists, although sociological knowledge has been applied by some social workers. As a sociology of social welfare, this book has shown that social welfare means different things to different people. Within the framework of the legitimization function of the state, policy makers consider it to be an item of expenditure and evaluate its social consequences in that light. Struggling with "maximum caseloads and minimum resources in a social context of optimum disparagement" (Timms and Timms, 1973, p. 3), social workers personify the best impulses of humanitarianism. Cynicism and despondency therefore result when social welfare clients verbalize their experience as one of social control.

Similarly, the welfare state can also be studied in different academic disciplines. A psychologist, a historian, or an economist will see the entire phenomenon quite differently from the sociologist. This book's sociological analysis has shown that the needs, wishes, and demands of people in the area of welfare are articulated within established social arrangements. The social structures impinge upon people's perceptions and choices, although these may be changed by people's efforts in the process.

A sociological analysis is more than an explication of the relationship between individuals and the larger society. It also entails an examination of the interrelationships among various social institutions. Social welfare is intermeshed with the economy, and the major legal and political institutions of society. It is also linked to the family, religion, and other societal institutions. A sociological analysis will, hopefully, help to dispel the myth that social welfare is the concern only of politicians, social workers, and social assistance recipients. Everyone has a stake in social welfare.

References

Adams, I., Cameron, W., Hill, B., & Penz P. *The Real Poverty Report*. Edmonton: M.G. Hurtig Ltd., 1971.

Adams, P. Social control or social wage: On the political economy of the 'welfare state'. *Journal of Sociology and Social Welfare, 1978, 5* (1): 46–54.

Armitage, A. *Social welfare in Canada: Ideals and Realities*. Toronto: McClelland and Stewart Ltd., 1975. Citation used by permission of the Canadian Publishers, McClelland and Stewart Limited, Toronto.

Armstrong, P. & Armstrong, H. *The double ghetto: Canadian women and their segregated work*. Toronto: McClelland and Stewart Ltd., 1978.

Atkinson, A.B. *The economics of inequality*. Oxford: Clarendon Press, 1975.

Badgley, R.F. & Charles, C.A. Health and inequality. In S.A. Yelaja (Ed.), *Canadian social policy*. Waterloo: Wilfrid Laurier University Press, 1978.

Bailey. R. & Brake M. *Radical social work*. New York: Pantheon Books, 1975.

Baines, B. *Women, human rights and the constitution*. Ottawa: Canadian Advisory Council on the Status of Women, 1980.

Baldus, B. The study of power: Suggestions for an alternative. *Canadian Journal of Sociology, 1975, 1* (2): 179–201.

Baldus, B. & Tribes, V. The development of perceptions and evaluations of social inequality among public school children. *Canadian review of sociology and anthropology, 1978, 15* (1): 50–60.

Banting, K. *The welfare state and Canadian federalism*. Kingston: McGill–Queen's University Press, 1982.

Bell, D. and Tepperman, L. *The roots of disunity*. Toronto: McClelland and Stewart Ltd., 1979.

Bergeron, M. *Social spending in Canada: Trends and options*. Toronto: Canadian Council on Social Development, 1979.

Beveridge, W.H. *Full employment in a free society*. London: Allen and Unwin Ltd., 1944.

Birch, A.H. *Federalism, finance and social legislation*. London: Oxford University Press, 1955.

Bliss, M. Preface. In L. Marsh, *Report on social security for Canada 1943*. Toronto: University of Toronto Press, 1975.

Boadway, R. *Intergovernmental transfers in Canada*. Toronto: Canada Tax Foundation, 1980.

Briggs, A. The welfare state in historical perspective. In C.I. Schottland (Ed.), *The welfare state*. New York: Harper and Row, 1967.

Butler, P.M. and Buckley, P.C. *Living on work and welfare: A closer look at linkages between income security and the world of work*. Halifax: Institute of Public Affairs, Dalhousie University, 1978.

Canada. Central Mortgage and Housing Corporation. *Special $200 million low-cost housing program: Interim report.* Ottawa: Government of Canada, 1970.

Canada. Department of Finance. *Government of Canada tax expenditure account.* A Conceptual Analysis and Account of Tax Preferences in the Federal Income and Commodity Tax Systems. Ottawa: Department of Finance, 1979.

Canada. Department of Manpower and Immigration. Employment Strategy. Notes for a Speech by the Honourable Bud Cullen, Minister of Manpower and Immigration in the Throne Speech Debate. Thursday, 21 October 1976.

———. *Canada manpower industrial training program.* Ottawa: Supply and Services Canada, 1981a.

———. *Labour market development in the 1980s.* Ottawa: Supply and Services Canada, 1981b.

———. *Unemployment insurance in the 1980s.* Ottawa: Supply and Services Canada, 1981c.

Canada. Department of National Health and Welfare. *Notes on welfare services*. Ottawa: National Health and Welfare, 1967.

———. *Income security for Canadians*. White Paper presented by John Munro, Minister of National Health and Welfare. Ottawa: Queen's Printer, 1970.

———. *Working paper on social security in Canada*. Orange Paper presented by Marc Lalonde, Minister of National Health and Welfare. Ottawa: National Health and Welfare, 1973.

———. *Status of day care in Canada.* A Review of the Major Findings of the National Day Care Study 1980. Ottawa: National Health and Welfare, 1980.

Canada. Federal-Provincial Ministers of Welfare. *Communique, meeting of federal-provincial ministers of welfare.* Ottawa, 3–4 February 1976.

Canada. Federal-Provincial Study Group on Alienation. *The world of the welfare recipients*. Ottawa: Federal-Provincial Conference of Ministers of Welfare, 1971.

Canada. Government of Canada. *Report of Royal Commission on Dominion-Provincial Relations*. Ottawa: Queen's Printer, 1940.

———. *Income security and social services*. Working Paper on the Constitution by Prime Minister P.E. Trudeau. Ottawa: Queen's Printer, 1969.

———. People in action. Report of the National Advisory Council on Voluntary Action. Ottawa: Supply and Services Canada, 1977.

———. The income security system in Canada. Report for the Interprovincial Conference of Ministers Responsible for Social Services. Ottawa: Canadian Intergovernmental Conference Secretariat, 1980.

———. *The Canadian Constitution* 1981. A Resolution adopted by the Parliament of Canada, December, 1981. Ottawa: Supply and Services Canada, 1981.

Canada. Special Senate Committee on Poverty. *Poverty in Canada*. Ottawa: Information Canada, 1971.

Canada. Statistics Canada. *Income distribution by size in Canada*. (Cat. 13–207) Annual. Ottawa: Statistics Canada.

———. *Income after tax, distribution by size in Canada*. (Cat. 13–210) Annual. Ottawa: Statistics Canada.

———. *Distributional effects of health and education benefits*. Ottawa: Information Canada, 1974.

———. *Canada year book 1976–77*. Ottawa: Supply and Services Canada, 1977.

———. *Perspectives Canada III*. Ottawa: Supply and Services Canada, 1980.

Canadian Advisory Council on the Status of Women. *Wife battering in Canada, the vicious circle.* Ottawa: Supply and Services Canada, 1980.

Canadian Civil Liberties Education Trust. *Welfare practices and civil liberties: A Canadian survey*. Toronto: Canadian Civil Liberties Education Trust, 1975.

Canadian Council on Social Development. *Social security for Canada 1973*. A Report of the Task Force on Social Security of the Canadian Council on Social Development. Ottawa: Canadian Council on Social Development, 1973.

———. *Social policies for the eighties*. Ottawa: Canadian Council on Social Development, 1981.

Carrier, J.-G. Social spending: C.C.S.D. slams budget. *Perception* 1981 4 (Jan.-Feb.).

Carter, N. *Volunteers: The untapped potential*. Ottawa: Canadian Council on Social Development, 1975.

Caskie, D.M. *Canadian fact book on poverty*. Ottawa: Canadian Council on Social Development, 1979.

Chapin, H. *Tapping the untapped potential: Towards a national policy on volunteerism.* Ottawa: Canadian Council on Social Development, 1977.

Clement, W. A political economy of regionalism in Canada." In J. Harp & J. Hofley (Eds.), *Structured inequality in Canada*. Scarborough, Ontario: Prentice-Hall of Canada, Ltd., 1980.

———. *Hardrock mining*. Toronto: McClelland and Stewart Ltd., 1981.

Cloutier, J.E. *The distribution of benefits and costs of social security in Canada 1971–1975*. Economic Council of Canada Discussion Paper No. 108. Ottawa: Supply and Services Canada, 1978.

Corrigan, P. & Leonard, P. *Social work practice under capitalism*. London: Macmillan Press Ltd., 1978.

Craib, P. & Bowles, R. Canada: Economy, opportunity and class. In J. Fry (Ed.), *Economy, class and social reality*. Toronto: Butterworth and Co. (Canada) Ltd., 1979.

Crysdale, S. & Beattie, C. *Sociology Canada*. Toronto: Butterworth and Co. (Canada) Ltd., 1977.

Cuneo, C.J. State, class and reserve labour: the case of the 1941 Canadian Unemployment Insurance Act. *Canadian Review of Sociology and Anthropology, 1979, 16* (2): 147–170.

Davis, K. & Moore, W.E. Some Principles of Stratification. *American Sociological Review, 1945, 10* (April): 242–249.

Day, S. Affirmative action: an explanation of its evolution, part I. *Saskatchewan Human Rights Commission Newsletter, 1980a, 9* (1): 1–2.

————. Affirmative action: the objectives of special programs, part II." *Saskatchewan Human Rights Commission Newsletter, 1980b, 9* (2): 1–2.

Dickeman, M. The integrity of the Cherokee student. In E.B. Leacock (Ed.), *The culture of poverty: a critique*. New York: Simon and Schuster, Inc., 1971.

Djao, A.W. Social welfare in Canada: ideology and reality. *Social praxis, 1979, 6* (1/2): 35–53.

Drover, G. Income redistribution. In A. Moscovitch & G. Drover (Eds.), *Inequality: essays on the political economy of social welfare*. Toronto: University of Toronto Press, 1981.

Drover, G. & Gartner, D. The growth of welfare expenditures in Canada. *The Social Worker, 1980, 48* (2): 63–67.

Economic Council of Canada. *People and jobs: a study of the Canadian labour market*. Ottawa: Information Canada, 1976.

Elias, P.D. *Metropolis and hinterland in Northern Manitoba*. Winnipeg: Manitoba Museum of Man and Nature, 1975.

Freire, P. *Pedagogy of the oppressed*. Harmondsworth: Penguin Books, 1972a.

————. *Cultural action for freedom*. Harmondsworth: Penguin Books, 1972b.

Friedman, M. *Capitalism and freedom*. Chicago: University of Chicago Press, 1962. Citations reprinted by permission of the University of Chicago Press, copyright 1962.

Galbraith, J.K. *The new industrial state*. Boston: Houghton Mifflin Co., 1967.

————. *The affluent society*. Boston: Houghton Mifflin Co., 1969.

Galper, J.H. *The politics of social services*. Englewood Cliffs, New Jersey: Prentice-Hall, Inc., 1975.

————. *Social work practice: a radical perspective*. Englewood Cliffs, New Jersey: Prentice-Hall, Inc., 1980.

Galtung, J. A structural theory of imperialism. *Journal of Peace Research, 1971,* 2: 81–117.

George, V. & Wilding P. *Ideology and social welfare*. London: Routledge and Kegan Paul, 1976.

Gillespie, I. *In search of Robin Hood: the effect of federal budgetary policies during the 1970s on the distribution of income in Canada*. Montreal: C.D. Howe Research Institute, 1978.

The Globe and Mail. B.C. legal aid study finds savings with staff lawyers; public defenders in five provinces called efficient, successful; legal aid systems vary among 10 provinces. Toronto: 18 January 1982.

Gough, I. Theories of the welfare state: a critique. *International Journal of Health Services, 1978, 8* (1): 27–40.

————. *The political economy of the welfare state*. London: Macmillan Press Ltd., 1979.

Gould, J. & Kolb, W.L. (Eds.), A dictionary of the social sciences. Compiled under the auspices of the United Nations Educational, Scientific and Cultural Organization. London: Tavistock Ltd., 1964.

Greenaway, W.K. Crime and class: unequal before the law. In J. Harp & J. Hofley (Eds.), *Structured inequality in Canada*. Scarborough, Ontario: Prentice-Hall of Canada, Ltd., 1980.

Guest, D. *The emergence of social security in Canada*. Vancouver: University of British Columbia Press, 1980.

Harding, J. & Riches, G. Social welfare, human justice and mineral resources: a Saskatchewan case study 1971–81. Paper read at the Conference of the Western Association of Sociology and Anthropology, Saskatoon, Saskatchewan, 11 February 1982.

Harp, J. Social inequalities and the transmission of knowledge. In J. Harp & J. Hofley (Eds.), *Structured inequality in Canada*. Scarborough, Ontario: Prentice-Hall of Canada, Ltd., 1980.

Hawrylyshyn, O. The economic nature and value of volunteer activity in Canada. *Social Indicators Research, 1978, 5* (1): 1–71.

Hayek, F.A. *Individualism and economic order*. London: Routledge and Kegan Paul, 1949.

————. The decline of socialism and the rise of the welfare state. In *The constitution of liberty*. Chicago: University of Chicago Press, 1960. Excerpt reprinted by permission of the University of Chicago Press. Copyright © 1960.

Hepworth, H.P. *Personal social services in context*. Personal Social Services in Canada: a review. Vol. 9. Ottawa: Canadian Council on Social Development, 1975.

Hobsbawn, E. Karl Marx's contribution to historiography. In R. Blackburn (Ed.), *Ideology in social science*. Glasgow: Fontana Collins, 1972.

Hofstadter, R. *Social Darwinism in American thought*. Boston: Beacon Press, 1955.

Johnson, L.A. The development of class in Canada in the twentieth century. In G. Teeple (Ed.), *Capitalism and the national question in Canada*. Toronto: University of Toronto Press, 1972.

———. The capitalist labour market and income inequality in Canada. In John Fry (Ed.), *Economy, class and social reality*. Toronto: Butterworth and Co. (Canada) Ltd., 1979.

Jordan, Z.A. The concept of inequality in the social sciences. In J. Harp & J. Hofley (Eds.), *Structured inequality in Canada*. Scarborough, Ontario: Prentice-Hall of Canada, Ltd., 1980.

Kellough, G. From colonialism to imperialism: the experience of Canadian Indians. In J. Harp & J. Hofley (Eds.), *Structured inequality in Canada*. Scarborough, Ontario: Prentice-Hall of Canada, Ltd., 1980.

Kelly, M. The new social services legislation—what next? *The Social Worker, 1977, 45* (4): 156–160.

Kerr, C., Dunlop, J.T., Harbison, F.H. & Myers, C.A. *Industrialism and industrial man*. Cambridge, Mass.: Harvard University Press, 1960.

Kinloch, G.C. *Sociological theory: its development and major paradigms*. New York: McGraw-Hill Inc., 1977.

Kostach, M. Fighting for control: the rape issue in crisis. *This Magazine, 1982, 15* (5–6): 8–13.

Kravitz, S. The dilemma of accountability. *Journal of Voluntary Action Research, 1973, 2* (1): 36–47.

Leacock, E.B. Introduction. In E.B. Leacock (Ed.), *The culture of poverty: a critique*. New York: Simon and Schuster, Inc., 1971.

Leonard, P. *Sociology in social work*. London: Routledge and Kegan Paul, 1966.

———. Toward a paradigm for radical practice. In R. Bailey & M. Brake (Eds.), *Radical social work*. New York: Pantheon Books, 1975.

Lewis, O. *La Vida*. New York: Vintage Books, 1965.

Loney, M. A political economy of citizen participation. In L. Panitch (Ed.), *The Canadian State*. Toronto: University of Toronto Press, 1977.

Mandell, B.R. (Ed.) *Welfare in America: controlling the "dangerous classes"*. Englewood Cliffs, New Jersey: Prentice-Hall, Inc., 1975.

Marsh, L. *Report on social security for Canada 1943*. 1943. Reprint. Toronto: University of Toronto Press, 1975.

Marshal, T.H. *Sociology at the crossroads and other essays*. London: Heinemann Ltd., 1963.

———. *Social Policy*. London: Hutchinson University Library, 1965.

———. *Value problems of welfare-capitalism. Journal of Social Policy, 1972, 1* (1): 15–32.

———. *Class, citizenship and social development*. Westport, Conn.: Greenwood Press, 1973.

Martin, W. B. & Macdonell, A. J. *Canadian education, a sociological analysis*. Scarborough, Ontario: Prentice-Hall Canada, Ltd., 1982.

Martindale, D. *The nature and types of sociological theory*. Boston: Houghton Mifflin Co., 1960.

Marx, K. Wages, Price and Profit. In *Karl Marx and Frederick Engels Selected Works*. Moscow: Progress Publishers, 1970.

————. *Capital, a critical analysis of capitalist production*. Vol. 1. Translated from the third German edition by S. Moore & E. Aveling. Frederick Engels (Ed.), Moscow: Progress Publishers, 1972.

————. *Grundrisse, an introduction to the critique of political economy*. Translated with a foreword by M. Nicolaus. Harmondsworth: Penguin Books Ltd., 1973.

Maslove, A. *The pattern of taxation in Canada*. Ottawa: Economic Council of Canada, 1972.

McParland, B. *Forty-nine children*. New Westminster: British Columbia Ministry of Human Resources, 1978.

Melichercik, J. Children and Youth. In J. Turner & F. Turner (Eds.), *Canadian social welfare*. Don Mills, Ontario: Collier MacMillan Canada Inc., 1981.

Midgely, J. *Professional imperialism: social work in the third world*. London: Heinemann Educational Books Ltd., 1982.

Miliband, R. *The state in capitalist society*. London: Weidenfeld and Nicolson, 1969.

Mishra, R. *Society and social policy: theoretical perspectives on welfare*. London: Macmillan Press Ltd., 1977.

————. *Society and social policy: theories and practice of welfare*. Revised Second Edition. London: Macmillan Press Ltd., 1981.

Moscovitch, A. The Canadian economy and inequality. In A. Moscovitch & G. Drover (Eds.), *Inequality: essays on the political economy of social welfare*. Toronto: University of Toronto Press, 1981.

National Council of Welfare. *The hidden welfare system*. Ottawa: National Council of Welfare, 1976.

————. *Jobs and poverty*. Ottawa: National Council of Welfare, 1977.

————. *Bearing the burden, sharing the benefits*. Ottawa: National Council of Welfare, 1978a.

————. *The refundable child tax credit*. Ottawa: National Council of Welfare, 1978b.

————. *The federal government and social services*. Ottawa: National Council of Welfare, 1978c.

————. *The hidden welfare system revisited*. Ottawa: National Council of Welfare, 1979a.

————. *In the best interests of the child*. Ottawa: National Council of Welfare, 1979b.

————. *The working poor: people and programs*. Ottawa: National Council of Welfare, 1981.

————. *Measuring poverty: 1982 poverty lines*. Ottawa: National Council of Welfare, 1982.

————. *Revised 1982 poverty lines*. Ottawa: National Council of Welfare, 1982.

O'Connor, J. *The fiscal crisis of the state*. New York: St. Martin's Press, 1973.

Oommen, T.K. The theory of voluntary association in a cross-cultural perspective. *Sociological Bulletin, 1975, 24* (2): 163–180.

Panitch, L. The role and nature of the Canadian state. In L. Panitch (Ed.), *The Canadian state*. Toronto: University of Toronto Press, 1977.

Pinker, R. *Social theory and social policy*. London: Heinemann Educational Books Ltd., 1971.

Piven, F.F. Social science and social policy. In P. Roby (Ed.), *The poverty establishment*, Englewood Cliffs, New Jersey: Prentice-Hall, Inc., 1974.

Piven, F.F. & Cloward, R.A. *Regulating the poor: the functions of public welfare*. New York: Vintage Books, 1971.

Poulantzas, N. The problem of the capitalist state. *New Left Review, 1969, 58* (Nov.-Dec.): 67–78.

Quebec Commission of Inquiry on Health and Social Welfare. *Report of Quebec Commission of Inquiry on Health and Social Welfare.* Quebec: Government of Quebec, 1971.

Rabinovitch, V. Policy choices for workplace health and safety in the 1980's. *Perception, 1982, 5* (4): 14–15.

Regush, N. *Welfare: the social issues in philosophical perspective*. Pittsburgh: University of Pittsburgh Press, 1972.

Rein, M. *Social science and public policy*. Harmondsworth: Penguin Books Ltd., 1976.

Riches, G. Which way for personal social services in Canada, now? *The Social Worker, 1977, 45* (4): 185–191.

————. Saskatchewan's social spending: conservatism in practice. *The Social Worker, 1980, 48* (1): 12–14.

Rinehart, J.W. *The tyranny of work*. Don Mills, Ontario: Longman Canada Ltd., 1975.

Robertson, I. *Sociology*. Second Edition. New York: Worth Publishers Inc., 1981.

Room, G. *The sociology of welfare: social policy, stratification and political order*. Oxford: Basil Blackwell and Martin Robertson, 1979.

Ross, D.P. *The Canadian fact book on income distribution*. Ottawa: Canadian Council on Social Development, 1980.

————. *The working poor: wage earners and the failure of income security policies*. Toronto: James Lorimer and Co., 1981.

Ryan, W. *Blaming the victim*. Second Edition. New York: Vintage Books, 1976.

Schottland, C.I. Introduction. In C.I. Schottland (Ed.), *The welfare state*. New York: Harper and Row, 1967.

Smucker, J. *Industrialization in Canada*. Scarborough, Ontario: Prentice-Hall of Canada, Ltd., 1980.

Spitzer, S. Toward a Marxian theory of deviance. *Social Problems, 1975, 22* (5): 638–651.

Splane, R. Whatever happened to the G.A.I.? *The Social Worker, 1980, 48* (2): 86–87.

Stevenson, G. Federalism and the political economy of the Canadian state. In L. Panitch (Ed.), *The Canadian state*. Toronto: University of Toronto Press, 1977.

Steward, J.H. *Contemporary change in traditional societies, Vol. I, Introduction and African tribes*. Urbana: University of Illinois Press, 1967.

Taman, L. *The legal services controversy: an examination of the evidence*. Ottawa: National Council of Welfare, 1971.

Thatcher, R.W. The political economy of Canada's 'war on poverty'. Paper read at the Conference of the Western Association of Sociology and Anthropology, Saskatoon, Saskatchewan, 11 February 1982.

Timms, N. & Timms, R. *Perspectives in social work*. London: Routledge and Kegan Paul, 1977.

Titmuss, R.M. *Essays on 'the welfare state'*. London: George Allen and Unwin Ltd., 1958.

———. *The gift relationship*. New York: Pantheon Books, 1971.

———. *Social policy*. B. Abel-Smith & K. Titmuss (Eds.). London: George Allen and Unwin Ltd., 1974.

United Nations. *Human rights: a compilation of international instruments*. (ST/HR/1/Rev 1), 1978.

Valentine, C.A. *Culture and poverty*. Chicago: University of Chicago Press, 1968.

Wallace, E. The origin of the social welfare state in Canada, 1867–1900. *Canadian Journal of Economics and Political Science, 1950, 16*: 383–393.

Warham, J. *Social policy in context*. London: B.T. Batsford Ltd., 1970.

Watson, D. Welfare rights and human rights. *Journal of Social Policy, 1976, 6* (1): 31–46.

Wax, M.L. & Wax, R.H. Cultural deprivation as an educational ideology. In E.B. Leacock (Ed.), *The culture of poverty: a critique*. New York: Simon and Schuster, Inc., 1971.

Wilensky, H.L. & Lebeaux, C.N. *Industrial society and social welfare*. New York: The Free Press, 1965.

Wolfe, D. Social policy issues absent in constitutional debate. *Perception, 1980, 3* (Nov.-Dec.): 13–15, 17.

Wolff, R.P. Liberty. In R.P. Wolff (Ed.), *The poverty of liberalism*. Boston: Beacon Press, 1968.

Wright, E.O. *Class, crisis and the state*. London: New Left Books, 1978.

Yelaja, S.A. What is social policy? Its assumptions, definitions and uses. In S.A. Yelaja (Ed.), *Canadian social policy*. Waterloo: Wilfrid Laurier University Press, 1978.

Zeitlin, I.M. *Marxism: a re-examination*. New York: Van Nostrand Reinhold Co., 1967.

———. *Rethinking sociology: a critique of contemporary theory*. Englewood Cliffs, New Jersey: Prentice-Hall, Inc.; 1973.

Zetterberg, H.L. *On theory and verification in sociology*. New York: Bedminster Press, 1965.

Index